GW00720611

Pocket Lawyer

Related titles in this series:

The Pocket Economist
Rupert Pennant-Rea and Bill Emmott

The Economist Pocket Banker
Tim Hindle

The Economist Pocket Accountant
Chistopher Nobes

The Economist Pocket Guide to Marketing
Michael Thomas

The Economist Pocket Guide to Defence
Michael Sheehan and James H. Wyllie

Pocket Lawyer

Stanley Berwin

Basil Blackwell
and
The Economist

Jointly published 1986 by
Basil Blackwell Ltd
108 Cowley Road, Oxford OX4 1JF, UK and
The Economist Publications Ltd
40 Duke Street, London W1A 1DW

First published in USA 1987

Basil Blackwell Inc.
432 Park Avenue South, Suite 1503
New York, NY 10016, USA

British Library Cataloguing in Publication Data
Berwin, Stanley
The Economist pocket lawyer.
1. Law — Great Britain — Dictionaries
I. Title
344.108′6 KD313
ISBN 0-631-15194-X

Library of Congress Cataloging in Publication Data
Berwin, Stanley.
Pocket lawyer.
1. Law—Great Britain—Terms and phrases.
2. Commercial law—Great Britain—Terms and phrases.
I. Title.
KD313.B47 1987 340′.03′21 86–22356
ISBN 0–631–15194–X

Typeset in 10/12pt Bembo
by Oxford Publishing Services, Oxford
Printed in Great Britain by
Billing & Sons Ltd, Worcester

To my darling wife Rosalie

Preface

I have endeavoured to assemble a collection of terms, concepts and phrases, some of which make the law mysterious to the layman and, in defining them, present a readable and practical guide to civil and commercial law. Hopefully the essential compression has not led to distortion. By its very nature the collection cannot be comprehensive, many of its subjects merit – and some have achieved – a book, or even two or more volumes in their own right.

A different system of cross-referencing has been used in *Pocket Lawyer* from that established in *The Economist* Pocket Books to date. To be complete, the cross-referencing would have meant an enormously complex and massive book. I trust readers will find their way around the book by using the references in the individual entries. This is fun to do and possibly more informative than following a disciplined cross-referencing system.

In the use of the words 'he/him' this book relies on the provisions of section 61 of the Law of Property Act 1925 whereby the masculine includes the feminine (and vice versa) unless the context requires otherwise.

The following abbreviations have been used:

The Act	The Companies Act 1985
DTI	Department of Trade and Industry
Secretary of State	The Secretary of State for the Department of Trade and Industry
Registrar	Registrar of Companies
FSA	Financial Services Act
Memorandum	Memorandum of Association
Articles	Articles of Association

This book reflects the law as at August 1986. Except where expressly stated, all references are to English law.

My thanks to those who have helped in the production of this book. There are many of them. In particular, my colleagues at S J Berwin & Co for their research, contributions, comments and forbearance; to my long-suffering secretary Christine Heywood, assisted by Claudia Bent; to Gavin Lightman QC for his comments; to Christopher Hutton-Williams of *The Economist* for the idea, and to Tony Sweeney and Mary Robinson of Basil Blackwell, for their editorship. Any omissions or mistakes are, unfortunately, all my own making.

Whether you are the kind of reader who likes to browse around or read from end to end, I hope very much that you will enjoy the *Pocket Lawyer*.

A

ABUSE OF PROCESS. The improper use of legal proceedings.

ACCEPTANCE CREDIT. A transaction in which a bank agrees to 'accept' bills of exchange of a fixed amount drawn on it, i.e. to pay their face value to whoever presents them at the end of a specified period, usually between 30 and 180 days.

It is normally used to finance the sale of goods, when it takes the form of an irrevocable letter of credit allowing the seller to draw a bill on the accepting bank for the relevant amount to be paid on maturity and production of documents relating to the goods. The seller can discount the bill immediately (sell it for cash at a discount): the obligation of the purchaser of the goods to put the bank in funds arises only on maturity of the bill.

An acceptance credit is not a borrowing in law, and is sometimes used to overcome borrowing restrictions imposed by the Articles. See NEGOTIABLE INSTRUMENT.

ACCOUNTING PERIODS. Companies are required under the Act to prepare their accounts by reference to 'accounting reference periods', which are normally periods of 12 months. The date is significant because it determines the time of the annual general meeting at which the accounts are presented. A company may shorten its accounting period as much and as often as it likes, but cannot extend it beyond 18 months nor normally, unless it is an oversea company, more than once every five years.

A company must also have an accounting period for the purposes of corporation tax and this cannot exceed 12 months. The accounting period ends with the accounting reference date, which is fixed either by the company, or failing that, by law, as 31 March. Where the company's accounting reference period is longer than 12 months, the profits are apportioned between the financial years (1 April to 31 March) in which it falls.

ACCOUNTING STANDARDS (SSAP). Otherwise known as statements of standard accounting practice. They describe methods of accounting approved by the leading accountancy institutions for all financial accounts. They are not a 'comprehensive code of rigid rules'. They vary from country to country and this has led to the introduction of international accounting standards which seek to achieve harmonization.

ACCOUNTS. A balance sheet and profit and loss account made out to the accounting reference date in the case of a company, and consolidated in the case of a group in accordance with the Act. They must also comply with accounting standards. They are required to show a true and fair view of the company's profit or loss and state of affairs and must be filed with the Registrar. See ACCOUNTING PERIODS.

ACCUMULATIONS. Accretions of interest or other income produced by a particular fund. Until 1800 a person could direct that income should be accumulated for the whole of the perpetuity period; there was nothing to prevent 'compulsory hoarding on a mammoth scale'. As a result limitations were introduced under which a direction to accumulate was valid only if limited to precise periods of time. Any one of six periods can be chosen, the most common being a term of 21 years from the making of a disposition.

ACCUMULATION AND MAINTENANCE TRUST. A trust under which income is accumulated unless used for the maintenance, education or benefit of a beneficiary. There must be at least one beneficiary who will have the right to receive the income or capital at or before the age of 25. Used to save inheritance tax and reduce income tax. A gift to such a trust will be liable to inheritance tax only if made within seven years of the donor's death.

ACTING IN CONCERT. There is no such term in English law. The concept was introduced in the City Code to ensure that a shareholder could not evade his obligations either to make a compulsory bid or to limit his share purchases by acting with others. It therefore treats as a single shareholder persons who actively co-operate through the acquisition by any of them of shares in a company to obtain or consolidate control of that company.

The Code also categorizes persons who are presumed to be acting in concert unless the contrary is established: where now the maxim that a person is innocent until he is proved guilty? These categories include a company with other companies in the same group and their associated companies; a company with its directors, their close relatives and related trusts; and financial advisers with their client and certain discretionary investment accounts.

In a similar vein the Rules Governing Substantial Acquisitions of Shares require two or more persons acting by agreement or understanding to have their own holdings and acquisitions aggregated and treated as held by one person.

The Act treats directors, certain members of their families and trusts as one in relation to prohibitions upon dealing in share options, and the disclosure of shareholdings.

The obligation imposed by the Act to disclose an interest in the voting shares of a public company may arise from an agreement between two or more persons, which includes provision for the acquisition by any one or more of them of interests in that company's shares: the agreement need not necessarily be legally binding. See DISCLOSURE OF INTEREST IN SHARES.

ACTION. The pursuit of a right or claim in judicial proceedings.

ADMINISTRATION ORDER. A new procedure instituted by the Insolvency Act 1985 which may salvage a distressed company. The effect of the order is to bar any creditor taking legal proceedings to recover his debt and a secured creditor from enforcing his security without leave of the court. The order may be made by the court where the company is, or is likely to become, insolvent, but there are reasonable prospects of a return to profitability or a more advantageous realization of assets than by winding up. See ADMINISTRATOR.

ADMINISTRATIVE LAW. Professor Wade wrote that the primary purpose of administrative law is to keep the powers of government within their legal bounds so as to protect the citizen against their abuse. 'The powerful engines of authority must be prevented from running amok.' It is a body of general principles which govern the exercise of the powers and duties of government and public authorities. Even when a public authority acts without bad faith, it may abuse the power given to it by Parliament or subordinate legislation and the law can provide essential remedies, e.g. judicial review.

ADMINISTRATIVE RECEIVER. See RECEIVER.

ADMINISTRATOR. A person appointed under an administration order by the court, with powers to manage the affairs, business and property of a company, to dismiss and appoint directors and to call meetings of shareholders and creditors. The office was created by the Insolvency Act 1985 which regulates his conduct and functions.

The administrator must protect the company's assets, and submit proposals for the company's future for the approval of creditors. If the proposals are supported he has the task of putting them into effect.

ADMIRALTY. Formerly the High Court of Admiralty, now part of the Queen's Bench Division of the High Court, with jurisdiction relating to ships, cargo and aircraft. See *IN REM.*

ADVANCE CORPORATION TAX ('ACT'). The tax payable by a company when it pays a dividend; the amount is a fraction of the dividend (currently 29/71), which is permitted to be set off against mainstream corporation tax for an accounting period. ACT is payable 14 days after the quarter in which the dividend is paid. The adroit finance director will ensure that an extra three months' credit is obtained by paying dividends just after, rather than just before, the end of a quarter.

An individual shareholder is regarded as having paid basic rate income tax of an amount equal to the ACT paid on his dividend.

ADVOCATES, FACULTY OF. A corporate body founded in 1532

consisting of barristers in Edinburgh. All barristers in Scotland are known as advocates.

AFFIDAVIT. A written and sworn or affirmed declaration made before a person authorized to administer oaths used as proof or testimony of the facts it contains.

AFFIRMATION. A non-religious form of solemn declaration equivalent to a statement upon oath.

AG (*AKTIENGESELLSCHAFT*). The West German and Swiss form of public company, which may be contrasted with the GmbH which is the form of private company.

The shares of a West German AG are usually in bearer form and held in collective deposit by specialist depositary banks. A peculiar consequence is that the votes in respect of those shares are exercised by the banks in accordance with their own views, unless the owner gives specific contrary instructions.

A distinctive feature of the West German AG is its two-tier system of management: its board of directors (*Vorstand*) is itself subject to the control of a supervisory board (*Aufsichtsrat*) which appoints the directors and generally represents the interests of the shareholders in relation to the directors.

AGENCY. Is one of the basic legal concepts of Anglo-Saxon countries; without its existence much of modern commercial and financial activity would grind to a halt. The relationship exists when the principal consents to an intermediary, the agent, acting on his behalf in concluding a transaction with a third party. The principal becomes bound as if he and the third party had entered into the transaction themselves. The agent generally no longer has anything to do with the matter. The underlying idea is that a person need not always act personally to change his legal position: he may use the services of someone else.

The relationship is consensual: an agent agrees or consents to act under the control or direction of the principal. It is usually fiduciary, as the agent agrees to act for and on behalf of the principal. The agent is in no sense a proprietor entitled to the profits, nor is he expected to carry the risks.

An agency can arise by:

- express agreement: whether a legally binding contract or not; or
- implied agreement: where the court will infer the relationship from the conduct or situation of the parties; or
- estoppel: where a person represents by words or conduct that another person is his agent – he is not allowed to deny the agency to a third party dealing in good faith with the person held out as agent; or
- operation of law: under the doctrine of agent of necessity; or
- ratification: where the agent has no authority but purports to act on the principal's behalf and the principal later ratifies what the agent has done.

The only time it is necessary to have a written appointment is if the agent is to execute a deed, such as a lease of land, when he must be appointed by a power of attorney.

As a general rule, whatever a person has power to do himself he can do through an agent; but he cannot do through an agent what he cannot do himself. Thus, an infant can bind himself through an agent in respect of the purchase of necessaries; a company can only act or contract through an agent on matters within the normal objects of the company. See BREACH OF WARRANTY OF AUTHORITY.

AGENCY OF NECESSITY. There may be circumstances in which it is impracticable for an agent to communicate with his principal and action must be taken to safeguard the principal's property. Where the agent does so bona fide in the interests of the principal, an agency of necessity will arise even if the agent has exceeded his authority. For example, the master of a ship in times of emergency may contract for urgent repairs and bind the ship-owner to the contract.

The courts will not readily extend the doctrine to a person who is not already an agent.

AGENT. The functions that an agent can perform are restricted only by the imagination of man. In law he is not always what he is called in ordinary commercial parlance. For example an 'exclusive agent' is usually a relationship between seller and buyer and no contractual relationship arises between the appointor of the so-called 'agent' and third parties. A person is, in law, an agent only if he is employed to affect the legal relations of his principal and a third party.

An agent has many obligations to his principal. He must carry out his duties with reasonable care, skill and diligence; act personally and disclose to his principal all material facts. He must not disclose confidential information, accept a bribe, or make a secret profit out of his position.

The personal interests of an agent must not be allowed to conflict with the interests of his principal, even after the agency has ended, if the agent makes use of knowledge acquired while acting as agent.

An agent can claim an indemnity from his principal against all liabilities or expenses properly incurred on his principal's behalf, but has no right to any remuneration unless it has been expressly agreed or can be implied from the nature of the agent's services.

Subject to the terms of any agreement, where the principal receives the benefit of contracts with people introduced by the agent after termination, no commission is payable to the agent. Some foreign laws entitle an agent to claim compensation from his principal for the goodwill which he has created and which continues to accrue to the principal after termination of the agency.

Generally, any contract made by an agent with the authority of his principal, may be enforced by or against the principal whether or not his name was disclosed at the time of the contract; the agent is not required to disclose that he is acting as agent, but if he does not he may incur personal liability. See BREACH OF WARRANTY OF AUTHORITY, CONFLICT OF INTEREST and UNDISCLOSED PRINCIPAL.

AGREEMENT. Some agreements, in particular guarantees and those relating to land, are not enforceable unless made or evidenced in writing. Apart from these, an agreement can be made in writing or by word of mouth, but will not be legally binding unless the essential elements of contract are present. If made under seal it is known as a deed.

Legal warning: evidence required to prove an oral contract can be onerous.

ALTERNATE DIRECTOR. A person, whether a director or not, who is appointed by a director to act for him at any board meeting he is unable to attend. The Articles must permit the appointment and must be strictly complied with. In the usual case an alternate director is not a director as such, although he may be given that status by the Articles. However, if he actively directs a company's affairs, he may become a shadow director.

AMALGAMATION. See RECONSTRUCTION AND AMALGAMATION.

AMERICAN BAR ASSOCIATION. A private voluntary association of which over one-half of the attorneys in the USA are members. Influential. A person cannot be licensed as an attorney unless he has graduated at a law school accredited by the ABA.

AMERICAN DEPOSITARY RECEIPT. The route through which most non-US companies have issued equity in the USA. ADRs are receipts held by large depositary banks (such as Morgan Guaranty, Chase Manhattan and Irving Trust) which represent underlying shares. Through this system, dividends are paid to US investors in dollars; and dividend payments, annual reports and key news releases are distributed by one source, the depositary, who is the shareholder of record. Morgan Guaranty has 90 per cent of the ADR market. Both large and small issues have been completed from $278 million for British Telecom to a $4 million issue for Universal Money Centres plc of the UK. It is not necessary to have a new issue of shares nor to be a listed company in order to have ADRs.

***AMERICAN LAWYER*, THE.** The *Private Eye* type magazine of the US legal profession. Sometimes scandalous, often revealing and widely read.

AMERICAN RULE, THE. The name given to the usual position that the cost of a US attorney is a non-recoverable expense of litigation, as it is deemed to be 'one of the incidents of (US) citizenship'. In the UK costs are in the discretion of the court, but normally follow the outcome of a case.

ANNUAL GENERAL MEETING. The general meeting of shareholders held once in each calendar year by a company. It is convened by the directors on not less than 21 days' written notice. Anything that can be done at an extraordinary general meeting can be done at an AGM.

The tendency is for the number of members present to be in inverse proportion to the company's success: the better a company does, the fewer attend.

ANNUAL REPORT. See DIRECTORS' REPORT.

ANNUAL RETURN. A form filed by a company with the Registrar within 42 days after its annual general meeting giving details of its registered office, share capital, register of members and debenture holders, secured borrowings, directors and secretary.

ANTICIPATORY BREACH. A breach of contract caused by the repudiation of obligations before they are to be performed. Such a repudiation occurs when a person indicates by words or conduct that he does not intend to honour his obligations when they fall due. It entitles an innocent party to an immediate cause of action, but he has an option: he can either wait until the day for performance arrives, or immediately treat the contract as discharged and sue for damages. If he waits and refuses to accept the breach as a discharge of contract, the contract remains in being for the future on both sides and each party has the right to sue for damages for present and future breaches.

It is not unknown for intervening circumstances to operate against an innocent party who waits; for the measure of damages will depend upon values at the time designated for performance, not at the date of repudiation.

ANTI TAKE-OVER DEVICES. Dependent upon one's perspective, the UK is an infant and the USA mature, or vice versa, in the use of defences against the unwelcome take-over. In the UK, principles of company law, regulations of The London Stock Exchange and the City Code all impinge on the freedom of action of directors of a listed company involved in take-overs: they cannot enter into transactions which could result in an offer being frustrated or shareholders being denied the opportunity to accept or reject an offer.

This is not so in the USA where the business judgment rule enables directors to employ defensive tactics, without reference to shareholders. The most prominent are the 'white squire' technique of issuing new shares to a friendly person; the sale or grant to a friendly party of options over valuable assets, grotesquely known as 'crown jewels'; 'poison pills' and 'shark repellents', which are conditions attached to shares to make them unappealing.

The white knight is a defence not a device. The City Code allows confidential information to be given to a preferred offeror. The hostile offeror is not entitled, by asking in general terms, to receive all the information given to his competitor.

ANTITRUST. A term generally used for agreements or actions which are likely to interfere with competition in the market or which are discriminatory against certain parties thus affecting free competition.

The USA used to take its antitrust law quite seriously. The Sherman Act of 1890, which is the fundamental antitrust statute, was spoken of by the Supreme Court as the 'Magna Carta of free enterprise . . . as important to the preservation of economic freedom and our free enterprise system as the Bill of Rights is to the protection of our personal freedoms.'

Any person injured in his business or property by an antitrust violation of the Sherman Act can recover three-fold the damages sustained, plus the costs of the suit, including an attorney's reasonable fee: a significant exception to the American Rule. Violation is also a criminal offence which can attract substantial fines (up to $1 million for a company) and imprisonment. Any agreement violating antitrust laws is illegal and cannot be enforced.

A violation under the Sherman Act arises under section 1 which prohibits contracts, combinations or conspiracies in restraint of trade or commerce and section 2 which prohibits monopolization, a combination or conspiracy to monopolize or attempts to do so in any part of the trade or commerce or the foreign commerce of the USA. Monopolization means having sufficient economic power to control prices and exclude competitors.

Although the Sherman Act applies to mergers and acquisitions, the principal US law governing them is the Clayton Act, which makes them unlawful where their effect may be substantially to lessen competition or tend to create a monopoly in any line of commerce. A foreign company will be subject to the Clayton Act, even if it is not doing business in the USA, if it is engaged in the foreign commerce of the USA. A foreign company attempting to acquire a US corporation would come within its scope as would a US company acquiring a foreign company. Under these provisions American Gillette Co. was prevented from acquiring Braun, the German electric razor manufacturer; and the Federal Trade Commission obtained an injunction requiring British Oxygen (a manufacturer of industrial gases) to maintain Airco (also a manufacturer of industrial gases) as an independent company and to refrain from voting the 35 per cent of the common stock of Airco it had acquired, on the principle that an acquisition can be unlawful because it removes a potential competitor (in this case British Oxygen) from entering the market. See ARTICLES 85 AND 86 EEC TREATY, COMPETITION LAW, HART-SCOTT-RODINO, RESTRAINT OF TRADE and RESTRICTIVE TRADE PRACTICES.

ANTON PILLER ORDER. A surprise visit to home or office by a solicitor to take possession of documents which are vital evidence before they are destroyed may now be commonplace, but the first orders enabling plaintiffs in an action so to do were not granted until 1974. Not long after, a West German firm called Anton Piller KG bequeathed its mellifluous name to English legal language by being the plaintiff in the first case in which the Court of Appeal approved such orders and laid down guidelines.

Before an order is made the plaintiff must show the High Court that he has a very strong *prima facie* case, that his potential or actual damage is very serious, that the defendant has relevant material and that there is a real danger he will destroy or dispose of it if not prevented. The essence of the order is surprise and accordingly the application is heard in camera and *ex parte*.

The order is particularly useful in copyright cases involving pirating and in complex financial fraud. It does not amount to a search warrant, so that the plaintiff cannot use force to enter premises but must have the defendant's permission. If this is refused, the defendant may be in contempt of court.

APPEAL. It is said that old solicitors never die, they just lose their appeal. Unlike judicial review, appeals are usually rehearings of the case, with notes or transcripts of the evidence given in the inferior court and legal argument being presented to the court. Civil courts normally only review points of law and only interfere with findings of fact where there is a clear error, or a decision is shown to have been reached contrary to the weight of the evidence. It is unusual for an appellate court to come to a new decision as to the facts, or to substitute its discretion for that of an inferior court, unless the discretion was based on a misunderstanding or ignorance of the true facts.

In spite of contrary impressions, relatively few cases in the USA are appealed. US appellate courts do not review facts, but only review and correct errors of law. See COURT OF APPEAL and HOUSE OF LORDS.

ARBITRATION. Commonly, but not necessarily correctly, regarded as a cheap and speedy method of resolving disputes before a tribunal of the parties' own choosing. Conciliation is cheaper. Some arbitrations are imposed by statute but normally arbitrators derive authority from a written agreement between the parties. Oral agreements are valid but are not subject to the Arbitration Acts. This can result in evidential difficulties and either party can resort to the courts at any time before the arbitrators' award is made.

Arbitration can be expensive as an arbitrator charges for his time (a judge does not), and institutional arbitrations impose administrative costs which can be substantial. There can also be delays as an arbitrator cannot compel a party to comply with his directions unless he is given power so to do by the court.

In England an arbitrator will seldom be an experienced lawyer; thus when mixed questions of fact and law or purely legal questions are involved in commercial disputes it can be cheaper and quicker to appoint a judge of the commercial court as sole arbitrator. Alternatively, the commercial court is capable of conducting speedy trials where it is imperative that a decision is obtained urgently.

The advantages of arbitration lie in its informality, as the strict rules of the court do not apply; in its privacy, as the award is published only to the parties and the hearing is private and informal. In cases where there are technical issues in dispute, the arbitrators can be selected from persons with the requisite technical knowledge.

It is no more difficult to enforce an arbitration award than a court judgment and indeed, internationally, it is sometimes easier to enforce an award.

The courts still play a significant part in English arbitration although the right of appeal from an award is limited by the Arbitration Act 1979. See EXCLUSION AGREEMENT, INTERNATIONAL ARBITRATION and UMPIRE.

ARBITRATOR. The person to whom disputes are referred under an arbitration agreement. Any person can be appointed an arbitrator provided that he is of sound mind. If the arbitration clause requires that the arbitrator shall have certain qualifications, he must possess them. For instance, if the requirement is for a 'commercial man', a practising barrister is not *per se* eligible for appointment.

An arbitrator is not justified in departing from normal rules of procedure even if the arbitration is a commercial one; he must act fairly to both parties; not hear one party or his witnesses in the absence of the other party or his representative, and he must decide the dispute presented to him: neither more nor less.

ARTICLED CLERKS. The Dickensian relationship which existed between the trainee solicitor and his principal has been overtaken by obligations which bind both for two years and require the solicitor to instil into the clerk a working knowledge of at least three legal disciplines before he is set loose to practise on the unsuspecting public.

ARTICLES OF ASSOCIATION. The internal regulations of a company and the equivalent of the bye-laws of a US corporation. Together with the Memorandum they form the company's 'constitution' and are available for inspection on the public record at the Companies Registry. They constitute a contract between the company and each of its members, but can be amended by special resolution (which does not require the approval of all members).

ARTICLES 85 AND 86 EEC TREATY. These provisions of the Treaty of

Rome prohibit agreements, concerted practices, and abuses of monopoly power by undertakings which perceptibly affect competition within the EEC.

Examples of agreements or concerted practices prohibited by Article 85(1) are those which directly or indirectly fix purchase or selling prices or other trading conditions, limit or control production, markets, technical development or investment, share markets or sources of supply, or apply discriminatory or anti-competitive conditions.

There is a limited exception to the basic prohibition against restrictive agreements and practices where it can be shown that they contribute to improving the production or distribution of goods, or promote technical or economic progress, while allowing consumers a fair share of the resulting benefit.

The European Commission, which administers EEC competition policy, has enacted a number of block exemptions in areas such as exclusive distribution and patent licensing agreements.

The prohibition against an abuse of a dominant position contained in Article 86 prevents the abusive or anti-competitive exercise of monopoly power in the Common Market. The existence of a 'dominant position' will depend on how the 'relevant market' is defined. Case law points to a narrow definition; for example, bananas constitute a separate market from other types of fruit and each vitamin category a distinct market from the other. See ANTITRUST and COMPETITION LAW.

ASSIGNMENT. An outright transfer of rights, for example intellectual property rights, leasehold interests in land or rights under contracts, from one person to another. Many rights, including the rights of a book publisher and of a software user, are 'personal' rights which may not be freely assigned unless the contract otherwise provides. This may cause difficulties on the sale of a business. See CHOSES IN ACTION.

ASSIGNMENT OF CONTRACTS. The benefit of contractual rights is capable of being assigned and transferred except those that involve personal skill or confidence. An assignment gives the assignee a right of action against the assignor and, once notice has been given, the debtor. A debtor cannot assign the burden of his obligations under a contract unless the creditor agrees: such an assignment is known as novation.

ASSOCIATED COMPANY. A salt and pepper phrase with a variety of meanings. Generally it distinguishes companies linked by a shareholding ranging from 20 per cent up to 50 per cent from companies which are subsidiaries.

For corporation tax purposes, they are companies one of which has control over the other or both of which are controlled by the same person. The Act applies the term to fair dealings by directors, where an associated company is one in which a director has at least 20 per cent of the voting power or equity share capital.

There is exemption from stamp duty for transfers of property between associated companies, one of which owns at least 90 per cent of the other or both of which are at least 90 per cent owned by a third company.

In accountancy, a company is associated if, broadly, an investing company can exercise significant influence over it. There is a presumption that a 20 per cent holding carries significant influence; a smaller holding does not.

The City Code regards a company and its associated companies (and, indeed, the associated companies of its associated companies) as all acting in concert with each other, the relevant test being ownership or control of 20 per cent or more.

ATTACHMENT. The execution of a judgment over assets of the defendant. There are various forms, depending upon the type of asset concerned, including: against goods or cash, by writ of *fieri facias* in the High Court; against land, securities, partnership interests and funds held by the court, by charging order; against debts due to the defendant, by garnishee order. Attachment is also a method used by the High Court for the punishment of contempt of court.

ATTESTATION. An essential element when a bill of sale, deed, will or power of appointment is signed, but not for other purposes. It is the witnessing and subscription by a person of another's signature for the purpose of testifying as to its genuineness. In the case of a will and bill of sale, failure to comply with the statutory requirements for attestation invalidates the document.

ATTORNEY. A US lawyer, of whom there are about 650,000. He is an officer of the court as well as agent of his client. He has to be licensed by the state in which he practises, which also qualifies him to practise in the federal courts. Being licensed in one state does not carry the right to practise in other states.

Alternatively, a synonym for an agent, appointed by some formal document, usually under seal. See POWER OF ATTORNEY.

The top ten US law firms (by gross revenue)

	gross revenue in 1985
	$Million
Skadden Arps Slate Meagher & Flom, NY	129
Baker & Mackenzie, Chicago	121
Shearman & Sterling, NY	107
Vinson & Elkins, Houston	106.5
Gibson Dunn & Crutcher, LA	101
Davis Polk & Waldwell, NY	91
Finley Kumble Wagner Heimer Underberg & Casey, NY	91
Cravath Swaine & Moore, NY	82
Jones Day Reavis & Pogue, Cleveland	82
Sidley & Austin, Chicago	81.5

ATTORNEY-GENERAL Member of Parliament and barrister who is the principal law officer of the Crown and head of the English bar. Makes infrequent court appearances as prosecutor in important criminal cases and on behalf of the Crown in constitutional cases.

In the USA the Attorney-General is a member of the cabinet appointed by the President. He is the head of the Justice Department and the government's lawyer. The best known Attorney-General was probably Robert F. Kennedy.

AUDITORS. One of the safeguards for investors and creditors of a company is its auditors who act independently of management in examining and reporting to the members upon its books and accounts and whether the directors' report is consistent with the accounts. All companies (unless dormant) must have an auditor whose report must be read out at the annual general meeting. An auditor must be a member of the accountancy profession and cannot be a director or secretary of the company.

Their independence of management is, hypothetically at least, safeguarded by enabling them to make representations to shareholders if they are removed. The procedure for their resignation is also, theoretically, designed to ensure that they cannot do so in order to avoid exposing a scandal.

However, auditors normally also act as financial advisers. Accordingly, they suffer from an inherent conflict of interest in that they are often passing judgment on matters on which they advised.

The degree of skill and care which an auditor has to display has been significantly increased in recent years. Consequently, as one New South Wales judge cautioned, in view of the more exacting standards which now prevail, one should beware of 'the slavish use of judicial observations'. But it is from decided cases that one can opine that an auditor's vital task is to see that errors are not made. If there is anything calculated to excite suspicion he should probe it to the bottom. But he is not bound to be a detective and is justified in believing trusted employees of the company. He is a watchdog but not a bloodhound.

His contractual duty is to the company, not the members, but he may be liable in tort for negligence to a member or prospective investor if he gives false information or unsound advice about the company's prospects, knowing that it is intended to be acted upon. See PROFESSIONAL NEGLIGENCE and SPECIAL NOTICE.

AUTHORIZED CAPITAL. The capital of a company authorized by its Memorandum or subsequently increased by shareholders' resolution. It is divided into shares of a fixed nominal amount. The authorized minimum capital of a public company is £50,000, of which at least 25 per cent must be paid up. There is no minimum for a private company. See ISSUED CAPITAL.

AUTHORIZED INVESTMENT TRUST. See INVESTMENT COMPANY.

AUTHORIZED UNIT TRUSTS. Authorization has nothing to do with the quality of investment performance. It relates to compliance with the many conditions required by the DTI or the Securities and Investment Board. It gives tax advantages to an investor. Unauthorized unit trusts can only be marketed in the UK to professional securities investors. Under the proposed FSA 1986, trusts can be 'authorized', if their managers are authorized investment businesses, regardless of what they invest in.

AVOCAT. Attorney admitted to practise before the courts of Belgium, France and the French-speaking area of Switzerland. Has right of audience in all courts and will generally be involved in both advising and planning on legal issues. Certain issues are reserved for notaries, such as establishing companies and making wills.

Other similarly qualified lawyers are avvocato in Italy, abogado in Spain, advogado in Portugal, advokat in Denmark and Sweden, and advokaat in Holland.

AVOIDANCE AND EVASION. Tax avoidance is lawful; tax evasion is illegal. If a person emigrates to reduce his tax burden he is avoiding tax; if he tells the Inland Revenue that he has emigrated when he has not, that is tax evasion. (The difference is sometimes cynically defined by reference to the quality of the professional advice that a particular taxpayer can afford.)

There are specific measures which enable the Inland Revenue to tax a transaction unless it can be shown that there was no tax avoidance motive, but there is no general anti-avoidance provision in the UK.

The basic approach of the UK tax system until 1984 was that stated in the Duke of Westminster case by Lord Tomlin: 'every man is entitled if he can to arrange his affairs so that the tax attaching under the appropriate Acts is less than it otherwise would be . . .'. By a process stemming from the decision in *Ramsay* v *IRC* in 1981 and ending – at least for the time being – in *Furniss* v *Dawson* in 1984, the Westminster doctrine is at least in doubt and at best diluted, as a concept of 'unacceptable' tax avoidance now applies.

The House of Lords decided that they were not going to stand still while the techniques of tax avoidance were improving. Thus courts now ignore any steps inserted without commercial purpose in a pre-ordained series of transactions or a single composite transaction. In consequence, the 'real' transaction is exposed and taxed accordingly.

AWARD. The decision in an arbitration by the arbitrator or umpire. In order to be a valid, and hence enforceable, award, a number of requirements have to be satisfied. Among these are that it must be a final decision on all matters requiring determination by the arbitrator, although an arbitrator may render an interim or partial award on a preliminary point. The award must also be supported by reasons where requested by either of the parties, and to comply with international practice most awards are today given with reasons. A valid award is conclusive evidence of the facts found by it as between the parties: evidence cannot be given to contradict it unless it is impeached by action in the courts.

B

BAILMENT. The delivery of goods into the possession of a person with an express or implied condition that they are to be returned in accordance with instructions when the purpose for which delivery was made has been fulfilled. Examples are, taking clothes to the cleaners, family jewels to the pawnbroker, or shares to a bank for safekeeping.

A bailee must take reasonable care of the goods. If he departs from the terms of the bailment, he will be liable for their loss or damage – unless he can show that the loss would have happened anyway.

BANK. Virtually the only things a bank owes to its customers (apart from their money!) are duties of care, skill and confidentiality. While it may provide many services, its essential characteristics are keeping current and deposit accounts and collecting cheques for and honouring cheques drawn by customers. UK banks, unlike those in the USA, can engage in underwriting and deal in securities. An institution may not call itself a bank nor accept deposits unless it is recognized under the Banking Act 1979.

The accounts and disclosure provisions of the Act applicable to banks are in some respects different from those of other companies. Banks can, for example, keep 'hidden' reserves, a privilege which they guard jealously.

John Maynard Keynes once observed that, if you owe your bank £1,000, you have a problem; but, if you owe them £1 million, they have a problem. See BANKING ACT 1979, DEALERS IN SECURITIES and SET-OFF.

BANK OF ENGLAND. Sometimes reviled, more often revered, it is England's central bank which acts as lender of last resort; it is the equivalent of the US Federal Reserve as it influences monetary policy. It was a private bank until 1946, when it was nationalized. Although its Governor is appointed by the Prime Minister, and the Chancellor of the Exchequer can direct its policy, it is constitutionally independent of government. In practice, however, it behaves as instructed – unlike the US Fed it does not have an independent role in monetary policy.

It controls capital-raising in the City of London, administers the Banking Act and regulates the gilt-edged market. It also acts informally as spokesman for city interests. After Big Bang and the acquisition of Stock Exchange member firms by banks it has become even more involved with the securities industry.

BANKERS' BOOKS EVIDENCE ACT 1879. A bank which is not a party to an action or arbitration can only be compelled to produce its books on the order of a judge. The order overrides the bank's duty of confidentiality.

The court may allow parties to legal proceedings to inspect and copy entries in bankers' books for those proceedings alone. The court's powers must be exercised in conformity with the law of discovery which, contrary to US practice, does not allow 'fishing' for evidence.

BANKER'S DRAFT. A promise to pay on demand, issued by a clearing bank. Although not technically a cheque, it can be thought of as a cheque drawn by a clearing bank on itself. It is a false belief to think it is irrevocable: it can be 'stopped' just like an ordinary cheque. Unlike a cheque, however, it will immediately be debited to the customer's account, and will be accepted by the recipient as if it were cash.

BANKING ACT 1979. This statute regulates the acceptance of deposits. Except for banks recognized as such by the Bank of England, all deposit-takers have to be licensed by the Bank unless an exemption applies, whether by reference to the deposit-taker (such as members of The Stock Exchange) or the type of deposit (such as certain corporate bonds).

The Bank of England administers the Banking Act, and at present applies it to companies who issue debt securities on a regular basis and to securities dealers who retain for their own account interest earned on clients' funds held while awaiting investment. It forbids domestic institutions calling themselves 'banks' unless they are recognized. Other deposit-taking institutions, including English branches of foreign banks, must refer to themselves as a licensed institution.

Because of the Johnson Matthey affair in 1985 where the supervision of that bank, as well as others, became suspect, it is intended to tighten regulation of both recognized banks and other deposit-taking institutions. Moreover, an advisory board has been appointed to advise the Bank of England on its banking supervisory role.

BANKRUPTCY. On 11 November 1761, John Perrott, a bankrupt, was hanged at Smithfield for concealing part of his effects. The law is now more lenient; some would say too lenient, for it is by no means unknown for the unscrupulous to seek bankruptcy as a way of being relieved of debts they have no intention of paying.

Bankruptcy is the state of personal insolvency, which often starts with a debtor failing to satisfy a demand for an outstanding debt and leads to his property and affairs being put in the hands of a trustee, who realizes assets and distributes them for the benefit of creditors.

The Insolvency Act 1985 has simplified the former administrative maze of procedures, enabling creditors' meetings and public examinations to be avoided and introducing a personal voluntary arrangement procedure, whereby a debtor can avoid bankruptcy altogether by getting his creditors to accept a scheme or proposal.

The 1985 Act also provides a system of automatic and early discharge from bankruptcy. Restrictions on undischarged bankrupts still prevent them from obtaining credit, disposing of property or becoming directors, solicitors, MPs or local councillors.

BARRISTER. A lawyer-advocate (sometimes called 'counsel') who is a member of one of the Inns of Court and has the exclusive right of audience in the High Court (a right which is being challenged and in time will probably disappear). Probably because they cannot sue for their fees, they are often called the gentlemen of the legal profession, much to the annoyance of solicitors, without whose instructions they may not appear in court. They cannot practise in partnership and are therefore very conscious of their health. A person intending to become a barrister must join one of the Inns of Court. He must eat dinners there and pass exams, which are both of minimal quality (which barristers deny!).

A solicitor is, in general, not bound to accept instructions from a particular client. It is a general principle of the code of conduct which a barrister must observe that he is bound to accept any brief to appear before a court in a field in which he professes to practise at a proper fee except in exceptional circumstances such as conflict of interest.

Junior barristers (who are sometimes senior) wear gowns of stuff. Their seniors, known as Queen's Counsel (QC), wear silk gowns and must have practised for a minimum of eight years with (normally but not always) a certain amount of distinction. Judges of the High Court are drawn exclusively from members of the bar. On 1 January 1986, there were 5,367 practising barristers in England and Wales.

A solicitor who takes, and acts upon, competent counsel's opinion will be protected from a claim for negligence; but he should choose carefully, as the range of competence and experience at the bar is very wide. Except for top specialists, barristers undercharge (relatively) for opinions, and then make up for it by their charges for courtroom work. See BRIEF.

BATTERY. See TRESPASS TO THE PERSON

BEARER SECURITIES. Shares or bonds which can be transferred by delivery without endorsement or any other formality, ownership being evidenced by a certificate. Anyone who claims payment or ownership need only present the certificate. Coupons are usually attached, which are presented against payment of interest or dividends.

The owner remains unknown to the tax man and the issuer alike; thus they have an international appeal.

Bearer shares can be issued by a UK company on payment of the appropriate stamp duty and can thereafter be transferred free of transfer duty.

BEAR-HUG. An expression demonstrating the unsurpassed ability of Americans to ascribe colourful nouns to prosaic actions. Bear-hug is a pre-bid approach to directors to acquire their company. The approaches are varied in firmness and forcefulness, e.g. 'teddy-bear-hug' is a soft approach, without publicity.

BENEFICIAL OWNER. The person entitled to the benefit of property, as distinct from a legal or nominal owner who merely holds property on trust. If a person tranfers property 'as beneficial owner' it implies covenants as to the validity of title and for quiet enjoyment in favour of the transferee.

BENEFICIARY. A fortunate person for whose benefit, whether alone or with others, property is held by one or more trustees (who may include the beneficiary).

Alternatively, the person on whose behalf a letter of credit is issued.

BIG BANG. The New York Stock Exchange did it in 1976; The London Stock Exchange followed in October 1986. It is the name given to the abandonment of the system of fixed commissions, which was intended in part to protect the smaller broker.

This dealt a death blow to insistence on single capacity by The Stock Exchange under which firms which dealt as principal for their own account (jobbers) could not also deal as agents on behalf of clients (brokers). Big Bang therefore includes the introduction of dual capacity on The Stock Exchange. This has led to the need for additional capital by market makers, which is one of the reasons for the revolution in the grouping of brokers, bankers and jobbers in the City of London. They will be subject to self-regulation under the proposed FSA 1986, which rivals the complexity of any taxing statute. See CONFLICT OF INTEREST and DEALERS IN SECURITIES.

BIG TICKET LEASING. The leasing of high value assets such as ships and aircraft.

BILL OF EXCHANGE. Defined in the Bills of Exchange Act 1882 as an unconditional order in writing, addressed by one person to another, signed by the person giving it, requiring the person to whom it is addressed to pay on demand or at a fixed or determinable future time a sum certain in money to or to the order of a specified person, or to bearer. An instrument which does not comply with these conditions, or which orders any act to be done in addition to the payment of money, is not a bill of exchange. See NEGOTIABLE INSTRUMENT.

BILL OF LADING. A receipt for goods delivered to and received by a shipper and the document which gives title to the goods during transit. The bill must be signed by the shipper or his agent. The buyer obtains the goods by presenting his copy of the bill to the master of the ship.

A clean bill of lading indicates that the goods are 'shipped in apparent good order and condition'. A foul or dirty bill notes that the goods have been put on board in a defective condition.

When goods are carried by air, the bill is referred to as an 'airway bill'.

BILL OF SALE. An assignment of goods under seal, usually as security for a mortgage, or a gift, where the donor remains in possession of the goods. The Bill of Sale Acts do not apply to charges given by companies.

Warning: this form of security should be avoided as failure to comply strictly with the formalities will invalidate the transaction.

BLUE SKY LAWS. US state governments started regulating the securities industry when Kansas, in 1911, first required registration of securities salesmen to protect the unsophisticated investor. State securities acts were nicknamed 'blue sky' laws because they were intended to prevent 'speculative schemes which have no more basis than so many feet of "blue sky" '.

Alien corporations wishing to issue securities in the USA must comply with state government regulations. Unlike federal regulations, state laws vary widely from state to state, but must be complied with in each instance in which there is no applicable exemption. In one case a Japanese company followed a common Japanese business practice of making loans to officers and employees. Its securities could not be registered in many states because this practice contravened applicable blue sky laws.

BOARD COMMITTEE. If empowered by the Articles, directors may delegate their powers to committees. One director can constitute a committee.

It is now good practice in the UK, following in that respect the USA, to ask non-executive directors to sit on committees where disinterested supervision is needed. Typically, these are the compensation committee, with responsibility for approving the remuneration of top management, and the audit committee, which reviews the accounts and auditing matters. An important committee in the USA which does not seem to exist in the UK is the nominating committee, which has responsibility for recommending persons to fill board vacancies.

Certain matters are, as a matter of law or practice, not capable of delegation to a committee. The Articles, for instance, may provide that the decision to allot shares is one that can only be taken by a full board. A major decision, such as the issue of a prospectus, should be taken by a full board, although final revision may be entrusted to committee.

BOARD OF DIRECTORS. The Articles usually delegate the company's powers and management of its business to the directors, acting as a board. Notice of meetings must generally be given to all directors in the UK. The length of notice varies according to the practice of the company: in some cases hours or even minutes would suffice. Notice need not be in writing, nor need it state the purpose of the meeting. Despite contrary desires by his colleagues, a director should not be excluded from board meetings.

Minutes of the meetings must be taken, but otherwise their conduct is largely a matter for the directors themselves. See BOARD COMMITTEE.

BONA FIDES. See GOOD FAITH.

BONA VACANTIA. Property which does not belong to anyone. On a dissolution of a company its undisposed-of property vests in the Crown as *bona vacantia*, subject to the Crown's right to disclaim. Royal fish, shipwrecks, treasure trove, waifs and estrays (valuable animals) found without any apparent owner also belong to the Crown.

BOND. A document, sometimes signed under seal, by which a person binds himself to do certain acts, e.g. to repay borrowed money on a stated date. Governments, and corporations, issue bonds to raise money on international markets. See BEARER SECURITIES.

BONUS ISSUE. After approval by shareholders in general meeting, reserves, including undistributed profits, are used to pay up unissued shares. These are distributed to ordinary shareholders without any payment by them. The purpose is either to bring the issued share capital of a company into line with the capital employed in its business or to make its shares more marketable.

While 'bonus' may connote an element of bounty, there is, in fact, none; each holder's proportion of equity in the company remains the same both before and after the issue, although he has a higher number of shares.

Alternatively called a scrip issue or capitalization issue, which were in common use in the 1960s to avoid provoking trade unions, for the word 'bonus' was regarded as inflammatory. Known in the USA as a stock dividend.

BOOTSTRAP BID. An attempt to achieve control of a US company by someone with limited financial resources. It involves the conditional sale of the assets of the company by the intended bidder before the bid is made, in return for being provided with the money to enable him to make the bid.

BORROWING. An agreement to borrow and lend is essentially no different from any other contract. The obligations of a borrower may be void or unenforceable, if the loan agreement is unlawful. If it causes a breach of another loan agreement the lender may be liable for any loss suffered by the other lender.

The Act prohibits a company from making a loan to a director or a director of a holding company and from providing a guarantee or security in connection with such a loan. The restriction extends to transactions in favour of connected persons. A public company must not provide financial assistance, including loans, for the purpose of purchasing its own shares.

It is unlawful for a UK company to permit a foreign company over which it has control to create or issue any debentures unless the UK Treasury consents. See TRACING and USURY.

BORROWING POWERS. A company may borrow money only if it is authorized to do so by its Memorandum and does so for the purposes of its objects. It would be unusual in the extreme for a trading company not to have power to borrow for the purposes of its business.

The ability of a company to borrow is restricted not only by its creditworthiness, but also by any limit on the amount of borrowings imposed by its Articles, as well as by any undertakings given in connection with any prior borrowings made by it.

There are safeguards for the innocent lender whose loan to a company exceeds the borrowing limits in the Articles. However, if the limit can only be exceeded by the authority of a special or extraordinary resolution, a lender is deemed to have constructive notice of their existence or absence. If a lender does not act in good faith and the authority to borrow is not properly given, the loan will be invalid.

BRANCH. A secondary establishment through which a company carries on its business. A branch is part of a company, not a separate entity. A foreign company carrying on business in the UK through a branch will have to register as an oversea company. Profits from a trade carried on in the UK by a branch of a company resident outside the UK are liable to UK taxation but have the benefit of any double tax convention between the UK and the home territory of the company.

BREACH OF CONTRACT. An innocent party is always entitled to bring an action for damages for a breach of contract and in some circumstances he has the right to specific performance.

Where a broken obligation is of significant, as opposed to minor, importance, the innocent party is entitled to claim that he is discharged from further liability: there has, in legal terms, been a fundamental breach.

Delightful metaphors have been used by judges in their attempts to formulate a test for a breach of major importance. Their favourite for over 150 years has been 'the root of the contract' so that a breach will not discharge a party from further liability unless it goes to the whole root, and not merely part, of the contract.

Where there is a fundamental breach, the innocent party may elect to treat the contract as continuing. In that event, he must perform his obligations and can recover damages for any loss he may sustain. If he chooses to accept the breach as discharging the contract, he can take action for a declaration that the contract is terminated, which will confirm (or not) that he was right. He may sue for damages, but if the value of any work done exceeds the amount that would have been due to him had the contract been performed, he will be better advised to claim a *quantum meruit* for the value of the work. See ANTICIPATORY BREACH and DAMAGES.

BREACH OF WARRANTY OF AUTHORITY. A person who acts, or purports to act, as an agent is deemed to warrant to persons with whom he deals that he has due authority from his principal. If the authority does not exist, and even if he acts in good faith, he is liable for any loss caused to persons who relied on the warranty.

When a director negotiates he impliedly warrants that he has authority to bind the company as its agent. If he lacks the authority he is personally liable, for instance if he accepts a bill of exchange in the company's name when the company did not have power so to do by its Memorandum or if he negotiates a loan to the company which results in it exceeding its borrowing powers.

The warranty may be excluded expressly. It does not apply where a person knows that the agent's authority is limited.

BRIBERY. A gift made to someone of influence with the intention of inducing him to show favour (or even not show disfavour) towards a particular person. If store buyers, company directors and other agents, never mind local councillors, were aware that the giving or acceptance of bribes could have both criminal and civil law consequences, would they accept the poisoned gift?

Any agent who accepts a bribe, and anyone who bribes an agent, so as to influence the affairs or business of his principal, commits a criminal offence if he does so corruptly i.e. with an evil mind or intention. If the bribe is to a person employed by the Crown or any government department or public body, and relates to a contract with that person, it is deemed to have been given or accepted corruptly. The maximum penalty is seven years' imprisonment.

The agent who, unknown to his principal, allows himself to be bribed in the conduct of his principal's business must account to his principal for the amount of the bribe, and is liable in the tort of deceit for any loss suffered by the principal as a result of entering into the transaction to which the bribe relates. Normally, the person who offered the bribe is similarly liable.

BRIEF. A misnomer for a sometimes lengthy statement of a client's case prepared by a solicitor for the benefit of the barrister.

When miniskirts were fashionable, a notice was displayed in the Inns of Court requesting lady barristers to wear skirts of decent length; it was annotated with the words 'This is to prevent the premature disclosure of instructions endorsed on Counsel's briefs'.

BROKER. Nothing esoteric: it is merely another name for an agent.

BULLDOG ISSUE. A sterling denominated Eurobond issue sold into the domestic UK market. A Euro-sterling issue is sold to non-residents of the UK.

BUNDESKARTELLAMT. The Federal Cartel Office in Berlin which administers and enforces the West German law against restraints on competition (*Gesetz gegen Wettbewerbsbeschränkungen*), the most wide-ranging competition law in Europe. It has very extensive powers to make investigations and impose orders and fines.

BURDEN OF PROOF. 'He who alleges must prove'. The burden of proof in any trial is usually on the person claiming the remedy:

he must prove the facts, and show that those facts constitute a breach of contract, negligence or whatever else he is alleging. But some facts do not need to be proved because they are presumed; for example, that a person is dead if he has not been heard of for seven years.

To discharge the burden of proof, and win the case, facts need to be proved to a particular standard: in civil cases, the judge must be satisfied 'on the balance of probabilities'; in criminal cases the magistrates or jury must be satisfied 'beyond reasonable doubt'. However, the burden of proof may be 'shifted' to the other side by certain presumptions or if evidence sufficient to establish a *prima facie* case is adduced.

BUSINESS EXPANSION SCHEME. It allows an individual to deduct from taxable income, and not merely from capital gains, new, full risk, share investments of up to £40,000 per annum in unquoted trading companies. Investment may also be made through one of the many BES funds which, for a fee (often for several very generous fees), invest in a range of companies, thus spreading what has, in practice, proved to be a high risk.

The relief is subject to many detailed conditions being satisfied both by the investor and the company in which the investment is made. In particular, the shares must be held for at least five years but can then be sold free of any capital gains tax.

BUSINESS JUDGMENT RULE. A fundamental principle of US corporate law that the business and affairs of a corporation are governed by its board of directors rather than its shareholders. The doctrine was developed because the courts are reluctant to substitute their judgment for that of directors acting in good faith on corporate business decisions. It has the incidental advantage of enabling corporations to attract as directors suitably qualified people, who would otherwise be put off by the threat of litigation from shareholders disagreeing with the board.

The rule creates a strong presumption of propriety in favour of the board. It bars judicial enquiry into actions of corporate directors taken in good faith and in the exercise of honest judgment in the lawful and legitimate furtherance of the corporation's purposes. The rule, therefore, goes further than the English court's normal reluctance to substitute its own commercial judgment for that of directors.

BUSINESS NAME. Not all companies carry on business under their corporate names, or partnerships under the surnames of all the partners. The name which they use to identify themselves is called a business name. It is a criminal offence for a business name to be used if it is likely to give the impression that the business is connected with the government or any local authority.

The law is contained in the Business Names Act 1985, which requires the disclosure of the name of each partner and, in the case of a company, its corporate name, in all business communications. There are certain exceptions in the case of a partnership of more than 20 persons. SEE PASSING-OFF.

BUY-BACK. A form of countertrade or barter transaction in which an exporter delivering goods, usually plant or machinery, to an importer receives in full or partial payment goods produced by that plant or machinery. It was under a buy-back agreement that Levi Strauss sold a foreign plant and the design of its famous jeans to Hungary, with 20 per cent of the payments for the plant and technology consisting of finished products from the Hungarian plant.

BYE-LAWS. See ARTICLES OF ASSOCIATION.

C

CALLS ON SHARES. A demand by a company for all or part of the outstanding amount of the issue price of partly-paid shares. Calls must generally be made equally on all shareholders of the same class and, when made, create a debt between the company and the shareholder.

CAPACITY. See CONTRACTUAL CAPACITY.

CAPITAL DUTY. A stamp duty payable on the raising of capital by limited companies and limited partnerships. The duty is payable on the value of assets contributed at a rate of £1 per £100 or part of £100. It raised over £130 million for the UK revenue in 1985.

A company can apply for exemption from the duty when it acquires, in exchange for its shares, at least 75 per cent of the issued share capital or all or part of the business of another company. The exemption may be lost if the holding is subsequently reduced.

The duty is not payable on the issue of loan stock, but will arise on the conversion of convertible loan stock.

CAPITAL GAINS TAX. Was introduced by a Conservative government as a short-term gains tax. It is now payable at the rate of 30 per cent on all capital gains realized by UK residents. Companies pay corporation tax on realized capital gains.

Capital gains (or losses) are generally calculated on the difference between the consideration received on the disposal of an asset and the aggregate of the cost of acquiring the asset, the expenditure incurred to enhance its value and costs incidental to its disposal.

It is quite a big money spinner for the UK revenue, who collected about £497 million in assessments made in 1984 on 84,900 individuals and companies. They did much better two years earlier when they collected £728 million.

CAPITAL REDEMPTION RESERVE. In order to protect creditors when a company redeems or purchases its shares out of profits, a sum equal to the amount by which its issued share capital is diminished by the cancellation or redemption has to be tranferred to the capital redemption reserve. The reserve is treated for all purposes as if it were paid-up share capital but may be used to pay up unissued shares on a bonus issue.

CAPITAL TRANSFER TAX. A combination of gift tax and death duties to be abolished by the Finance Act 1986 and replaced by an inheritance tax. The Capital Transfer Tax Act 1984 has been retrospectively named the Inheritance Tax Act. All references in wills and other documents to capital transfer tax are construed as referring to inheritance tax.

CAPITALIZATION ISSUE. See BONUS ISSUE.

CARRIED INTEREST. An incentive arrangement for the management of (usually) an investment fund to participate in the capital, or sometimes revenue, profits of the fund: commonly given in the venture capital industry and investment partnerships.

The participation usually operates after the investors have received a return equal to their initial investment and, in some cases, a notional interest rate or an amount equal to the increase in the retail prices index (the addition being described as a 'hurdle rate'). The amount of the carried interest is typically between 10 per cent and 25 per cent of growth.

CASE STATED. A form of appeal from a suspect judgment of a court or tribunal. A concise statement of the facts (which is supposed to be prepared by the tribunal or court but is, in practice, drafted by the appellant) is presented to a superior court which determines whether or not the decision was well founded in law.

It is also the correct form of appeal to the High Court or Court of Appeal from decisions of government ministers and tribunals in administrative matters as diverse as planning, taxation, and mental health, as well as on a point of law from a Magistrates' Court.

CAUSATION. In a claim for damages for negligence, the plaintiff must prove that the defendant's negligence was a cause, and not too remote a cause, of his loss or injury.

The problem is to determine what is not too remote, and is judged on a common-sense view: 'causation is to be understood as the man in the street, and not as either the scientist or the metaphysician, would understand it'.

CAVEAT. A notice lodged at a probate registry which prevents probate of a will being granted without first notifying the person who lodged the notice.

This enables a person who disputes the validity of a will, or wishes to claim an interest under it, to make enquiries, and bring his claim before the courts, before the will is proved.

CAVEAT EMPTOR. Let the buyer take care. The common law rule under which the buyer must satisfy himself as to the quality of goods and the seller need not disclose defects known to him.

The rule has been substantially eroded by statutes which imply warranties in favour of the buyer. It is still relevant where the sale is not made in the course of the seller's business, e.g. when a car is bought from a friend rather than a second-hand dealer.

CERTIFICATE OF INCORPORATION. The birth certificate of a company issued and signed by the Registrar. It is conclusive evidence that all the requirements of registration have been complied with and that the association is a company authorized to be registered and is registered. It avoids the US problem where defectively formed corporations have been a fruitful source of litigation for attorneys.

CERTIFICATION TRADEMARK. A trade or collective mark which distinguishes goods not by the identity of their supplier but by reference to their peculiar characteristics, such as their material, mode of manufacture, quality or accuracy. Examples are the International Woolmark and Harris Tweed. The goods have to be certified by the owner of the mark as conforming to the relevant distinguishing characteristic.

The marks can be protected in some 94 countries who are parties to the International Convention for Protection of Industrial Property.

CERTIORARI. See JUDICIAL REVIEW.

CHAIRMAN. The chairman has no greater power than that of any other director. He presides at meetings of the board of directors and at general meetings of the company. He does not have a second or casting vote in the event of a tie unless the Articles so provide. It is his personality, political skill or personal achievements which endow his leadership with authority.

CHAMBERS. The office of a judge or barrister.

CHANCELLOR OF THE EXCHEQUER. Political head of the government department known as the Treasury, which deals with revenue and disbursement of payments on behalf of the public services of the UK. The Inland Revenue comes under his authority. His annual moment of (hopeful) glory is when he delivers his budget speech.

CHANCERY DIVISION. A division of the High Court. It springs from the former Court of Chancery, which was presided over by the Lord Chancellor. From the sixteenth century it developed and applied the principles of equity so as to grant relief from the rigours of the common law.

All High Court actions concerning company law, taxation, patents, copyright, probate, trusts and mortgages are assigned to the division. It deals with approximately one action to every 25 dealt with by the Queen's Bench division: in 1984 approximately 7,500 actions were commenced in Chancery compared with 190,000 in Queen's Bench.

CHAPTER 11. A US procedure by which a US insolvent corporation can reorganize and settle its accounts under the supervision of the US Bankruptcy Court and one or more committees composed of its creditors, without going into liquidation.

All unsecured creditors are bound by the terms of an approved plan of reorganization. The plan does not need to provide for payment to creditors in accordance with strict priority of claims: so a superior creditor need not get 100 cents in the dollar before lower tier creditors. The plan has to be approved by the court, and by a majority in number and two thirds in amount of each class of creditor.

The procedure gives a corporation an opportunity to rise from ashes: a feat accomplished by Wickes Companies Inc. in three years after going into Chapter 11 in 1982, as probably the biggest ever US corporate insolvency. Recently it has been used to avoid penal litigation (such as in asbestos cases) and to reject onerous labour and other contracts (as with Continental Airlines in respect of labour contracts of pilots and mechanics).

CHARGES. Synonym for mortgages over a company's assets. There are nine categories of charge created by companies which have to be registered with the Registrar, although the government is now reviewing the whole question of registration.

If priority over subsequent charges is to be maintained, registration may also be required in other registers, e.g. charges over patents with the patent office, those over ships in the ship's port of registry, a mortgage over an aircraft in the registry of air mortgages, those over real property at the land charges registry or the land registry. See CHARGES REGISTER, FIXED CHARGE and FLOATING CHARGE.

CHARGES REGISTER. Registrable charges over the assets of a company must be entered in a charges register kept at its registered office and available for inspection by the public, as well as in the charges register of the company kept by the Registrar. Failure to register a charge with the Registrar within 21 days of creation may result in the charge being void against other creditors and any liquidator. See DEBENTURE and SLAVENBURG REGISTER.

CHARGING ORDER. A means of execution to secure payment under a judgment. It is effected by a court imposing a charge over land, securities, money in court or any interest under a trust. This does not always give the creditor the cash he wants, so he must enforce the charge in the normal way. In the case of land, the court can help by appointing a receiver to enforce the charge.

CHARITY. A trust or company established for exclusively charitable purposes, based on the statute 43 Eliz. 1 c.4 of 1601. Most charities must be registered with the Charity Commission. Charities are exempt from income and capital gains taxes on their investments, but not from tax on trading profits unless the trade is closely related to the charity, e.g. charities for the blind selling goods made by the blind. Gifts and bequests to charities are exempt from inheritance tax.

There must be an element of public benefit involved in the object of the charity: the court is sometimes called upon to judge whether or not a charitable bequest is for the benefit of the public, as in *re Pinion*, where Harman LJ in the Court of Appeal observed, 'I can conceive of no useful object to be served in foisting upon the public this mass of junk. It has neither public utility nor educative value.' See CY-PRES.

CHARITY COMMISSIONERS, THE. A Department of State headed by three Commissioners who are responsible to the Home Secretary. They are the watchdogs, overseers and advisers of charity trustees. When they approve charitable objects the Inland Revenue will almost certainly grant tax benefits. The department is helpful and conscientious.

CHEQUE. It is doubtful that many people who sign the perforated paper in their cheque book, as an alternative to paying cash or using a plastic card, realize that it is a bill of exchange payable on demand which is drawn on a bank.

The cautious customer will cross his cheque 'account payee' or 'account payee only' which will put his bank to the trouble of making stringent enquiries before it is collected for the account of anyone other than that of the payee. If the cheque is crossed '& Co.', it may only be presented through a banker; if the words 'not negotiable' are added it is still transferable, but the recipient cannot acquire greater rights than the transferor.

A bank may refuse to pay a cheque if the drawer subsequently stops it, or if the sum exceeds the credit in the account and any agreed overdraft, or if the bank is exercising a right of set-off. The use of a cheque card amounts to a warranty by the bank that the cheque will, within the limits of the card, be honoured in any event.

CHIEF EXECUTIVE OFFICER. The US equivalent of managing director. The term has become fashionable in the UK to connote someone who is superior to the managing director.

CHINESE WALLS. Self-imposed barriers within financial conglomerates but, as Professor Gower says, he has never seen a chinese wall without a grapevine growing over it. They are intended to protect investors by preventing the dissemination of price-sensitive information between separate functions within the same company or group. Their efficacy is doubtful (even if, for example, the investment management arm is physically separated, or kept in a separate company, from the corporate finance arm). If they do work they militate against the integration of function, regarded as one of the advantages of financial conglomerates.

Under the proposed FSA 1986, the Secretary of State (or a designated agency) may require a chinese wall to be erected.

CHOSES IN ACTION. All personal rights to property which are not capable of being physically possessed and which can only be claimed or enforced by action. They include debts, shares, rights under contracts and the share of a trust fund.

In the early seventeenth century, no choses in action could be assigned, except by or through the King, or with the debtor's consent. They may now be assigned, either in a manner dictated by statute (as in the case of shares) or – in the case of an interest under a trust – in writing, or in certain other cases, orally.

CIF. Cost, insurance and freight: a contract for the sale of goods under which the seller agrees at his own expense to procure and tender the appropriate shipping documents to the buyer; normally a bill of lading, sea insurance policy and the commercial invoice for the goods. It is the most widely used contract in seaborne commerce and is derived from the custom of merchants.

Ownership in the goods *prima facie* passes to the buyer when he pays the seller against delivery of the documents. The risk of loss or damage is assumed by the buyer from the time the goods effectively pass the ship's rail at the port of shipment.

It has been said that a cif contract is not a sale of goods, but a contract for the sale of documents relating to goods. Mr Justice Donaldson (now Master of the Rolls) observed in one case: 'the contract called for chinese rabbits cif. Their obligation was, therefore, to tender documents, not the rabbits themselves. If there were any chinese rabbits afloat, they could have bought them.'

CIRCUMSTANTIAL EVIDENCE. A series of circumstances leading to the inference or conclusion of guilt in the absence of direct evidence. The term is used to describe the fact which is proved, and the means of its proof.

In a murder trial, the testimony of an eye-witness who saw the victim stabbed to death is direct evidence. Evidence that the accused person had threatened the victim, had bought a knife, and that the death was caused by stabbing from that knife, which bore the finger-prints of the accused, are all items of circumstantial evidence.

Circumstantial evidence may carry as much, if not more, weight than direct evidence which may sometimes be more easily fabricated or inaccurate.

CITATION. Reference to or quotation from a case, statute or other source of law.

In probate, it is a notice issued by the court, normally requiring those entitled to a grant of administration in priority to the applicant to enter an appearance or lose their rights by default.

CITIZENSHIP. British citizenship is governed by the British Nationality Act 1981 which created three types of citizens out of those who previously constituted the citizenship of the UK and Colonies: British Citizens, British Dependent Territories Citizens, and British Overseas Citizens. Status within these groups depends on the birth, adoption, descent, registration or naturalization of the individual concerned.

The Nationality Act has many critics who feel it does not cover many issues such as civic rights and duties, and access to employment. Such rights can only be found piecemeal in legislation and common law. The only such right which the statute unequivocally confers is the right of a British citizen to entry, abode and settlement in the UK.

CITY CODE, THE. The City Code on Take-overs and Mergers is published and enforced by the City Panel. The Code, which has recently been revised to regulate the avoidance of conflicts of interest after Big Bang, regulates the way in which take-over offers may be made. It applies to all (listed or unlisted) UK resident public companies, and to certain categories of private UK and Irish companies.

The Code has no sanctions apart from ostracism by the City and The Stock Exchange. Its provisions are as a general rule observed despite the odd protestation from lawyers and merchant bankers.

CITY PANEL. The City Panel on Take-overs and Mergers, which is the UK non-statutory regulatory authority on the City Code. It operates in a charmingly British manner, sometimes citing the spirit of the rules when applicants quote the letter and vice versa.

CIVIL LIABILITY. Liability to pay damages or to be injuncted as a result of committing a tort, breach of contract or trust, or under a statute; to be contrasted with criminal liability, which is punishable by fines and/or imprisonment.

CLASS ACTION. A law suit instituted by one party on behalf of himself and several (often many) other parties with respect to common questions of law and fact. Once the principle of liability is accepted or rejected by the courts it applies equally to all the parties as the issue for them all is the same. The advantage of a class action is that all the claimants can join together to fight the principal issue of the dispute and to share in the legal costs and risk, rather than for each claimant to fight his own case with a fragmentation of arguments and positions. Normally the defendant agrees with the plaintiff to accept the final decision of the court and to give effect to it with respect to all the claimants, in return for their agreeing not to institute a plethora of legal actions all at the same time.

A class action is particularly appropriate for issues of product liability and, in the USA, securities issues. A typical example was the litigation concerning the rights of the thalidomide children against Distillers, the manufacturers of the drug taken by their mothers during pregnancy. See CONTINGENT FEE and COUNTERCLAIM.

CLASS RIGHTS. Exist where the shares of a company are divided into different classes with different rights, or members have different rights. Unless the rights are specifically conferred, the basic rights are those of dividends, capital and voting.

A variation of rights clause providing a procedure for the variation of rights is, itself, a class right, as are rights attached to a class of share by the terms of issue. See MODIFICATION OF RIGHTS.

CLAYTON'S CASE. See TRACING.

CLOG. See EQUITY OF REDEMPTION.

CLOSE COMPANIES. A company is close if it is under the control of generally not more than five shareholders and their associates, or of its directors. A listed company is not close if 35 per cent or more of its voting shares are owned by the general public. A UK subsidiary of an oversea parent company is close if the parent would have been close if resident here.

The Inland Revenue tends to view them as vehicles for tax avoidance. However, contrary to the usual rule, interest on certain loans to a close company made by shareholders or management is deductible for tax purposes.

CODE OF PRACTICE. Rules of conduct which are normally not in themselves legally binding but which establish standards to be met as good practice by the persons to whom they apply – e.g. dealers in securities or employers. They are issued by government, trade associations and self-regulatory organizations.

Failure to observe particular codes may be *prima facie* evidence of a criminal offence, or of the breach of governmental regulations, or the rules of the association or organization concerned. Breach of the rules of conduct of self-regulating organizations under the proposed FSA 1986 may entitle persons prejudiced by the breach to damages.

COLD CALLING. An unsolicited call by personal visit or telephone with a view to persuading non-professional investors to purchase insurance policies, securities, commodities or financial futures. It is intended under the proposed FSA 1986 that cold calling will be prohibited, except where the contract may be cancelled after a 'cooling off' period, or with a person with whom the caller has a written agreement.

Contravention will not constitute a criminal offence, but the resulting contracts will be unenforceable.

COLLATERAL CONTRACT. In order to do justice where a contractual relationship would otherwise not exist – e.g. to enforce a promise which induced someone to enter into a contract – the courts have developed the concept of implying the existence of a dependant or collateral contract, the consideration for which is the making of another contract. In the words of Lord Denning, 'when a person gives a promise or an assurance to another, intending that he should act on it by entering into a contract, and he does act on it by entering into the contract, we hold that it is binding.'

Collateral contracts, and the intent to form them, must be proved strictly and must not conflict with the main contract. The principle has been relied on to circumvent privity of contract and to enforce 'side' letters varying the terms of a contemporaneous agreement.

COLLATERAL SECURITY. The cautious creditor will not always be satisfied with the security offered him by a debtor and may ask for additional security to be given either by the debtor or a third party. The additional security is known as collateral. In the USA collateral means the property used as the security for an obligation.

COMFORT LETTER. An informal written statement concerning some fact or intention. The letter may, or may not, be legally binding upon the writer as a contract, representation, or guarantee: it depends on its content, not on its title.

COMMERCIAL COURT. Has five judges, its own administration, and is part of the Queen's Bench Division of the High Court. The court hears about 140 commercial cases each year relating to the carriage of goods, insurance, re-insurance, banking, and arbitration. There is a two-year waiting list, as the average case takes about six days.

COMMISSION . Remuneration paid to an agent. Commissions paid by a company for placing and underwriting share issues may not be paid out of capital unless the payment is authorized by the Articles, is not more than 10 per cent of the share price and is disclosed in the prospectus or listing particulars.

COMMISSIONER FOR OATHS. All solicitors can now administer oaths, but a commissioner is a solicitor appointed by the Lord Chancellor to do so. See AFFIDAVIT.

COMMITTEE OF INSPECTION. A committee appointed at a creditors' meeting to represent the creditors and supervise and assist in the administration of the liquidation of a company (other than in a members' voluntary winding up). A liquidator must receive the prior consent of the committee (or the court) for a number of matters including compromising claims and taking his own remuneration.

If any person, other than the Official Receiver, is appointed as trustee of a bankrupt's estate he will be subject to control by a committee of inspection.

COMMODITY TRADING. In holding that a commodity broker owed his client a duty to exercise reasonable skill in carrying out his instructions, a judge referred to the 'man-made jungle of the commodity markets'. A broker's duty does not extend to ensuring that his client is protected from losses and, as many have found, to lose money in commodity trading is one of the easiest things to do.

Formal commodity markets can be traced to the sixteenth century. They provide merchants, producers and consumers with a method of insuring against price movements; this has become known as 'hedging'. A producer might sell his coffee crop for future delivery at a particular price to safeguard himself against a fall in the market price. A consumer will buy on the futures market to insulate himself against a rise in price.

Physical commodities may be purchased or sold for their 'spot price', which is the price ruling on that day. Futures contracts are for delivery on any trading day within a period of three months in the future, because it used to take about that time for a sailing boat to travel from Chile to the UK. The forward contract price is geared to the spot price plus factors representing interest and warehousing costs. In normal market conditions the forward price will be in excess of the spot price: this interest differential is known as 'contango'. If the forward price is less than the spot price, it is known as 'backwardation'. A broker will normally require only 10 per cent of the contract value as collateral security against a forward contract. This is known as 'a margin'. The broker is entitled to call for an additional deposit known as 'a margin call' should the price of the commodity move against the speculator.

COMMON LAW. The primary unwritten law of England and Wales, whose history began in the time of Henry II in the late twelfth century with the creation of England's first central system of courts. It is the shared legal heritage of the common law countries such as Canada, Australia, New Zealand and the USA. It stands in contrast to civil law (prevalent in continental Europe and based on Roman law and the Napoleonic Code), to statute law and to equity.

COMMON SEAL. See SEAL.

COMMON STOCK. Ordinary shares of a US corporation.

COMPANY. A legal person in its own right which is regarded as an entity distinct from its shareholders. Originally, corporate personality could be acquired only by a special Act of Parliament or by Royal Charter, both slow and expensive procedures. Incorporation is now achieved under the Act and is speedy and inexpensive.

English company law is not codified; the Act is merely a new consolidation of preceding statutes. Behind the Act is a general body of law and equity, applying to all companies, which is found in case law and not in statute. The first attempt at a statute regulating companies was passed in 1720 and was known as 'the Bubble Act'. It deliberately made it difficult in practice for joint stock societies to assume a corporate form and made no rules for their conduct. It was not until 1844 that a worthwhile statute was passed, and since that time the numbers of companies have increased dramatically, as have the problems they pose, and the wealth they are responsible for creating.

COMPENSATION. Any payment to make up for loss or personal injury. Somewhat wider than the term damages, which is generally confined to sums awarded by a court in cases involving some fault.

COMPENSATION FOR LOSS OF OFFICE. Normally arises in relation to the termination of a director's service contract although the principles are equally applicable to any employee. Removal from the board of directors does not of itself give rise to a claim, although it may put the company in breach of contract.

No compensation will be payable upon termination of a director's contract where:

- he is in fundamental breach of his contract so as to justify summary dismissal without notice;
- the contract is terminated by proper notice, or a fixed-term contract expires; or
- he resigns, unless the reason for his resignation is that the company is in fundamental breach of contract which justifies his resignation.

Basically the director is to be compensated for what he would have earned during the balance of his contract, less what he has actually earned or it is anticipated he will earn during that period. He may also be entitled to a redundancy payment and/or compensation for unfair dismissal. See CONSTRUCTIVE DISMISSAL.

COMPETITION LAW. The body of law developed to regulate the results of the inevitable failure to achieve the Utopian state of perfect competition. The principal threat is perceived to be the monopoly which has the power to increase prices and slow technological progress.

In the UK, there was early legislation on monopolies, resulting in the development of patents and case law on contracts in restraint of trade. More recently there has been a spate of legislation including: Fair Trading Act 1973, Resale Prices Act 1976, Restrictive Trade Practices Acts 1976 and 1977, Competition Act 1980, together with other provisions in the Patents Act 1977 and Copyright Act 1956. Also, the UK is now subject to EEC competition laws, notably Articles 85 and 86 of the Treaty of Rome.

Under present law:

- company mergers leading to reduced competition may be disallowed;
- existing monopolies are regulated or even split;
- agreements for limiting or distorting competition (such as exclusive trading or licensing agreements), partitioning of markets, refusal to supply or selection of outlets and for holding up prices of goods or services may be declared illegal;
- agreements for controlling retail prices (except those of books and medicaments) are void; and
- other anti-competitive practices may be reviewed.

See ANTITRUST, MERGER CONTROL and RESTRICTIVE TRADE PRACTICES.

COMPROMISE. An agreement between parties to a dispute to settle an action out of court.

COMPULSORY ACQUISITION. The provisions contained in section 428 of the Act (formerly section 209) – are being replaced under the proposed FSA 1986. An offeror (which will include joint offerors) who acquires not less than nine-tenths in value of the shares in a company to which his offer relates (excluding those he holds at the date of the offer and those acquired by any associate of his) may acquire the balance of the shares compulsorily. New provisions include: an offeror need not be a company; market purchases are excluded and convertible loan stock, warrants and options are treated as classes of shares.

COMPUTER LAW. While there is no separate law relating to computers, this phrase is increasingly used as the generic term describing various heads of law and equity which happen to relate to computer databases, software, integrated circuits, the design and performance of hardware and computer fraud.

Computer databases and software are protected under the law of copyright and confidence. Works used in the manufacture of integrated circuits are probably also protected by copyright, and there are proposals for a new law to give additional protection. Hardware may be protected by patents and copyright.

Computer fraud presents both legal and evidential problems. Where the result is theft of money there is usually a clear remedy but if data is abstracted from a computer system the remedies may be uncertain under current law. See DATA PROTECTION.

CONCILIATION. The cost of litigation and arbitration, which is sometimes greater than the award to the winning party, has led to a proliferation of non-judicial methods of resolving disputes. Conciliation is one such method and the conciliator helps the parties to agree: their agreement is as binding as any other contract. Many such settlement procedures are operated by trade or professional organizations.

In international trade, conciliation has also become increasingly favoured to overcome differences of economic, political and legal background. To assist in the procedure for conciliation the International Chamber of Commerce (ICC) and the United Nations Commission on International Trade Law (UNCITRAL) have developed specialized international conciliation rules. See 'MINI-TRIAL'.

CONDITION PRECEDENT . An external fact upon which the existence of an obligation depends. Contracts are often made which are 'subject to' some future event or performance of an act by a stranger to the contract: a binding contract will not arise until the fulfilment of the condition. A condition precedent is not, however, limited to contracts: e.g. a gift may be made to John provided that he marries: no gift is intended at all until the condition is fulfilled and John does in fact marry.

If an agreement is 'subject to contract' there is no contract at all because the parties have agreed not to be bound until the execution of a formal contract. An agreement 'subject to the purchaser obtaining a satisfactory mortgage' is void because of the uncertainty of the condition.

While there is a clear distinction between a promise which, if broken, can be sued upon and a condition upon which an obligation is dependent, the same matter may be both a promise and conditional. This is known as a promissory condition. If land is sold 'subject to planning permission' the courts will imply a promise by the purchaser to use his best endeavours to obtain that permission. If a condition is solely for the benefit of one of the parties to an agreement, he may waive it and make the contract unconditional.

A conditional sale is a contract for the sale of goods where the property is not to pass to the buyer until he has fulfilled the condition of paying the price.

CONDITION SUBSEQUENT. Where a contract is to end upon the happening of some event, it is said to be subject to a condition subsequent. See CONDITION PRECEDENT.

CONDITIONAL CONTRACT. See CONDITION PRECEDENT.

CONFIDENCE. Breach of confidence may give rise to an action for damages and an injunction, if information is given to the defendant in circumstances which create an obligation of confidence on his part and improper use is made of that information. An obligation to treat information as confidential may be implied from the circumstances, e.g. an inventor discussing his plans with a possible developer, or from employment.

Remedies will not be granted when it would be contrary to public policy so to do, or the obligation is an unreasonable restraint of trade.

CONFIDENTIAL INFORMATION. Information not readily available to the public which there is a duty not to disclose or exploit. The duty can arise whenever information is obtained in confidence or through a position of trust or even improperly.

Certain categories of confidential information are protected by specific statutes such as the Official Secrets Act (a blunderbuss whose notorious section 2 is indiscriminate in its scope, but permits leaks authorized by Ministers of the Crown) and the Company Securities (Insider Dealing) Act 1985 aimed at preventing the misuse of unpublished price-sensitive information.

Although confidential information in a letter may not be disclosed, there is no basis, at least in law, for the controversial new proposition in the 1986 Westland Helicopters saga that the very existence of a letter marked 'confidential' must not be divulged. See EMPLOYER AND EMPLOYEE and SPRINGBOARD PERIOD.

CONFIRMING HOUSE. Otherwise known as an export house. It acts as agent for overseas buyers. The sale contract is between the overseas buyer and the seller of the goods and the house is not liable for the price; however, it may undertake personal responsibility for the price. In that sense the house adds confirmation to the bargain.

CONFLICT OF INTEREST. An agent or any other person in a position of trust must not allow his personal interests to conflict with the best interests of any person for whom he acts. This is one aspect of the principles underlying fiduciary duties.

While, generally speaking, a person should not act where a conflict arises or put himself into a position where a conflict might arise, it is sometimes possible to do so if, after full disclosure of all relevant facts, consent is given by the people concerned. Where a solicitor acts for two clients and a conflict arises between the interest of those clients, he must cease to act for both. If an agent sells to a company of which he is a director and large shareholder, the sale is not binding on his principal. If a trustee buys trust property the beneficiaries can avoid the sale.

A company having a potential conflict of interest between its relationship with a substantial corporate shareholder and its duties to the remaining shareholders may be denied listing on The Stock Exchange. The area of conflicts of interest in the investment and securities industry receives particular attention under the proposed FSA 1986.

CONFLICT OF LAWS. Also known as private international law. In England it relates to cases having any sort of contact with a system of law other than English law. Scottish and Northern Irish law may be treated as foreign laws.

In the conflict of laws there are four general questions to be dealt with by the English courts. Firstly, their limits of jurisdiction in matters which arise abroad in connection with foreign transactions. Secondly, if within English jurisdiction, which system of law to apply to the matter. Thirdly, if a foreign court has already given a judgment on an issue before an English court, what effect that foreign judgment should have on the English proceedings. Fourthly, the reciprocal enforcement of judgments between the UK and other countries.

Unlike public international law, the rules in the conflict of laws differ widely from country to country. English courts, for example, give jurisdiction a much higher priority than do European courts. A European court would tend to concentrate on the choice of law aspect. US conflict of laws differs from both as it has mainly been developed in conflicts between states within the USA rather than in international conflicts cases.

Knowledge of foreign law is not imputed to an English judge. Therefore any foreign law which is to be relied upon by any party must be pleaded specifically as fact; otherwise it will be assumed to be the same as English law. Foreign law can be applied in English courts where it is relevant, but no foreign law or judgment will be recognized or enforced which repudiates the policy of English law, or is of a penal or revenue nature. See PROPER LAW.

CONGRESS. One of three branches of government in the USA, the other two being the Judiciary and the Executive. It is composed of the Senate (two Senators elected by each state) and the House of Representatives (elected by the states according to population). If Congress constitutionally exercises legislative power on any subject, it invalidates a state law. In the words of one judge, 'the sword and the purse, all the external relations, and no inconsiderable portion of the industry of the nation, are entrusted to its government.'

CONNECTED PERSONS. Under company law, a person is connected with a director if he is a spouse, child under 18, a 20 per cent associated company, a trustee of a trust (including a discretionary trust) of which the director is a beneficiary, a partner of the director or of any person connected with him.

The definition is applied to stop the wily director receiving an indirect benefit from his company by extending certain restrictions upon a director to persons with whom he is related – but not, surprisingly, his adult children.

CONSIDERATION. Is a concept which separates those promises which should be enforced from those which will not be enforced by the courts. It is one of the essential elements in all contracts, except those made by a deed, and is 'the price for which the promise of the other is bought'.

It is sometimes difficult to apply what are complex rules. It is hoped that the following scenario will help.

If John promises Jane to give her £100 for nothing, there is no consideration and no contract. If John promises to give her the packet of cigarettes which is in the kitchen if she fetches it, there is no consideration, it is merely a condition precedent to the operation of his bounty. If John tells Jane that he will give her £100 if William stops smoking and William does stop, Jane has still not given consideration. If John tells Jane that he will give her £100 if she stops smoking for one week and she does so, she may enforce John's promise because she has suffered what she may perceive to be a detriment. The courts do not enquire into the economic adequacy of consideration, but it must be something of worth: it does not matter how little. It therefore follows that consideration is insufficient if it involves doing something which a person has already done, or is bound to do.

The consideration and the promise must be substantially part of the same transaction. There is an exception to this where services are rendered at a person's request on a tacit understanding that they are to be paid for and no price is fixed. If at a later date a promise is given to pay a definite sum, that is treated as merely fixing the price, and is regarded as part of the original transaction.

Many technical rules embellish what is essentially a bargain between persons, e.g. the consideration must be given by the person who wishes to enforce the contract. See VARIATION OF CONTRACT.

CONSOLIDATION OF MORTGAGES. A lender holding several mortgages from the same borrower who is in default may consolidate them and refuse redemption of one unless redemption is made of all. The exercise of the right is subject to some qualifications and is now excluded by statute unless expressly retained by a clause in the mortgage document.

CONSOLIDATION OF SHARES. Where shares in a company are combined into a lower number of shares of higher nominal amount, e.g. the conversion of four 25p shares into one £1 share.

CONSORTIUM. A number of companies, otherwise unrelated to one another, which together own a company or enter into a joint venture. For corporation tax purposes, a company which is at least 75 per cent owned by a consortium is treated, broadly, as if it were a member of the same group as each of the consortium companies, provided none owns less than 5 per cent of its shares.

In a different sense, a husband may sue for loss of consortium with his wife resulting from her being injured by another's negligence, but a wife (having, of course, no property in her husband) has no corresponding right!

CONSTITUTION. The supreme law of the land enshrined in writing. Perhaps the most famous is the US Constitution, but other countries such as Switzerland and France also have written constitutions. The UK does not. See CONSTITUTIONAL LAW.

CONSTITUTIONAL LAW. The law concerning the government of the country. In the UK there is no formal constitution, but a loosely defined body of rules and conventions governing the exercise of political power: these amount to an unwritten constitution. The fundamental rule is that of the sovereignty of Parliament, for there is no limit to its legislative power. No Act of Parliament can be held by the courts to be invalid and there is, in theory at least, no rule or Act of Parliament which cannot be changed by Parliament. This has led to philosophical conundrums about such matters as whether an Act can be made irrevocable unless a special procedure enshrined in that Act is followed, or indeed at all.

The position in the UK contrasts with that in the USA, where the US Supreme Court can overturn state or even federal laws or policies on the grounds of inconsistency with the Constitution as interpreted by the court.

CONSTRUCTIVE DISMISSAL. Termination of employment by the employee, where he is entitled to end it without notice because of the employer's conduct. It is regarded as a dismissal by the employer; the employee has the same rights as if he had actually been dismissed (although the question of whether the dismissal is fair or unfair is a separate one).

It is not sufficient that the employer's conduct was so unreasonable that the employee could not be expected to tolerate it. There must be a breach of contract, either amounting to a repudiation or being so serious as to entitle the employee to terminate under the law of contract. However, there is usually an implied term in employment contracts that an employee will not be treated capriciously, arbitrarily or inequitably, so that very unreasonable conduct will, in effect, be a breach of contract. See COMPENSATION FOR LOSS OF OFFICE.

CONSTRUCTIVE NOTICE. A rule of evidence which avoids the need to prove knowledge of facts contained in or relating to a legal document, such as the Memorandum and Articles or the contents of title deeds to land. A person is deemed to have knowledge of all facts of which he would have been aware had he taken reasonable steps of enquiry.

CONSTRUCTIVE RESIGNATION. Termination of employment by the employer following conduct by the employee amounting to a repudiation of the contract. This does not constitute a dismissal but merely acceptance of the repudiation. Accordingly there can be no valid claim for wrongful or unfair dismissal.

CONSTRUCTIVE TRUST. There is no satisfactory definition of a constructive trust, and perhaps there never will be; for its limitations are obscure and its concept uncertain. The trust is imposed in order to satisfy the demands of justice and good conscience where property has been acquired in such circumstances that the holder should not be entitled to retain it and is thus treated as the trustee for another.

CONSUMER CREDIT. The Consumer Credit Act 1974 regulates the activities of those who provide an individual (but not companies) with credit in some form, and the conduct of credit transactions in order to protect the consumer. Credit includes loans, credit card purchases, budget accounts, hire purchase, conditional sales and credit sales. The statute (among other things) controls traders concerned with the provision of all consumer credit by licensing requirements, regulation of advertising and canvassing. These are policed by the Director General of Fair Trading. Control of individual credit agreements is more complex and detailed regulation is contained in Statutory Instruments.

CONSUMER PROTECTION. Consumer protection is often thought of as a recent phenomenon. In fact the law has long been concerned with the regulation of certain business practices, even those of innkeepers. However, there has been a proliferation of statutes over the past 20 years dealing with the rights of consumers and remedies available to them. These have been inspired partly by the increasingly complex nature of goods, whose faults may not be detectable on examination by the purchaser, and partly by social and political trends.

Consumer protection is a varied branch of civil law, but its chief concerns are: the basic duties of a supplier to pass title, to deliver the goods contracted for, to deliver goods of the right quality and fitness and to deliver them at the right time; a manufacturer's liability in negligence or on a guarantee; exclusion of liability, including exemption clauses, and the remedies available to consumers. The major statutes are the Sale of Goods Act 1979, the Unfair Contract Terms Act 1977, the Fair Trading Act 1973 and the Trade Descriptions Act 1968; the safeguards they provide are referred to under appropriate headings. See CONSUMER CREDIT, CONTRACT FOR SERVICES and MANUFACTURERS' WARRANTIES AND GUARANTEES.

CONTEMPT OF COURT. The failure to comply with an order of the court, or an act of resistance or insult to the court, or the judges, or conduct likely to impede the fair trial of an accused person. The maximum penalty for contempt is imprisonment for two years and an unlimited fine; but in 1631 when a prisoner threw a brick bat at the Judge of Assize in Salisbury his right hand was cut off and fixed to the gibbet, after which he was hanged in the presence of the court. See SEQUESTRATION and SUBPOENA.

CONTINGENT FEE. A method of tying the lawyer's remuneration to the success of the action, i.e. a percentage of the amount of tax or damages recovered. It is condoned in the USA and largely condemned in the rest of the world. Generally the lawyer agrees to act for nothing, or for his out of pocket expenses only, in return for an agreed fee if a particular result is achieved, or most frequently a percentage of the amount recovered, reducing as the size of the award grows. It is particularly popular for class actions and personal injury cases. It is said to promote justice for the poor in the absence of a proper legal aid system, to encourage 'ambulance chasing', and to induce lawyers to want to win at all costs, depending on one's point of view.

CONTINGENT INTEREST. An interest under a trust which does not vest until an uncertain future event occurs or a qualifying condition is met. For example, if property is left on trust for John subject to attaining the age of 21, John does not receive it until he becomes 21. However, the interest can be sold while still contingent, and it can also be insured.

CONTRACT FOR SERVICES. A person providing a service is expected to carry out his functions with reasonable skill and diligence and to charge a fair price. The Supply of Goods and Services Act 1982 codifies these principles and sets out the conditions implied when a person provides a service. These implied terms relate to the care and skill to be used, the time to be taken and the price to be charged.

Also the term applied to a contract with an independent contractor. See EMPLOYER AND EMPLOYEE and EXEMPTION AND EXCLUSION TERMS.

CONTRACTS. Virtually every aspect of society is affected by the law of contract. The everyday life of individuals is ordered by its existence. It applies when a person goes shopping, goes to work, buys a home, reads an advertisement, or borrows money. People remain blissfully ignorant of the relationship until things go wrong. Obviously, contract law enters into all aspects of national and international trade.

The fundamental idea of a contract is that of a bargain and it can be expressed in writing or verbally or implied by law. The lawyer talks about it as being formed by an 'offer and acceptance', with 'consideration', 'intention to create legal relations' and 'capacity to contract'. These are all essential elements required to create a valid enforceable contract.

What this boils down to in layman's terms is that the parties have to agree upon contractual terms which should be established with reasonable clarity, and which are intended to be enforceable by a court if either party fails to comply with their obligations.

A contract may be unenforceable or may be vitiated by mistake, misrepresentation or undue influence. It may be void because of illegality or on grounds of public policy. It may be discharged by frustration or breach. Its ability to confer benefits or impose liabilities upon strangers depends upon privity of contract; however, obligations and benefits under contracts may be varied or capable of assignment. The remedies for a breach of contract are damages, specific performance or injunction. All these are noted under separate headings.

CONTRACTUAL CAPACITY. The law recognizes that certain classes of person are not competent to contract or their ability to do so should be limited. See BANKRUPTCY, MINOR and *ULTRA VIRES*.

CONTRIBUTION. A doctrine developed by equity to ensure that a trustee could claim from other trustees if he paid more than his share of a liability for breach of trust. The doctrine has been extended by statute and now applies where two or more persons are liable to pay some damage or debt.

Whatever the legal basis of the liability and whether it be in tort, breach of contract, or breach of trust, the amount each must pay is fixed at the figure a court considers just and equitable, having regard to the extent of each contributor's liability for the damage (Civil Liability (Contribution) Act 1978). Guarantors are not covered by the statute, but where one of them pays all or more than his proportion of the debt, he has a right of contribution from his co-guarantor. There is no right of contribution in a case of debt unless the parties are liable to a common demand.

CONTRIBUTORY. Anyone liable to contribute to the assets of a company being wound up. Includes, in particular, present and past shareholders (although no further contribution can be required once the shares are fully paid up), but not a mere debtor of the company.

CONTRIBUTORY NEGLIGENCE. See NEGLIGENCE.

CONTROL. There can clearly be more than one view as to what constitutes control of a company, and the various minds of the legislature seem to have adopted most of the possibilities at one time or another. Generally it means the power to determine how the company's affairs are conducted.

The Act deems directors to control a company if they have more than 50 per cent of the voting power. Under the City Code, it means 30 per cent of voting power. In relation to newspaper mergers, it is 25 per cent of the votes, but otherwise merely the ability to exert material influence on the company's policy. See TAKE-OVERS.

CONTROL OF BORROWING ORDER. The principal Order under which the Treasury exercises its wide powers to control borrowing and the issue and offer for sale of securities. Contravention attracts penalties but does not invalidate the transaction. The Order adopts the approach beloved of authorities that everything is forbidden unless there is an express exemption or consent. Bank borrowings in the ordinary course of business and transactions involving less than £3 million are generally exempt. Where £3 million or more is to be raised, the consent of the Bank of England as to the timing and amount of the transaction must be obtained.

CONTROLLED FOREIGN CORPORATIONS. In the UK, anti tax-haven measures apply to foreign companies that are resident outside the UK, controlled by residents of the UK and subject to a rate of tax in the country of residence that is less than one half of the corresponding UK tax. Comprehensive tax legislation has been introduced by a number of countries, including the UK, USA, France, Germany and Japan, to prevent domestic source income being diverted to tax-haven corporations and the accumulation of income in those corporations.

The legislation generally taxes the resident shareholders on their *pro-rata* share of the undistributed income of controlled foreign corporations.

CONVERSION. A tort which consists of dealing with goods in a way inconsistent with the rights of the owner and depriving him of possession. The defendant need not act in bad faith or intend to deny the owner's rights: it is enough that his conduct is inconsistent with those rights.

Conversion should be contrasted with Trespass to Goods which is direct interference with an owner's possession of goods without asserting title to them. The two torts co-exist where there is interference with possession which implies denial of title. Under the Torts (Interference with Goods) Act 1977, a co-owner commits conversion if he wrongfully destroys goods or disposes or purports to dispose of the entire property in the goods.

CONVERSION RIGHTS. Rights attaching to debentures, shares or other securities of a company enabling them, often subject to conditions, to be converted into shares or another class of shares. Shares of UK companies may not be converted into redeemable shares nor may convertible debentures be issued at a discount in order to circumvent the rule against issuing shares at a discount.

CONVERTIBLE STOCKS. Usually unsecured loan stock of a company carrying a lower than market rate of interest because it entitles the holders to convert the stock into shares of the company in the future, and therefore has a speculative value. If conversion takes place, equity capital will have been raised at a premium over the original market price of the shares.

When listed loan stock carries outstanding conversion rights, The Stock Exchange requires that the value of the rights is not diluted, that there is always sufficient unissued capital to cover the rights and that they are clearly identified as being convertible. Holders are normally entitled to convert the stock into shares in the event of a take-over. Interest on loan stock is tax deductible by a company – dividends are not. See DEBENTURES and CONVERSION RIGHTS.

CONVEYANCING. The art and practice of that part of the law relating to the ownership of freehold and leasehold property. It is intended that the monopoly of solicitors in this area of the law should end; and as there were in 1983 approximately 201 million property transactions valued at £4,422 million, the potential loss is self-evident.

CO-OWNERSHIP. Co-ownership of land or goods exists where they are owned by more than one person, either as joint tenants, or as tenants in common.

On the death of a joint tenant, his rights pass to the remaining joint tenant: this process continues until there is only one survivor who becomes the sole owner. Hence, on the death of a joint tenant his share of land does not form part of his estate for it no longer belongs to him. Tenants in common each own a specific share in the land: any one of them can therefore dispose of his share as he likes. It is possible to convert a joint tenancy into a tenancy in common, e.g. by written notice.

Partners always own property as tenants in common and it is treated as goods, or personal estate. Therefore if a partner makes a will in which he leaves realty to one person and personalty to another, the person to whom he leaves realty will not be entitled to the deceased's interest in the partnership land.

COPYRIGHT. A right created by statute which affords the originator of an original literary, artistic or dramatic work the exclusive right to carry out, or authorize, certain defined restricted acts in relation to that work, for example reproducing the work in a material form or broadcasting or publishing it. Separate rights of copyright also subsist in secondary works such as films, sound recordings, television and cable programmes. Unlike in many countries, UK copyright extends to designs applied industrially and to computer programs.

Copyright comes into existence automatically without the need for registration and, by virtue of Copyright Conventions, most foreign nationals are also entitled to UK copyright. In the case of primary works (other than engravings and photographs) copyright continues until the end of the 50th year following the death of the author and, in the case of secondary works, engravings and photographs, the end of the 50th year following publication.

Copyright does not subsist in ideas; only in works reduced to a material form. It gives no monopoly right and so, in any legal proceedings, the plaintiff must establish both objective similarity and a causal link between the two works.

Remedies include injunction, damages and, in certain cases, delivery up or recovery of the value of the infringing goods. Infringement can also be a criminal offence.

COPYRIGHT CONVENTIONS. International agreements which require a member country to afford minimum standards of copyright protection under its domestic law to citizens of other member countries.

The UK is a party to:

- the Berne Convention, which requires no formalities for protection;
- the Universal Copyright Convention, under which countries may require use of the familiar © symbol and provide a shorter term; and
- the Rome Convention, which relates only to public performance, phonograms and broadcasts.

Most countries are members of one or more of the Conventions.

CORPORATE OPPORTUNITY. There is a hope that, if a director who takes advantage of his position cannot keep the benefit he gets, he will not be tempted to take advantage of that position. Even an unsophisticated director is likely to realize that he cannot use the company's assets as if they were is own. He may not be aware that he must not use information or opportunities coming to him because of his position as a director. The rule is very strictly applied.

However, subject to the Articles, a director may participate in investment opportunities or deals in which his company is participating, provided the board of the company has independently decided on the amount of its investment, and the overall size of the transaction requires the participation of other investors on no more favourable terms than those offered to his company.

CORPORATE UMBRELLA. This term is used in relation to companies in a group who shelter under the protection of a licence or authorization of another company in the same group (usually a holding company) to refer to the extended protection of that licence or authorization. Sometimes, for example under the proposed FSA 1986, the licence or authorization cannot in fact be so extended.

CORPORATE VEIL. Of the persons who have entered the history of company law, perhaps none is so significant as Mr Salomon who carried on business as a leather merchant. In 1892 he decided to incorporate a company which purchased his business for £39,000. It was 'a sum which represented the sanguine expectations of a fond owner' rather than an objective estimate of value. The company went bust a year later: the judge held that the company was a sham and nominee for Salomon, the real proprietor, who should be liable for its debts. The House of Lords unanimously overruled the decision. The company was in law, they said, a different person altogether from its members. The corporate veil was born.

Since then, there have been many attempts to lift the veil and to fix directors and shareholders with personal liability for the debts and obligations of a company. There are statutory exceptions, e.g. when the number of members falls below two, where group accounts are necessary, or where there has been fraudulent trading. There have even been occasions when the veil has been lifted in favour of shareholders by statute. Judges have lifted the veil and refused to allow the corporate entity principle to be used as a creature of fraud or in relation to associated companies. The veil has also been pierced to look at the economic reality of some situations – but has not yet been shredded.

CORPORATION. It may be difficult to believe, but it is true, that your Bishop is a corporation sole (not soul!), as is the Queen of England. A local authority or a university is a corporation aggregate, as are the Dean and Chapter of your local cathedral. So, a corporation possesses the character of perpetuity, its succession being constantly maintained by new individuals replacing those who die, retire or are removed. A corporation aggregate is in law considered as one person, although it may consist of many.

A trust corporation is of a different breed, although the Public Trustee, who is also a corporation sole, is among their number. They are corporations appointed by the court or entitled to act as a custodian trustee under the Public Trustee Act 1906. A trust corporation can be the sole trustee of a trust and give valid receipts for capital money.

In the USA the term 'corporation' is generally used for a company.

CORPORATION TAX. It cannot be said of many English institutions that they are modelled on the French, as is the imputation system of UK corporation tax which raised £8,341 million for the UK revenue in 1984–85; about 7 per cent of all taxes. Other features of the imputation system are the payment of ACT, when profits are distributed, and the associated tax credit in the hands of a shareholder.

A company resident in the UK is liable to corporation tax on its profits wherever arising and whether distributed or not, as are the UK profits of a foreign company which trades in the UK through a branch or agency. A company is resident in the UK, no matter where incorporated, if its central management and control are exercised in the UK.

COUNSEL. Another name for a barrister-at-law. In the USA a lawyer is described as being 'of counsel' if he is not qualified to practise under the state law, or if he has outside activities and is not engaged full time with the practice of the firm which employs him. US law firms practising in England are increasingly employing practicing barristers, and they are also referred to as 'of counsel'.

COUNTERCLAIM. A claim brought by a defendant in any action against the plaintiff. A counterclaim, unlike a set-off, need not be merely a defence to the original claim. It can be any claim whether related or not, whenever and however arising and for any kind of remedy, which could have been brought as a separate action.

The procedure is a useful means of avoiding multiplicity of

actions. It has an advantage for the defendant for he may normally delay any payment he is ordered to make in the original claim, up to the amount of his counterclaim, until the counterclaim has been resolved. See CLASS ACTION and CROSS ACTIONS.

COUNTERPURCHASE. Has been around for a long time and is a form of barter. The Dutch West India Company acquired Manhattan Island for $24 worth of glass beads in 1626. More recently jumbo jets have been exchanged for oil. The resurgence of countertrade in the 1980s has resulted from the liquidity problems of many Third World countries, who could not obtain finance from banks to enable them to trade on a pure cash basis because of their indebtedness to Western banks generally.

COUNTERTRADE. A form of trading in which an export of goods or services to a particular market is made conditional upon undertakings from the exporter to accept imports from that market. Numerous transactions are encompassed under the countertrade label e.g. 'counterpurchase', 'swap', and 'barter'.

COURT. The place and the judges who administer justice, and not merely the palace where a monarch resides with her retinue of courtiers.

COURT OF APPEAL. Consists of the Lord Chancellor, the Master of the Rolls, the Lord Chief Justice, the President of the Family Division and 18 Lords Justices of Appeal.

The Civil Division, headed by the Master of the Rolls, hears appeals from the High Court, judges in chambers, the Divisional Court in civil matters, the County Courts and various tribunals; leave to appeal is not normally required. The Criminal Division hears appeals from convictions on indictment in the Crown Court (leave to appeal is needed unless only a question of law is involved) and points of law referred by the Attorney General following an acquittal.

Appeals from the Court of Appeal are made to the House of Lords, but leave to appeal is required.

The Court of Appeal with the High Court and the Crown Court constitute the Supreme Court of Judicature of England

and Wales. The House of Lords, although superior, is not part of the Supreme Court. See LEAP-FROGGING APPEAL.

COVENANT. A clause in an agreement under seal (or deed) under which a person promises to do, or not to do, some act; or warrants the truth of facts; or undertakes that a certain state of affairs exists.

CREDIT. To give someone credit is to allow them to incur a debt or defer a payment in the hope, which is sometimes misplaced, that it will be paid in the future. In this sense, for example, an undischarged bankrupt may not obtain credit of more than 50 without disclosing his status. Credit can also mean trustworthiness, as in the context of cross-examination as to credit of a witness in court. For the purposes of the consumer credit legislation, credit is widely defined to include any form of financial accommodation.

CREDIT SALE. A sale where the seller hands over ownership and possession of goods to the buyer in exchange for a promise by the buyer to pay at a later date, or in instalments.

The distinguishing feature of a credit sale is that, despite non-payment, the purchaser owns the goods and is therefore free to sell them; the seller is a creditor of the buyer. It differs from hire purchase where ownership of the goods does not pass until payment of the final credit instalment and exercise of the option to purchase. In a conditional sale ownership does not pass to the purchaser until some condition, such as payment of the price, is satisfied.

CREDITOR. A person to whom money is owed. In bankruptcy and liquidation the term includes anyone who has a claim which can be asserted, whether or not it is strictly a debt.

A preferential creditor is one whose claim is given priority by statute, such as the Inland Revenue, local authorities (for rates) and employees.

CROSS ACTIONS. Two separate actions brought between the same parties where the plaintiff in one is the defendant in the other and vice versa. Whether or not the actions relate to the same subject-matter, the court may stay the proceedings in one of the actions so that both may more conveniently be tried together. The stayed action will reappear as a counterclaim in the consolidated action.

CROSS BORDER LEASING. The structuring of leases of assets, across national boundaries, to take advantage of investment incentive credits, depreciation deductions, or tax exemptions, which are available where the lessor and lessee have different nationalities. Sometimes the lessor and lessee are in the same country, but a third party of a different nationality is concerned because, for example, he is the supplier of the assets to be leased.

CROSS EXAMINATION. The crux of the accusatorial system of the common law. Cross examination is generally directed to challenging the veracity of the evidence or the reputation or credibility of the witnesses of one party by the lawyer for the other. It is frequently viewed with distrust and fear by parties from civil law countries.

CROWN. In a legal sense it is not the jewelled hat put on a Sovereign's head at his coronation, but the Sovereign in an executive or public capacity acting by ministers and servants who must answer for their actions in Parliament and, in case of abuse, to the courts.

The Crown, as distinct from the Sovereign personally, is no longer immune from most actions in contract or tort, but is still not bound by a statute unless expressly mentioned.

CRYSTALLIZATION. That unfortunate moment of time when a floating charge over assets becomes a fixed charge attaching to assets owned by the company at the time. Depending on the terms of the charge, it will occur on the commencement of winding up, the appointment of a receiver, cessation of business and, normally, on any default under the charge.

CURRENCY SWAP. Because of sharp and too often unpredictable changes in exchange rates, companies are exposed to the risk of a serious reduction in profits. A currency swap transaction can reduce that risk. But its use is not limited to foreign exchange risk; swaps have become a tool of financing for a fixed term or at lower cost. This is done by companies, with mirror liquidity in two currencies, lending each other their 'surplus' currency either by parallel loans or a currency swap.

A straight currency swap is essentially an exchange between companies of two currencies, with an agreement between them to repurchase the same amounts at the same exchange rate at a fixed date in the future. The amount to be swapped is determined in one currency and the exchange rate to be applied to establish the amount in the other currency is its spot rate at the time of closing. The interest cost generally represents the difference between the prevailing rates in each country, and can be either a fixed or floating rate. At agreed times the company in the low interest rate country pays the interest to the one in the higher rate country.

CUSTOM. An unwritten rule having the force of law. A local custom in England and Wales is valid, even if contrary to the common law, if it is certain and reasonable, confined to a locality and has or can be presumed to have existed since 'time immemorial', which is defined by statute, with surprising precision, as the year 1189. Many trades and areas of commerce have particular customs which are binding, even though not necessarily ancient. Mercantile custom was the basis of the introduction into English law of negotiable instruments and many of the rules of partnership, agency and insurance.

It is well established that a term sanctioned by custom may be implied in all contracts, although the parties have not mentioned it. However, if the plain words of an agreement between commercial men who know of the custom do not take it into account, they must be supposed to have decided not to adopt it.

Custom is still an important source of public international law, which in many ways is at a stage comparable with that of domestic legal systems in the Middle Ages.

CY-PRES. If a charitable (as opposed to a private) trust is initially impossible or impracticable, or subsequently becomes so, the court will apply the property of the trust cy-pres, i.e. apply it to some other charitable purpose as nearly as possible resembling the original trust, in order to avoid the trust failing.

The doctrine was applied when trusts for Harvard College to teach Christianity to natives in or near the College and for the propagation of Christianity among the infidels in Virginia had become impossible of performance a century later. The scope of the doctrine was extended by statute in 1960 and, since the Charities Act 1985, a charity over 50 years old is given power to do a simple do-it-yourself cy-pres without going to the court.

D

DAMAGES. The monetary compensation awarded by a court for loss, damage, or injury suffered by a person following a breach of contract or the commission of a tort. Courts cannot avoid the task of assessing damages merely because it presents difficulties.

Damages for breach of contract are intended to place the plaintiff in the position he would have achieved had the contract been performed and, exceptionally, to return him to his position before the contract was made.

In tort the purpose is to place the injured party in the same position as if the tort had not been committed, although aggravated damages may be awarded where, e.g., the defendant has acted outrageously. Exemplary damages, which are punitive, may be given where, e.g., the defendant has calculated to make a profit from his wrongdoing which might well exceed the compensation normally payable to the injured party. Nominal damages, of as little as 1p in torts actionable *per se*, have been 'awarded' where the injury is considered to be minimal and the judge or jury wish to indicate their contempt for the plaintiff's case.

In contract and tort the plaintiff must take reasonable steps to mitigate his loss, and damages will take this into account. He need not, however, take steps which might injure his commercial reputation.

DATA PROTECTION. Increasing concern about the possible misuse of information about individuals, stored in computers, led to the Data Protection Act 1985. It is the first UK statute to address the use of computers.

It broadly requires persons who control and process personal data through computers and computer bureaux to register themselves, and the purposes for which data are held, with the data protection registrar. They are required to observe principles of good practice concerning the fair and accurate collection and processing of personal data, and restrictions upon their use and disclosure.

The principles give individuals the right to have access to data held about themselves as well as establishing new legal rights. Individuals may now be compensated for damage and any associated distress caused by the loss, destruction or unauthorized disclosure of data or inaccurate data, and they can apply for rectification or deletion of inaccurate data.

There is no parallel provision for manually-stored information.

DAWN RAID. See RULES GOVERNING SUBSTANTIAL ACQUISITION OF SHARES (SARs).

DE FACTO. In fact. For example the UK will recognize a regime of a foreign state as the *de facto* government if it has effective control over the state and its inhabitants. See *DE JURE.*

DE JURE. By right or law. For example, a foreign government will be recognized by the UK as the *de jure* government of that state if it commands the obedience of the mass of the inhabitants and has firmly established control. See *DE FACTO.*

DE MINIMIS NON CURAT LEX. The maxim that the law does not concern itself with very trifling matters. Thus insignificant departures from description or quantity when goods are sold are ignored. It has been held that 1 per cent is not *de minimis* but 1lb in 100 tons is. It has also given rise to improper limericks.

DEALERS IN SECURITIES. Until the proposed FSA 1986 becomes operative, any person who carries on the business of dealing in securities must be licensed by the DTI unless an exemption applies. The main exemptions are for members of a recognized association (such as the UK association of New York Stock Exchange members), banks and insurance companies, on the basis that they do not deal in securities as their main business. Exempted dealers are 'expected' to comply with the DTI's conduct of business rules for licensed dealers, but are not legally bound to do so and, indeed, are considered 'classier' than licensed dealers. This differentiation will disappear under the proposed FSA 1986, which will require all dealers in securities (and most other investment businesses) to be 'authorized' by membership of a recognized self-regulatory organization. Conduct of business rules will be promulgated to be observed by directly authorized businesses. Although this mirrors the present system for licensed dealers, a new requirement will be that recognized organizations themselves will have to introduce similar rules for their members. However, authorization need not be received each year. Banks (and other former exempted dealers) will therefore for the first time have to comply with detailed conduct of business rules, which will probably be something of a cultural shock. See INVESTOR PROTECTION.

DEALING COMPANY. One which buys securities or property with a view to making a profit on their sale rather than holding them as an investment for capital appreciation.

DEBENTURE TRUST DEED. Debenture and loan stocks are usually constituted by a trust deed with a trustee who acts for all the holders. It helps the company as it only has to deal with one person, the trustee, who can act speedily in connection with matters on behalf of the holders; and, if the debentures are secured, the power to enforce them is conveniently vested in one person. The deed includes the trustee's powers and authorities, the obligations of the company and the rights of the debenture holders.

The trustee is normally an insurance company or trust corporation. Banks acted as trustees until they realized, following a case in 1934, the conflict of interest and duty which might arise if they were both creditor in their own right and trustee. There is nothing to prevent the company acting as trustee itself, if it is not subject to Stock Exchange requirements, by making a deed poll.

DEBENTURES. Documents which evidence borrowing by a company. Academics have a great time debating their meaning; while companies enjoy using them to borrow money.

Unsecured debentures are called loan stock or notes. They can be secured by a mortgage, or a fixed or floating charge (or both) on company assets. They can be registered so that the legal title is vested in the person named in the register of debenture holders kept by the company, or bearer documents transferable by delivery. They may be convertible into shares of the company. The holder is a creditor and is entitled to interest on his loan, whether or not the company makes profits, and to repayment of the principal, in priority to shareholders' capital, if the company goes into liquidation. A company can create debentures which are subordinated to (rank after) the repayment of other creditors, or even shareholders' capital, in a winding up.

Debenture stock and loan stock are terms applied to a loan fund provided by a number of lenders. Each stockholder is given a certificate evidencing the amount of his loan and this is transferable in the same way as shares. See DEBENTURE TRUST DEED, FIXED CHARGE, INSOLVENCY, PRIORITY, RECEIVER and CHARGES REGISTER .

DECEIT. See FRAUD.

DECLARATION OF SOLVENCY. A statutory declaration made by a majority of the directors where it is proposed to wind up a company voluntarily. The declaration records the directors' opinion that the company will be able to pay its debts in full within a specified period not exceeding 12 months. It must be made within five weeks of the winding up.

If the declaration is made without reasonable grounds, its makers are liable to imprisonment or a fine as well as disqualification as directors under the Insolvency Act 1985.

DECLARATION OF TRUST. One of the principal ways of making an express (as opposed to a constructive) trust, the other being a transfer of property to trustees. It is simply achieved by the settlor declaring himself a trustee of property in favour of a beneficiary. The declaration need not be in writing unless it relates to land, but a clear intention to make the trust must exist.

DEED. An active anachronism in a modern society for its form overrides content. It is a written contract, agreement, or promise, which is executed under seal and delivered. Unlike a document executed without a seal, it is binding notwithstanding the absence of consideration. Not all documents which are sealed are deeds; for example, neither a share certificate nor a certificate of incorporation is a deed: they are evidential.

The seal is now a round red wafer (available from most stationers at reasonable cost) and delivery is, in practice, merely a matter of intention.

If a person executes a deed by stating that it has been 'signed sealed and delivered' without sealing it and another person relies on the deed to his detriment, the person executing the deed is estopped from denying it was sealed. See ESCROW, ESTOPPEL and EXECUTION.

DEED OF COVENANT. Usually it forms the basis of an income tax saving device under which income is paid to a person who does not pay income tax, e.g. charities or grandchildren with no income. The covenantor deducts and retains basic rate tax on the payment. The recipient reclaims that tax from the Inland Revenue if the gross amount of the payment, together with any other income, does not exceed the payee's personal allowance for tax purposes. The covenant must be capable of continuing for at least six years (four years to a charity). The scheme does not work between parents and infant children nor employer and employee.

DEED POLL. A deed under which the signatory creates rights in favour of third parties. Its obligations are legally binding upon the signatory.

DEEP DISCOUNT SECURITIES. Bonds and other securities whose issue price is much less than the amount payable on redemption; interest is 'rolled up' and paid as capital. The Inland Revenue are wise to this and, where the discount is, broadly, over 15 per cent, they tax the discount or 'premium' element as income on a disposal. Redemption proceeds can thus be paid free of withholding tax. Conversely, a UK issuer of the securities can get a yearly deduction as if interest had been paid. A court has yet to determine whether an investor may claim for the amount of the discount on the insolvency of the issuer: the problem has exercised legal minds in New York as well as in London.

DEFAMATION. The publication to a third person of words containing an untrue imputation against the reputation of another. If the publication is made in permanent form, is broadcast or is part of a theatrical performance, it is libel. If in some ephemeral form, it is slander. The law presumes that some damage will flow from the publication of a libel. For the publication of a slander to be actionable, some special damage must be proved to flow from it, unless the words:

- impute adultery or unchastity to a female; or
- are calculated to disparage the complainant in any office, profession, trade or business; or
- impute to the complainant a contagious or infectious disease; or
- impute a crime.

The place and time where the words are published is important. In the time of Charles II, it was actionable to call a person a Papist and to say that he went to Mass. In Quebec, it is actionable to say of a candidate for public office that he is a freemason. As Dean Swift said, you may 'convey a libel in a frown and wink a reputation down', but mere vulgar abuse is never defamatory.

Truth, privilege and fair comment are among the defences to an action for defamation. See QUALIFIED PRIVILEGE and TRADE LIBEL.

DEFENDANT. The person on the receiving end of a legal action (the opposite of plaintiff). In civil cases he may have a counterclaim against the plaintiff; if he appeals against a judgment he becomes an appellant.

DELAWARE CORPORATION. A US corporation incorporated under the laws of the state of Delaware. Minute in area, the state is a mammoth in the US corporate scene because its corporate charter is aimed at efficiency and ease in operation, and its application of state taxes makes it a comparative tax haven.

DEMERGER. The splitting up of a trading company or group in respect of which tax exemptions are available. The motivation to demerge is based on the hypothesis that the sum of the parts is greater than the whole. A demerger is effected by the distributing company paying a dividend to ordinary shareholders of the shares of the company/ies to be demerged. It must not be intended to enable persons other than members of the distributing company to gain control. Although it was thought on its introduction in 1980, to have been designed to enable a particular substantial company to split up different trades or trading subsidiaries, it is not limited to substantial companies.

DENNING, LORD. Master of the Rolls from 1962 until his retirement in 1982 aged 83. He became a judge of the High Court in 1944 and, by the date of his retirement, had served some 31 years in the Court of Appeal interrupted by a short interlude in the House of Lords. Highly regarded in the legal profession, he first became known to a wider audience as a result of his enquiry into the Profumo affair in 1963. An innovative judge who particularly championed the rights of the individual against abuses of power by the state, employers and trade unions. He had a scant regard for legal precedents in the interests of doing justice between the parties and, while this was acclaimed by the public and fascinated students of the law, his judgments did not always receive similar approbation in the House of Lords. His approach is typified in a judgment given in 1954 when he stated: 'If we never do anything which has not been done before we shall never get anywhere. The law will stand still while the rest of the world goes on; and that will be bad for both.'

DEPARTMENT OF JUSTICE. A non policy-making agency of US government founded in 1789 as the office of the Attorney-General. It advises the President and his cabinet on their constitutional and statutory powers, drafts laws and expounds the government's position in litigation involving federal, state, and human rights. It also enforces federal law concerning public interest points. Its investigative arm is the FBI.

DEPARTMENT OF TRADE AND INDUSTRY (DTI). An amalgam of the former departments of protection (Industry) and liberalization (Trade) which, according to critics, is fundamentally muddled. Carries out government policy with regard to industrial and commercial matters. Its responsibilities include merger references to the Monopolies and Mergers Commission, investigations into the affairs of a company, its membership and dealings in its shares and administering the various Lloyds and Insurance Companies Acts.

Under the proposed FSA 1986 the department will delegate its vigilatory functions, with regard to securities and investments, to a supervisory board of practitioners.

DEPONENT. From the latin verb deponere (to lay down or record) he is the maker of a written statement or, more specifically, an affidavit. In contrast, the maker of a declaration is a declarant and the maker of an oral statement is a witness. A deposition is a statement on oath made in judicial proceedings; the maker is called a witness – not a deponent!

DEPOSITION. A statement on oath taken from a potential witness, which can be used in evidence if the witness dies, goes insane or leaves the country before the trial. It is also a useful means of obtaining evidence from a witness living abroad who will not come to England.

DICEY. Albert Venn Dicey, 1835–1922, was an eminent jurist and for 28 years Vinerian Professor of English law at Oxford. During his lifetime he was best known as a constitutional lawyer both in the UK and in the USA, where he gave a course of lectures at Harvard. Dicey was disappointed with his major work *The Conflict of Laws*, and felt that academic opinion did not justify his efforts, but its continued success as one of the great authorities on the subject today (now as Dicey and Morris) proves him to have been wrong.

DIPLOMATIC PRIVILEGE. Immunity from criminal, civil and administrative proceedings is given to diplomats, on an hierarchical basis. Immunity may, of course, be waived.

DIRECTOR GENERAL OF FAIR TRADING. His responsibilities are so wide-ranging that one wonders whether he ever has time for dinner, never mind lunch. The office was established by the Fair Trading Act 1973 to protect the interests of consumers. He may make monopoly references to the Monopolies and Mergers Commission, whether for factual investigation or in order to have prohibitory orders made, and advises the government on the referral of mergers. He is responsible for dealing with restrictive trade practices, resale prices and, if all this is not enough, he must make annual and other reports, publish advice and information to consumers and encourage trade associations to prepare codes of practice for consumer protection.

DIRECTORS. Whether a person is a director of the largest company or of the smallest, his legal obligations are basically the same: it is the nature and extent of his responsibilities which differ. Professor Gower said that their duties of loyalty are exceptionally strict and their duties of diligence and skill exceptionally lax. This comment now requires considerable qualification for, since the Insolvency Act 1985, a finance director will almost certainly have a much higher duty in relation to a company's financial affairs than hitherto, and non-executive directors with special skills must take special care.

Directors are officers of the company. As such they are entitled only to the modest fees fixed by the Articles. Substantial salaries can be and are paid to them as employees or independent contractors. A director need not work full time for the company; he may be a non-executive director. Unlike a director of a US company, he can be a director of several companies, even if they compete.

Directors have the fiduciary obligations of agents and trustees to the company. They are collectively responsible for running the company through the board, though they may delegate their powers to committees or individual directors. They may not do any act which is illegal or *ultra vires* the company. Directors cannot be protected from negligence except by the court.

A private company must have at least one director; a public company at least two. There are no maxima. The shareholders in general meeting have the power to appoint directors, although vacancies can be filled, and additional directors can be appointed, by the directors. The directors usually cannot remove another director from office, but he can be removed at any time by a general meeting, subject to compensation for breach of contract. See BREACH OF WARRANTY OF AUTHORITY, CONFLICT OF INTEREST, CONNECTED PERSONS, CORPORATE OPPORTUNITY, DISCLOSURE, DISQUALIFICATION OF DIRECTORS, GOOD FAITH, INDOOR MANAGEMENT RULE, SUBSIDIARY COMPANY, *ULTRA VIRES*, WRONGFUL DISMISSAL and WRONGFUL TRADING.

DIRECTORS' REPORT. A report by directors concerning the general activities and finances of the company during the preceding financial year. It is circulated with the company's annual audited accounts.

DIRECTOR'S SERVICE AGREEMENT. An agreement containing the terms of employment of a director: motivated as much by the desire to give a director security of employment as it is to secure his services to the company. The term of employment must not exceed five years without the prior approval of an ordinary resolution.

Publicity requirements attend these contracts to ensure that members are aware of the company's liability to pay compensation if they are wrongfully terminated. Directors who think that they cannot be sued for damages for their breach of service contracts are living in a dreamworld! See WRONGFUL DISMISSAL.

DISCHARGE OF CONTRACT. The parties to a contract are absolved from further performance of their contractual obligations on satisfactory performance. Although as a general rule the law requires precise and exact performance, it recognizes that an innocent party may sometimes treat a contract as discharged by a breach of its terms and acquire a right of action against the defaulter.

The parties may also discharge a contract by deed; by the release of unperformed obligations in return for a monetary payment; by making a new agreement with the intention of extinguishing the original agreement; or by one party waiving the right to insist on strict performance of the other's obligations in return for doing something which he was not bound to do under the original contract. See BREACH OF CONTRACT and FRUSTRATION.

DISCLAIMER OF ONEROUS PROPERTY. A liquidator may now, by giving notice, get rid of onerous property, which is defined in the Insolvency Act 1985 as any unprofitable contract and any other property which is not readily saleable or which may give rise to a liability to pay money or perform any onerous act. The effect of the disclaimer is to terminate the rights, interests and liabilities of the company in the disclaimed property. A person who suffers loss or damage from the disclaimer is deemed to be a creditor and may claim in the liquidation.

DISCLOSURE. Whenever the relation between the parties to a contract is of a fiduciary or confidential nature, the person in whom confidence is reposed cannot bind the other party to the contract unless he satisfies the court that he has disclosed all material facts within his knowledge, and that the contract is advantageous to the other person. Where there is a duty to disclose a material fact, keeping silent or not disclosing it may have the same effect as saying it does not exist. The Act requires disclosure by directors of loans, interests in shares and interests in contracts with the company. See CONFLICT OF INTEREST, DISCLOSURE OF INTEREST IN SHARES, FIDUCIARY DUTY and GUARANTEES.

DISCLOSURE OF INTEREST IN SHARES. A director is obliged to notify his company within five days, of all acquisitions and disposals of shares in the company, and its holding or subsidiary companies. Disclosure extends to any 'interest' in shares, which includes contracts and assignment of rights in shares. Interest is widely defined in the Act.

A shareholder in a public company must notify it within five days if he acquires 5 per cent or more of its voting shares or any interest in them, and of any increase or decrease in that holding. See ACTING IN CONCERT.

DISCOVERY AND INSPECTION. In civil proceedings each party must produce to the other a list of documents and letters relating to the case which are or have been under their control (discovery). Those which are not privileged are made available for inspection and copying by the other side (inspection).

This assists each party to assess the strengths and weaknesses of both its own and the other's case. It may also reveal unknown facts and enable new lines of enquiry to be pursued.

DISCRETIONARY TRUST. A settlement giving a discretion to trustees to apply income and capital among a specified class of beneficiaries during the perpetuity period. It still serves its original purpose of keeping wealth within a family, despite occasional savage forays upon its benefits by the Inland Revenue.

There are now possibly as many discretionary trusts created outside the UK as there are in the UK because they are so strongly tipped as an insulation of funds against future exchange control restrictions. The trusts are also used by non-UK domiciled settlors, who intend to become resident in the UK, to insulate their assets against the ravages of inheritance tax – formerly capital transfer tax.

DISQUALIFICATION OF DIRECTORS. There are circumstances where, under the Articles, a director is disqualified from office because of involuntary actions on his part such as becoming 70, or suffering mental illness. Regrettably human error is a failing of some directors, and those who are fraudulent, dishonest or unduly reckless may be disqualified by the court for a period of five years. A register of these unfortunates is kept by the DTI. In 1985 there were 120 of them.

The number will undoubtedly increase, for the Insolvency Act 1985 will enable the court to make a disqualification order if a company goes into insolvent liquidation, or is the subject of an administration order, or has a receiver appointed, if it is shown that the directors' conduct renders them unfit to be concerned in company management. These provisions may be more lethal than they appear, for insolvency practitioners have to report to the DTI if it appears that directors have behaved in an unfit manner. Disqualification by the court may also follow an investigation by the DTI, wrongful trading or fraudulent trading.

The court proceedings under the new statute will be civil, not criminal, which will diminish the burden of proof and increase the possibility of disqualification.

DISSOLUTION. The process by which a company evaporates at the conclusion of its winding up, or by the Registrar striking its name off the register which he did with 50,914 companies in the UK in 1985. The latter method is cheaper than liquidation for a defunct company which has no assets. See *BONA VACANTIA*.

DISTRESS. A remedy by which a person is entitled, without legal process, to take into his possession the personal chattels of another person, to be held as a pledge to compel the performance of a duty or the satisfaction of a debt or demand. It is an important remedy for a landlord but its use is not confined to real property.

DISTRIBUTABLE PROFITS. The profits of a company available for distribution to its shareholders. They are its accumulated realized profits less its accumulated realized losses as shown in the latest accounts, or interim accounts filed with the Registrar. Profits include realized capital profits. Losses include realized losses not written off on a reduction or reorganization of capital.

As profits must be realized a company cannot revalue (upwards) its head office and pay a cash dividend out of the unrealized gain over cost but (although it may be a foul) the profit can be realized by selling the head office to another company in the group.

DISTRIBUTION. Has two meanings. Under the Act it is any payment of a company's assets to its members, whether in cash or any other form, except the issue of bonus shares, the redemption or purchase of a company's own shares, the reduction of share capital and the distribution of assets in a winding up. To ensure that a company maintains its capital intact for the protection of creditors it can only make a distribution out of distributable profits. A public company is subject to additional restrictions.

Distribution is also defined in wide terms in the Taxes Acts, and includes dividends and most other distributions out of the assets of a company made in respect of its shares, except bonus issues of non-redeemable shares. When a distribution is made by a company resident in the UK, the recipient is liable to income tax and the company must pay ACT.

DIVIDEND. The cash reward paid to shareholders by a company for the use of their capital. If the Articles permit, a dividend can be paid in other assets of the company. Shareholders cannot require the directors to pay a dividend, no matter how large the profits may be.

The final dividend is submitted for shareholders' approval at an annual general meeting and becomes a debt when it is declared. Shareholders have the right to reduce, but not to increase, the payment. The directors may declare an interim dividend without shareholder approval and may withdraw it before actual payment.

DIVISIONAL COURT. Two or more judges of the Queen's Bench

Division sitting together to hear applications for judicial review and certain appeals.

DOMICILE. A common law concept denoting permanent attachment to a country. Every person must have a domicile (cf. residence) which is either a domicile of origin, dependence or choice. Domicile of origin is acquired on birth from one's parents and even if abandoned in favour of a domicile of choice will revive if the domicile of choice is abandoned.

Domicile is the relevant criterion for determining liability to inheritance tax; its predecessor tax introduced the concept of deemed domicile which treats a person as domiciled in the UK if resident in the UK for 17 out of 20 years of assessment. Emigrants from the UK therefore have a three-year quarantine period before avoiding liability to inheritance tax. See CAPITAL GAINS TAX and INCOME TAX.

DOUBLE TAX CONVENTIONS. When the same item of income or capital gain is taxed by two separate countries under their different tax rules, double taxation arises. Double Tax Conventions are signed between countries. They override domestic tax laws and contain rules which determine which party to the Convention is entitled to the tax.

Conventions attempt to harmonize the internal laws of countries so that a common interpretation may be placed on important concepts such as residence and permanent establishment. Where, despite a convention, double tax results, provision is usually made for one or other of the countries to give credit against its own tax for tax paid to the other country. The UK has over 90 Double Tax Conventions.

DUAL RESIDENT COMPANY. Where a company is considered to be resident in more than one country in accordance with the domestic laws of the countries concerned, it may claim tax benefits in both. It is possible to establish a company resident in the USA and the UK, for the test of residence in the USA is incorporation while in the UK it is central management and control.

DUMPING. This arises when an exporter unfairly sells goods at less than their economic price in order to eliminate competition in an export market. Dumping is unlawful under EEC and US law.

The EEC commission has a wide discretion to impose duties on imports of a 'dumped' product. Application of its rules can be highly artificial; so when Timex instigated anti-dumping investigations in relation to Soviet watches, the European Commission imposed an anti-dumping duty by comparing prices and production costs of Hong Kong manufacturers and not those of the USSR. Timex appealed to the European court to force the Commission to re-open the basis on which Hong Kong was selected.

DURESS. An illegal threat, or threatened or actual violence, to a person. An illegal threat is one to commit a crime or a tort. A person cannot be held to a contract unless he consented to it, and it can barely be said that he is a free agent if he is 'persuaded' to contract by duress. To avoid a contract it must be established that the threats were a reason for entering into it, but they need not be the only or even the main reason. Duress is a defence to most criminal charges, but not to murder.

E

EDGE ACT CORPORATION. A corporation formed by a US bank to engage in foreign banking and financing.

EIUSDEM GENERIS. Literally 'of the same kind': a rule of construction which applies where a list of particular words is followed by general words (usually to cover any possible omission in the list): the general words must be restricted to things of the same kind as the specific words. For example, 'cats, dogs, horses, cows and other things' does not cover computers or buildings but there will be some question as to whether it is limited to domestic animals or all animals.

EMPLOYEE SHARE SCHEMES. Defined in the Act as a scheme for encouraging or facilitating the holding of shares or debentures in a company by, or for the benefit of, present or former employees or their spouses or minor children.

It does not have to be (but usually is) a formally-constituted scheme. They are normally:

1. Ownership (or profit-sharing) schemes, under which a company funds the acquisition by trustees of shares, and the trustees appropriate the beneficial interest to participants. Maximum annual participation for each individual: £1,250 or 10 per cent of salary (but not exceeding £5,000).
2. Savings-related (or SAYE) option schemes, under which an employee enters into an approved savings contract for five or seven years and at the same time is granted an option to subscribe shares at the end of the contract period. The employees are exempted from income tax. Maximum contribution: £100 per month.

Both schemes must be open on similar terms to all employees (subject only to a service qualification not exceeding five years).

A share option scheme, however, can be used on a discretionary basis to grant options over shares worth up to £100,000 or four times annual salary. The same tax exemption applies as in the case of SAYE schemes.

Outside these schemes (which must be approved individually by the Inland Revenue) any share acquisition by, or grant of a share option to, an employee is fraught with tax problems, sometimes of nightmarish complexity.

EMPLOYER AND EMPLOYEE. Identifying employment is not just an exercise for academics; important legal consequences flow from the employer–employee relationship. For instance, an employer is vicariously liable for a tort committed by an employee during the course of his employment; an employer is bound to operate PAYE.

Usually the existence of the relationship will be clear, but often the lawyer will have to determine whether there is a contract for services which applies to an independent contractor or a contract of service which applies to employment. Broadly employment exists if the employer determines the work to be carried out and controls how it is done.

Employees owe their employers a number of duties which are implied by law. These include the exercise of due skill and care, obedience to lawful instructions, acting in good faith and non-disclosure of confidential information. Patentable inventions made by employees as part of their duties will normally belong to the employer (subject in some cases to compensation) as will copyright works created in the course of their employment. Confidential information of an employer's business acquired by an employee in the course of his service may be used by him after the termination of his employment unless the information is classed as a trade secret or is of such a confidential nature that it requires the same protection as a trade secret.

Statute and the common law confer numerous rights on employees ranging through holiday pay to maternity leave, the provision of safe working conditions and written conditions of service. See REDUNDANCY, TRANSFER OF BUSINESS and UNFAIR DISMISSAL.

ENTICEMENT. As a cause of action, enticement no longer exists. It was the tort of unlawfully inducing a spouse to leave the plaintiff. It was abolished in 1970 along with other anachronistic actions such as breach of promise to marry.

The word is now used when an employee is induced to leave one employer to join another on more attractive terms. This can result in an action for procuring a breach of contract.

EQUITABLE CHARGE. Lord Chancellor Walker said in 1894, 'every charge is not an equitable mortgage, though every equitable mortgage is a charge'.

An equitable charge does not transfer any estate or interest in property. It creates rights over property because the property stands charged with the payment of a sum of money. For example, if John is contractually bound to pay a debt due to Jane out of his Woolworth shares, Jane has an equitable charge on those shares for the amount of the debt, whether either of them knew or intended that result.

The remedies of an equitable chargee are the same as an equitable mortgagee, except that, as there is no mortgage, he cannot foreclose, but a court will order a sale in lieu of foreclosure.

EQUITABLE INTERESTS. Rights of ownership, such as an interest under a trust, which will be enforced in equity but not in common law. They should be distinguished from 'mere equities' which is a procedural right, such as to have a transaction set aside for fraud or undue influence or to have a document rectified for mistake.

EQUITABLE JURISDICTION. The primary jurisdiction of equity is over a defendant personally and springs from the maxim that equity acts *in personam*. This is now of less significance than it used to be, principally because of the introduction of statutory powers. On this principle the court will hear an action concerning foreign property which is outside its jurisdiction, if the defendant is in England or can be served with proceedings outside England. So, in *Penn* v *Lord Baltimore* in 1750, specific performance was ordered of an agreement relating to land boundaries in America, as the defendant was in England.

EQUITABLE MORTGAGE. This arises when a loan is made on the security of property (it need not be land) without transferring the title to the property into the name of the lender; it is a mortgage without a transfer of the legal estate. The informality attached to its creation is little short of breathtaking. Although any agreement to create a mortgage over land is required to be in writing, the mere deposit of the title deeds to land with a lender as security for his loan, is sufficient to create an equitable mortgage. The deposit, as security for a loan, of a share certificate or an insurance policy, even without any written memorandum, is also an equitable mortgage.

The lender under an equitable mortgage has the same remedies as a legal mortgagee on default by the borrower, except that he cannot enter into possession of the property without a court order. As the lender cannot transfer the legal estate (because the title has not been transferred to him), the agreement usually contains a device, such as a power of attorney, to enable him to sell. Where the mortgage is by deed, the lender may sell or appoint a receiver; otherwise the court at his request may do so. See EQUITY OF REDEMPTION.

EQUITY. Developed in the Middle Ages by the Chancellor in his Court of Chancery, to temper the rigidity and harshness of the common law. Gradually equity became so systematized that its court was no longer one of conscience, but one with rules as fixed as those of common law. This led Lord Eldon, prior to his retirement as Chancellor in 1818, to state that nothing would inflict on him greater pain, than the reproach that the equity of his court varied 'like the Chancellor's foot'.

In England (as in the USA) until the late nineteenth century equity was distinguished from the common law not only by its historical origin but by four other characteristics: its application by a separate court which introduced new procedures, such as discovery; a procedure which did not use a jury; the discretionary nature of its remedies, such as an injunction, which supplemented those of the common law; and the application of rights, such as trusts, which the common law did not enforce.

In 1875, following a report that deep rooted mischiefs arose from separate courts proceeding on antagonistic principles, the Judicature Acts amalgamated the courts of common law and equity. Equity now prevails where there is any conflict or variance with common law. See MAXIMS OF EQUITY.

EQUITY OF REDEMPTION. The right of a borrower to redeem a mortgage, and his other rights in the mortgaged property. A debenture issued by a company can be irredeemable, but apart from that exception any agreement to prevent a borrower redeeming his mortgage is ineffectual. There must be 'no clog or fetter' on the equity of redemption.

ESCROW. Executing a deed and delivering it subject to a condition that it will only take effect on the satisfaction of a specified condition or event. Pending the happening of the condition or event, the escrow is irrevocable. The term is often wrongly applied to other documents whose exchange is subject to a condition precedent.

When a corporation seals a deed, that is evidence of delivery; it is therefore prudent, if operation of the deed is to be conditional, to execute a separate escrow agreement stating the conditions upon which the principal deed is to become operative.

ESTOPPEL. Derives from the old French 'estoupail' – a bung or cork which stops something from coming out. The doctrine is one of the most useful weapons in the legal armoury. In general it precludes a person from denying a statement of fact whether in reality it is true or not. Promissory estoppel applies where a person in a transaction, by his words or conduct, makes to another an unambiguous promise or assurance which is intended to effect legal relations (whether contractual or not) between them, and the other acts upon it altering his position to his detriment. The person making the promise or assurance will be bound by it.

It is not a cause of action but a rule of evidence; it is 'a shield not a sword'. But it can give rise to a binding obligation which, without estoppel, could not exist: e.g. a principal cannot be bound by a contract made without his authority; but, if the result of the principal's conduct is that a person who appears to be his agent makes a contract with a third person who relies on that appearance, the principal may be stopped from denying the existence of the authority.

Proprietory estoppel can establish a new and permanent right to property. It is principally concerned with land rights but can extend to other forms of property. It operates where a person has spent money on or suffered some detriment in relation to property, believing himself to have sufficient interest to justify what he did, and that belief has been fostered by another person. That other will be stopped from asserting his legal rights if it would be unfair for him to do so.

EUROBONDS. Bearer instruments, which are usually unsecured, issued as a means of raising money by corporate and unincorporated entities (e.g. governments). $135.4 billion were issued in 1985. They are listed on an internationally recognized stock exchange and are denominated either in dollars or other Eurocurrencies and, latterly, in ECUs. They are termed 'Notes' if issued with a maturity of under five years and 'bonds' if over but should not be confused with Euronotes.

It is conventional for interest on Eurobonds to be paid without deduction of tax. UK companies, since the Finance Act 1984, can pay interest gross on quoted Eurobonds and obtain tax relief for the interest if payment is made by or through a person not in the UK, the beneficial owner of the bond is non-resident and the bond is held in a recognized clearing system such as Euro-clear.

EURO-CLEAR. The most widely used clearance system for internationally traded securities, operated by Morgan Guaranty Trust Company of New York through its Brussels office. Its principal rival is Luxemburg-based Cedel. A high proportion of Eurobonds are physically deposited with Euro-clear (or one of the other systems), all subsequent trading being effected merely by book entries.

EUROCURRENCY MARKET. Eurocurrency is a national currency which is held by a person outside that country. The principal Eurocurrency is the Eurodollar.

The Eurocurrency market was born out of the dollars expended by the USA in Europe after World War II in development aid. The growth in the pool of offshore dollars was enhanced by the higher returns available in Europe and the exclusion of offshore deposits from regulatory reserve requirements imposed on US banks. The Euromarket (and the number of overseas branches of US banks) escalated when the 1964 US Interest Equalization Tax and related legislation cut off the US capital markets as a source of funds for operations outside the USA. The restrictions were lifted during 1974 but the Euromarket continued to flourish partly because it is largely free of the regulatory constraints which (albeit to a decreasing degree) apply in most relevant domestic markets and partly because the market provides an alternative (and possibly cheaper) source of funds.

EURONOTES. Short-term negotiable bearer instruments of up to six months duration, usually issued at a discount to par and generally (but not necessarily) denominated in dollars. They are not listed on a stock exchange but may be rated by Standard & Poor (one of the largest US credit rating agencies) under a specially devised system. Euronotes are the Euro-equivalent of US commercial paper.

EUROPEAN COMMISSION. The Commission of the European Communities and 'guardian' of the EEC Treaties. It is a collegiate body governed by a President and 17 Commissioners appointed by the governments of member states. Commissioners must remain independent and undertake not to take instructions from their national governments. It formulates proposals for Community policies, administers and enforces existing policies and legislates for the Community when required to do so by the Treaties.

The Commission is divided into Directorates General corresponding to the main areas of Community activity. Each Directorate-General is the responsibility of a Commissioner, and is administered by civil servants ('Eurocrats') recruited from the member states.

EUROPEAN COMMUNITIES. There are three groupings: the European Coal and Steel Community (ECSC), the European Atomic Energy Community (EURATOM) and the European Economic Community (EEC). The ECSC and EURATOM are limited to their eponymous sectors of the economy. The EEC covers most other areas of economic activity.

EUROPEAN CONVENTION ON HUMAN RIGHTS (1950). Designed to protect the basic tenets of individual rights as they are known to the Western world, such as freedom of expression and the right to a just trial. The Convention has been incorporated into the municipal laws of a number of signatory states. Attempts to incorporate the Convention into English law have been consistently avoided by successive governments although the UK is a party.

The Convention can be enforced by application to the European Human Rights Commission in Strasburg which is known as the Council of Europe. If no friendly settlement is reached the Commission refers to the European Court of Human Rights whose judgments are final and binding on signatory states.

EUROPEAN COURT OF JUSTICE. The court of the European Communities is the only court that can give a final and binding interpretation of Community law. It has exclusive jurisdiction in disputes between the member states and the Community, and between the Community institutions *inter se*, as well as exclusive competence to declare Community legislation invalid.

Courts or tribunals of member states may refer questions of interpretation of Community law to the court. National courts against whose decisions there is no appeal are obliged to do so.

Each member state appoints one judge for a term of six years. There are also six Advocates-General who have the same status as judges. They assist the court by giving opinions which are not binding but are usually followed.

EUROPEAN CURRENCY UNIT (ECU). The unit of account used in the European monetary system. The ECU is valued on the basis of specified amounts of currencies of certain EEC member states; both the currencies chosen and their respective weighting can be varied by EEC regulation. The ECU is becoming increasingly popular in Eurobond issues because, as a basket of currencies, it reduces the risk of volatility. Nevertheless, the ECU is not yet legal tender anywhere, although a small group of banks on both sides of the Atlantic have made the ECU one of the more actively traded currencies in the foreign exchange and deposit markets.

EUROPEAN DIRECTIVES. Legislative instruments proposed by the European Commission. Member states are required to implement the provisions of Directives in their national legislation within a period of two to four years from their adoption by the Council of Ministers. Failure to implement a Directive may mean that it takes effect in any event.

EUROPEAN ECONOMIC INTEREST GROUPING (EUREIG). By 1988 a new creature of the EEC of this name will exist: it is a form of cross-national partnership, based on concepts in French law, where members have joint and several liability for debts.

It will transcend the domestic laws of EEC members except those relating to employment. The object is to encourage the formation of partnerships between corporations to achieve a common business objective. Whether this form of grouping will be used, and how successful it will be, remains to be seen.

EUROPEAN JURISDICTION AND JUDGMENTS CONVENTION, THE. This will, when ratified, enable a judgment obtained in one EEC member state to be recognized and enforced in another, merely by registration in the enforcing jurisdiction, provided that it is not contrary to public policy.

It will apply to most civil and commercial judgments against a company or individual 'domiciled' (resident) in the Community; accordingly its scope of application will not be limited to nationals of EEC member states.

EUROPEAN RECOMMENDATIONS AND OPINIONS. A Recommendation can be given by any Community institution to any person in the EEC with the object of suggesting a particular course of conduct: no legal obligation is imposed. It can be given to a member state as a polite way of seeking a change in statute to conform with Community law, or to a company suggesting that it should abide by a particular law as a prelude to enforcement.

An Opinion is given by the Commission in consequence of

representations made to it, and contains a general appraisal of processes or a contribution to the preparation of legislation.

EUROPEAN REGULATION. A law which binds and is directly applicable in member states without any need for national legislation. They may be enacted by the European Commission or the Council of Ministers. For example, the Council has enacted regulations on regional development measures, and concerning public service in transport.

EVASION (TAX). See AVOIDANCE AND EVASION.

EX PARTE. Civil proceedings brought before a judge by one party alone, without first giving notice to the other. They are used in emergency cases where there is no time to go through the normal notification procedures and where an urgent and immediate remedy is required.

EX TURPI CAUSA NON ORITUR ACTIO. The maxim that 'out of an evil cause, no action arises' is one of the roots of many so-called illegal contracts where, in consequence, no rights or liabilities can originate.

EXCHANGE AND SALE. Exchange is not a sale. In both exchange and sale, ownership of an asset is transferred by mutual assent. To constitute a sale the consideration for the transfer must be in money or both money and goods having a fixed value. If the consideration is goods, or value of some other kind, the transaction is one of exchange. An exchange does not enjoy the protection of the Sale of Goods Act 1979.

Capital gains tax relief is available in certain situations where there is an exchange (but not a sale) of shares.

EXCHANGE CONTROLS. Regulations controlling movements of finance, property and services to protect a country's currency resources. Exchange controls in the UK were suspended in 1979. The UK courts recognize foreign exchange controls to the extent required by private international law. Monetary deals in currencies of any member of the 1945 Bretton Woods

Agreement which are contrary to the exchange control regulations of that member are unenforceable in the UK.

EXCLUSION AGREEMENT. A written agreement between the parties to an arbitration to exclude a reference to the court on a preliminary point of law or to review an award on points of law. It is valid only if it is made after the commencement of the arbitration in domestic and special category arbitrations.

A domestic arbitration is one which provides for arbitration in the UK to which broadly no foreigner is a party. A special category arbitration is one governed by the law of England and Wales which relates to a claim or dispute involving Admiralty jurisdiction or an insurance or commodity contract.

The parties can at any time, by what is known as a *Scott* v *Avery* clause, provide that an action shall not be brought into court until an award is made.

EXECUTION. The valid signing of a document. In favour of a purchaser a deed is deemed to have been duly executed by a company if it purports to have been sealed in the presence of and attested by a director and the secretary or by two directors.

EXECUTIVE DIRECTOR. A director who is employed to perform management duties in a company, usually on a full-time basis. Appointed for the skills he possesses rather than for the aura attaching to his name as is sometimes the case with non-executive directors.

EXECUTOR. See PERSONAL REPRESENTATIVE.

EXEMPT DEALER. See DEALERS IN SECURITIES.

EXEMPTION AND EXCLUSION TERMS. These are clauses in contracts by which one party attempts (sometimes successfully) to absolve himself from liabilities which would otherwise be his. They are usually found, in small print, in standard form contracts for the supply of goods or services where there is a 'take it or leave it' situation.

Statutes have reduced some of their worst effects, particularly in relation to private consumers. The Fair Trading Act 1973, for instance, stops an unscrupulous trader using a contract provision which is void in law: traders used to get away with it because the law is not generally known and legal advice is so rarely sought.

It is now impossible to exclude liability in negligence for death, personal injury or, unless the clause is fair and reasonable, any other loss caused by negligence.

An exclusion clause must be an integral part of the contract and drawn to the attention of the other party before the contract is made. In the case of private consumers it cannot exclude liability for fraud, or terms implied by statute.

There are no statutory controls on exclusion clauses contained in contracts for the international supply of goods. On the contrary, statute may impose exclusion clauses as in the carriage of goods by sea.

EXHIBIT. A document or object referred to in an affidavit, or produced to a court. The *White Book* contains detailed regulations on exhibits, e.g. very small articles 'must be enclosed in a sealed transparent container of such a nature that it could not be reconstituted once opened . . . '.

EXPERT. Defined in the Act as including an engineer, valuer, accountant and any other person whose profession gives authority to a statement made by him. When an expert's report appears in a prospectus, it must contain a statement that he has consented to the inclusion of his report in the form and context in which it appears and that the consent has not been withdrawn. It is a precaution against unscrupulous promoters who, in the past, were prone to putting fictitious reports from leading experts in prospectuses.

Except on a share exchange or merger an expert (who can be the company's auditor) must value a non-cash consideration when it is acquired by a public company for shares.

A person who is asked to assess a value as an expert is not an arbitrator.

EXTRAORDINARY GENERAL MEETING. Any meeting of shareholders other than the annual general meeting of a company. It may be convened by the directors whenever they wish.

Shareholders owning not less than one-tenth of the paid-up

capital carrying voting rights may require the directors to convene a meeting: but there is no statutory obligation to hold it (as opposed to convening it) within a specific time unless the Articles so provide. If the directors fail to convene the meeting within 21 days, the requisitionists may do so themselves at the expense of the company.

A meeting must be convened and held within specific time limits on the requisition of a resigning auditor; and within 28 days of the directors becoming aware that the net assets of a public company have fallen to one-half or less of the company's paid-up capital, to consider the measures to be taken: this may be too late to prevent penalties against the directors resulting from the Insolvency Act 1985. See EXTRAORDINARY RESOLUTION, ORDINARY RESOLUTION and SPECIAL RESOLUTION.

EXTRAORDINARY RESOLUTION. One passed by a majority of not less than 75 per cent of the members voting in person or by proxy at a general meeting of a company at which notice specifying the intention to propose the resolution as an extraordinary resolution has been given.

These resolutions are required, e.g., to wind up the company voluntarily or to give certain powers to the liquidator in a voluntary winding up. A copy of the resolution must be filed with the Registrar and annexed to the Articles.

See MODIFICATION OF RIGHTS, ORDINARY RESOLUTION and SPECIAL RESOLUTION.

F

FAIR COMMENT. Fair comment on a matter of public interest is a defence to an action for defamation. As the defence is in the nature of a general right it enables any publicly-spirited individual to comment on matters in which the public is legitimately concerned or interested. The comment must be fair, must not be a statement of fact, but may be an opinion based on accurate or reasonably believed facts. The comment must be made honestly and not actuated by malice: allegations of motive are particularly dangerous.

FALSE MARKET. The Stock Exchange considers it as any market in which the movement of a share price is brought about by contrived factors, such as a collaboration of buyers and sellers calculated to cause a price movement not justified by the company's assets, income or prospects. To thwart such conspiracies, members are prohibited from knowingly, or without due care, dealing in such a way as to promote or assist in promoting a false market.

The City Panel adopts a wider line and insists that all parties to a take-over must not make statements which may mislead shareholders or the market, and must endeavour to prevent the creation of a false market in the shares of the companies involved.

FAMILY PROVISION. The freedom of a individual to dispose of his property on death as he wishes is limited by the Inheritance (Provision for Family and Dependants) Act 1975. A court may increase the provision made for a surviving spouse, children and other persons dependent upon the deceased on the impersonal ground that the law or his will does not make reasonable financial provision for the applicant. The jurisdiction is used cautiously, if not sparingly, where luxuries are concerned but lavishly where bare necessities are needed.

FEDERAL COURTS, USA. The US consumer is faced with two different court systems: those of the 50 individual states and the federal system. There is substantial overlapping of jurisdiction.

The federal courts are, at the lowest level, the US District Courts, which have a territorial jurisdiction and a single judge; then 11 Courts of Appeals, where cases are usually heard by a

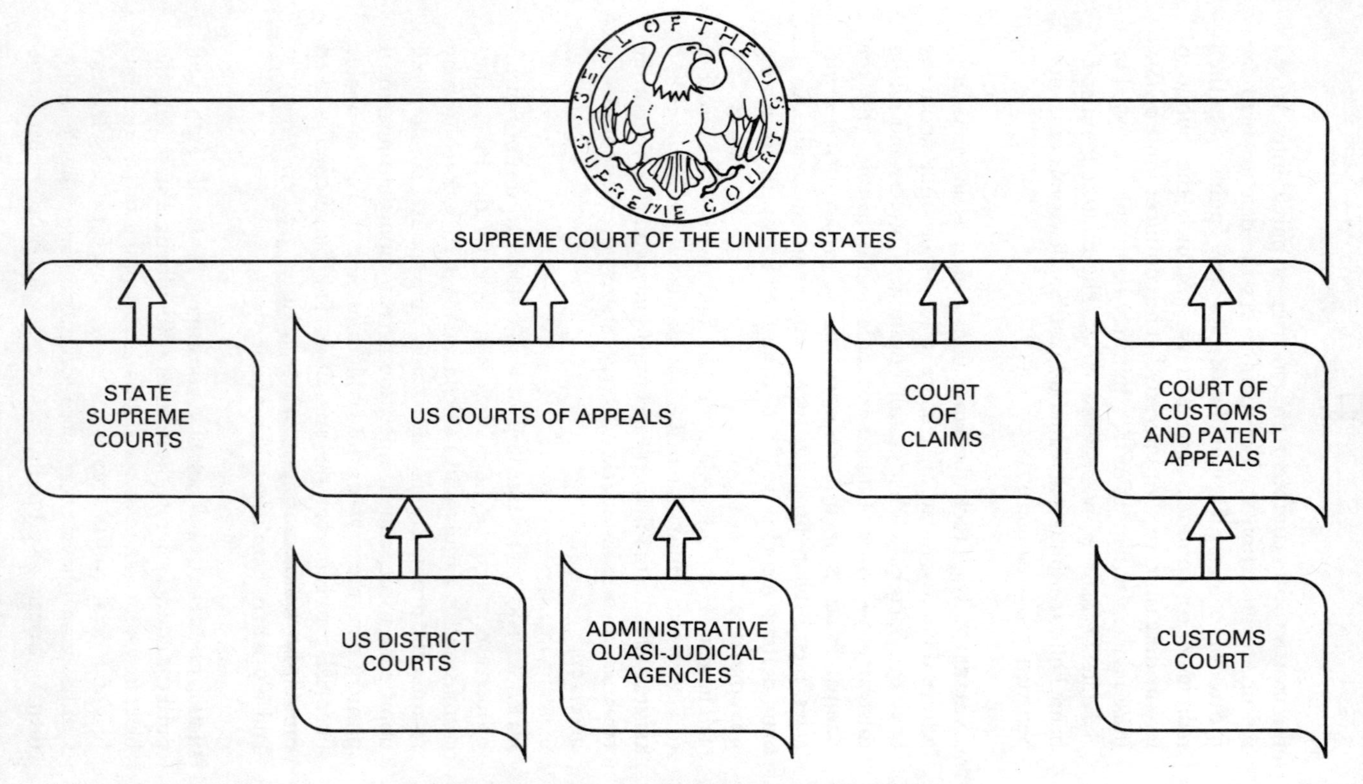

THE FEDERAL JUDICIAL SYSTEM OF THE UNITED STATES

panel of three judges. They review all final decisions of courts within their circuit except where, exceptionally, the law provides for direct review by the US Supreme Court. They may review decisions of the Tax Courts and federal and administrative bodies such as the Securities and Exchange Commission (SEC) and the Labor Relations Board.

Federal judges are appointed for life, subject to good behaviour, by the President with the advice and consent of the Senate.

In the USA it is estimated that corporations spend $80 billion a year on legal costs. To reduce these, the Federal Bar Council has introduced a scheme to eliminate pre-trial procedures and to have an award made on the merits of the case, without adopting the conventional US adversary procedure. English lawyers have not yet been seduced by this practice!

FEDERAL TRADE COMMISSION. An independent agency of the US government, whose role is analagous to that of the Office of Fair Trading in the UK.

FEE SIMPLE. The 'estate of fee simple absolute in possession'. It is the freehold interest in land which, to all intents and purposes, is everlasting. It is one of only two estates in land capable of existing in law, the other being a 'term of years absolute', or leasehold.

FIDUCIARY DUTY. Any person who is in a position of trust in relation to another has duties of loyalty and good faith imposed upon him. There is authority that this applies whenever a plaintiff has entrusted a job to the defendant to do. There may even be a fiduciary duty to 'gazump'. A fiduciary must not place himself in a position where there is a conflict between his duties and his personal interests. Good faith must not only be done but it must openly and clearly be seen to be done. Whether what a fiduciary does is fair or unfair is irrelevant. A fiduciary must not put himself into a position where his judgment is or is likely to be biased, nor can he avoid liability by asserting that he was not biased.

This principle of equity applies to a whole range of relationships including trustee and beneficiary, agent and principal, director and company (but not to an individual shareholder) and solicitor and client. All are liable to refund, with interest, all profits made by means of their position unless they were made after full disclosure, with the full knowledge and approval of the persons to whom they owed a duty. See UNDUE INFLUENCE.

FIERI FACIAS (FI-FA). Means 'cause to be done' and is the name given to a writ issued in the courts by a judgment creditor requiring the Sheriff to seize from the debtor sufficient goods and chattels to meet his judgment. The Sheriff auctions the goods he has received and accounts to the creditor. The notification to the creditor from the Sheriff that the money has been raised is called *fieri feci* 'done it'. 'Dunned' might be more apposite.

FINANCIAL SERVICES ACT 1986. This will come into force by stages beginning in early 1987 and will regulate the business practices of the financial services industry, including dealers in securities, brokers and investment managers and advisers.

The statute will apply to practically all investments (including unit trusts, and futures and long-term insurance contracts acquired or entered into for investment purposes) other than physical commodities or investments such as stamps and antiques. The statute will make it a criminal offence to carry on any investment business in the United Kingdom without authorization, which can be obtained either directly from a government-appointed supervisory agency (proposed to be the Securities and Investments Board) or by joining a self-regulatory organization recognized by that agency as competent to regulate its members. It will also control the issue of mailshots, advertisements and other marketing documents, which will normally have to be issued by 'authorized persons' except in the case of prospectuses containing prescribed disclosures.

FIRM. Persons who have entered into partnership with one another. A partnership can sue and be sued in the firm's name.

FIXED CHARGE. Security given by a borrower over present or future property. It fastens on existing property when the charge is executed and may fasten on future property when it comes into existence. Unless the charging document provides otherwise, the borrower is unable to deal with the property without the consent of the lender.

The Insolvency Act 1985 will adversely affect the holder of a fixed charge over a company's property: he cannot prevent an Administration Order being made, nor enforce the charge after the making of an Administration Order without the consent of the court.

A fixed charge, even if it has priority, can be overridden if an Administrative Receiver appointed under a floating charge satisfies the court that the sale of the secured property could promote a more advantageous realization of the company assets if it were sold free from the security. The chargee will receive the net proceeds of sale but this may lead to disputes where the property is sold with the rest of the business and the price requires apportionment. See RECEIVER.

FLOATING CHARGE. A security given by a company over all or any part of its existing and future undertaking or assets. The advantage to the company is that it can deal with its property without the consent of the lender until the charge crystallizes.

Preferential debts of a company in liquidation have priority to the repayment of holders of a floating charge.

An Administrative Receiver can be appointed by the lender if the borrower defaults and the charge is secured on all or substantially all of the company's property.

If the charge is given by the company without receiving full consideration (which can be money, goods, services) at the same time as, or after, the creation of the charge, it will be invalid as to the amount of the shortfall if it was created within twelve months of an administration order or winding up, or two years if it was given to a person connected with the company. See RECEIVER.

FLOM, JOE. A New York attorney who, because of his brilliance, is retained by numerous corporations to avoid his acting against them in a take-over. He has, in a short space of time, been responsible for building the firm of Skadden Arps Meagher & Flom into perhaps the largest law firm in the world. In the USA a take-over is not regarded as serious unless he and Martin Lipton are acting on opposite sides.

FLOTATION. There comes a stage in a successful company's existence when its proprietors decide to 'go public' by getting its shares listed on The Stock Exchange or dealt in on the Unlisted Securities Market. That they may subsequently regret doing so is irrelevant, at the time: few landmarks in a company's existence are as exciting. It provides a market for the company's shares, and raises capital for the company or the shareholders or both. It pleases the local bank manager and the Chancellor of the Exchequer, and is a delight to the Issuing House and brokers who sponsor the issue, and the professional advisers who do the work.

There are various methods by which a flotation is effected; each involves the issue of a prospectus and the sale or subscription of shares at a fixed price.

An offer for sale is made by an Issuing House, or stockbroker, which agrees to buy or subscribe shares in the company which it then sells to the public at a somewhat higher price. The Issuing House will insure against an unsuccessful issue by underwriting and is remunerated by the turn which it makes on the sale, or by a fee, or both. Alternatively the company may sell shares directly to the public by an offer for subscription without any intermediary. A merchant bank will usually underwrite the issue, but will not be involved as a principal.

Another method is a placing where either the Issuing House purchases the securities and sells them to its clients or procures their sale to its clients without purchasing. See OFFER FOR SALE BY TENDER.

FORCE MAJEURE. It has been said that 'this term has a clear meaning in law' and also 'the precise meaning of this term, if it has one, has eluded the lawyers for years'. Despite this dichotomy it is generally held to mean an event beyond the control of the parties: such as strikes, government restrictions, acts of God or war (cf. FRUSTRATION).

Force majeure clauses may either provide for the cancellation of the contract on the occurrence of the disturbing outside element or for an extension in the time of performance.

The phrase 'subject to force majeure' means that, in the event of force majeure, the parties will be excused from further performance of the contract, subject to their obligation to co-operate reasonably to ensure the performance of their bargain, such as by obtaining any licence.

FORECLOSURE. Foreclosure is one of the remedies of a mortgagee when the person to whom he has lent money upon the security of property defaults.

In foreclosing, the mortgagee asks the court to set a date by which the borrower has to repay all outstanding principal and interest, and the cost of the legal services involved. If the borrower fails to repay by the due date, the court's earlier foreclosure order *nisi* is made absolute and the property belongs to the mortgagee and the debt is discharged.

FOREIGN CORRUPT PRACTICES ACT OF 1977. A US federal body of law, designed to prevent the bribing of foreign governmental officials by companies or individuals subject to the laws of the USA. It requires certain companies to comply with books and records and internal accounting control provisions. Enforcement rests with the SEC and the US Department of Justice.

FOREIGN JUDGMENTS. It has been established for over a century that, if a foreign judgment has been given by a court of competent jurisdiction, it is conclusive and cannot be re-examined in England on its merits. The view taken by the courts is that the foreign judgment creates a simple contract debt between the parties. But fresh legal proceedings have to be instituted for its enforcement in the absence of a statute (of which there are a number) which makes judgments enforceable by, for example, production of a certificate of judgment or registration. Where a foreign judgment can be enforced under the simpler procedure of a statute, this will generally be pursuant to some multilateral (e.g. the European Convention on Civil Jurisdiction and Judgments) or bilateral agreements entered into by the UK.

There are four basic principles:

- the foreign court must have had jurisdiction according to a recognized principle of international law, such as the residence of the defendant in that country;

- the foreign judgment must be final and conclusive although enforcement proceedings may be brought in England despite the possibility of a future appeal in the foreign country;
- the judgment must be for a fixed sum: neither indefinite sums nor equitable remedies, such as specific performance, will be enforced;
- the English court is not entitled to consider whether the foreign court has been mistaken as to law, procedure, or fact, even if it got its English law wrong.

A defendant can escape liability if he proves that the foreign court had no jurisdiction, or the judgment was obtained by fraud, or was contrary to natural justice, or repugnant to English public policy.

FORUM NON CONVENIENS. A US and Scottish doctrine which, in theory if not in practice, is not recognized in English law. Under the doctrine, a court may decline to hear a case, or stay proceedings before it, on the ground that the action has been brought in the wrong country and should have been brought elsewhere.

***FOSS* v *HARBOTTLE*, THE RULE IN.** The general rule is that if a wrong is done to a company only the company itself can sue. The justification for its existence is the general principle that a majority of the members control the company and to allow the minority to sue could result in a multiplicity of actions. Moreover, if the alleged wrong is suffered by the company, it is logical that it should be the plaintiff in any action.

The rule is not of much help in the real world where sharp directors act illegally, or an individual's rights as a member under the Articles are deliberately disregarded. So judges, with good sense, have made exceptions to the rule, including the right of a minority of members to sue where there has been an abuse of power by controlling directors or shareholders.

Difficulties arise when directors do not control the company and a minority wish to sue them for something less than fraud or breach of fiduciary duty to the company. There are alternative minority rights. See FRAUD ON A MINORITY and INSPECTION AND INVESTIGATION.

FRANCHISE. A contract or licence for the exploitation of a right owned or concept created by the franchisor.

The franchisor usually receives an initial fee and continuing payments based on a percentage of turnover for his central management services which may include quality control, market research, centralized advertising, buying and supply.

A franchise may relate to a business format consisting of a product and a system of producing and selling that product, or merely give the right to exploit a product in a particular location.

In the USA, the antitrust authorities have generally taken a positive view of franchise agreements, and consider that the restrictions on competition are outweighed by the competitive benefits arising from them.

The European Court on 28 January 1986 held that territorial restrictions in franchise agreements in the EEC where the franchisee is given exclusive territorial protection and provisions which prevent franchisees from entering into price competition among themselves, infringe Article 85 and are accordingly void. In the present state of Community law, and in the absence of a block exemption applying to franchise agreements, notification to the Commission of such agreements must now be the prudent course.

FRAUD. In a civil, as opposed to a criminal, sense fraud, or deceit, is a false statement made knowingly or recklessly which the representor did not honestly believe to be true. The representor may be liable for damages even if the misrepresentation was made without a corrupt motive, and with no expectation of profit, if it was acted upon by the person to whom it was made.

If an agent innocently makes a statement which is known to his principal to be false, neither the agent nor principal is guilty of fraud unless the principal intended the agent to make the false statement.

Fraud, in a criminal context, is an element in a variety of offences. It is generally obtaining property, or a pecuniary advantage, by deception calculated to leave the criminal fraudster financially better off. See MISREPRESENTATION and UNDUE INFLUENCE.

FRAUD ON A MINORITY. English company law believes in majority rule. However a shareholder can challenge the actions of the majority who act in such a way as to perpetrate a fraud on the minority. This does not necessarily involve fraudulent behaviour, as the name suggests, but it does require that a minority of the shareholders is in some way unfairly prejudiced, which includes conduct by majority shareholders or controlling directors enabling an action to be brought under one of the exceptions to the rule in *Foss* v *Harbottle*.

The Act allows a minority shareholder to petition the court for an order that the company's affairs are being, or are proposed to be conducted, in a manner which is unfairly prejudicial to some part of the members. The court order may regulate the company's affairs in the future; require the purchase of the minority shares; enable civil proceedings to be brought in the company's name; or provide for the company's winding up.

FRAUD SQUAD. A branch of the Metropolitan Police designed to tackle the incidence of criminal fraud in both the private and public sectors. It operates from an address conveniently situated within walking distance of the House of Commons where it would appear that most of the available information on the incidence of fraud in London is collated and publicized.

FRAUDULENT PREFERENCE. Paying a lawful debt at its due date is neither illegal nor fraudulent but, if insolvency occurs soon afterwards and it was intended to give that creditor an advantage, the payment may be recovered by the liquidator for the benefit of all the creditors. The word 'fraudulent' is a misnomer. No fraud need be involved.

As part of its aim of enhancing the position of creditors generally, the Insolvency Act 1985 treats preferences of a broadly defined category of connected and associated persons more strictly. It extends from six months to two years the period prior to the winding up during which such transactions are vulnerable. It establishes a presumption in those cases that there was the necessary intention to prefer. The statute allows the court to make such order as it thinks fit for restoring the original position. The misleading term at the head of this entry is abolished. What was a fraudulent preference is now simply a 'preference', which applies as much to individuals as to companies.

FRAUDULENT TRADING. Knowingly carrying on a company's business with intent to defraud its creditors, or creditors of any other person, or for any fraudulent purpose. The most common example is that of a company continuing to incur liabilities when it is insolvent. It is a criminal offence for which the directors and other persons can be liable. They may also be held personally liable for all the company's debts and liabilities and disqualified from acting as officers of a company.

The degree of fraud has never been completely clear, but it has been held to involve 'actual dishonesty involving . . . real moral blame'. Consequently, fraudulent trading has been difficult to prove, as it is a valid defence that the directors genuinely believed that 'there was light at the end of the tunnel'. Fraudulent trading is supplemented (but not replaced) by the new offence of wrongful trading.

FRUSTRATION. In 1902 Mr Henry agreed to let his flat to Mr Krell to view the eagerly awaited coronation procession of King Edward VII. A deposit was paid. Unfortunately, His Majesty was impelled through illness to postpone the celebrations. Mr Henry sued for the balance of the rent. The Court of Appeal decided that the agreement was frustrated and the rent was irrecoverable.

Frustration occurs whenever the law recognizes that, without default of either party, a contract has become incapable of being performed because the circumstances in which performance is called for would render it radically different from the obligations originally undertaken.

From the date of frustration the contract is killed and it discharges both parties automatically. But what if the contract has been partly performed? This leads to difficult questions but in most cases the Law Reform (Frustrated Contracts) Act 1943 will apply to a contract governed by English law to enable the courts to adjust differences on the basis of justice and equity.

G

GARNISHEE. A person who owes money to someone who has had a judgment order made against him to pay a sum of money. The facility exists to require a garnishee to pay a debt owed to the judgment debtor directly to the judgment creditor, by an *ex parte* application to the court. A successful application leads to an interim or *nisi* order which, following service on the garnishee, has the effect of creating an equitable charge over the debt in favour of the garnishor until final judgment.

Banks are usually the subject of garnishee orders but the rules have equal application to most other persons owing money to judgment debtors.

GENERAL COUNSEL. The chief legal officer of a US corporation who, because of his powers of patronage, is sedulously courted by US attorneys anxious to pick up some business. Alternatively a firm of US attorneys which is retained to give general rather than specialist advice.

GIFTS. Everyone knows what a gift is, although they may not realize that in law it is the absence of consideration which distinguishes it from a contract. Consequently, the courts will not enforce a promise to make a gift unless it is made by deed. If a gift is not the subject of a declaration of trust and the donor has not done all that is necessary on his part to transfer it, the courts will not treat it as effective. As Lord Justice Turner said in 1862, 'there is no equity in this court to perfect an imperfect gift'. For instance, with land, the transfer must be in writing; shares must have a properly executed share transfer, and chattels, such as jewellery, must be delivered. A gift by cheque is not completed until it is paid and cleared.

But take comfort! A gift will be effective even if the recipient does not intend to accept it as a gift but, for example, as a loan.

Wealth warning: a gift can give rise to a charge to inheritance tax and capital gains tax.

GLASS-STEAGALL BANKING ACT 1933. A US federal statute prohibiting a commercial bank from undertaking investment banking activities.

GOLDEN HANDCUFFS. City slang for the legal restrictions imposed on members of firms of brokers and jobbers who have sold out to the big financial institutions. The object is to try to tie them in to the ongoing business by providing them with various future benefits if they remain with the enlarged organization for a specified period.

GOLDEN HANDSHAKE. The satiric description applied to the sometimes over-generous payments made to directors or employees as alleged compensation for loss of office. A voluntary payment made to a director in compensation is generally unlawful, unless disclosed to and approved by shareholders.

GOLDEN PARACHUTE. US contracts providing extra lucrative payments to top management either resigning or sacked after a change in control. While they may be justified as needed to retain the services of such persons during a take-over bid, they may deter a bidder and function as a defensive measure. They may work in the UK but at significant tax cost and institutional anger.

GOLDEN SHARE. The share that represents the residual influence of government in a former nationalized company which has been privatized. The rights attaching to the share will vary with the nature of the veto which the government wishes to retain over the running of the company's affairs.

GOOD FAITH. An act is performed in good faith if it is done honestly. There are many areas of the law where a person is required to show good faith. There are other areas where a person acting in good faith may acquire rights which would otherwise not be available to him. For instance, a purchaser acting in good faith may acquire a good title to goods if he is unaware that the person selling the goods has no title to them. Where a fiduciary relationship exists, good faith is merely one component of that relationship, e.g. a director can be in breach of his duty even if he acts in good faith. All the powers of a director must be exercised in good faith for the benefit of the company and not for some extraneous purpose. See FIDUCIARY DUTY and INSURANCE.

GOODMAN, LORD. Known to his intimates as Goodie. Born 21 August 1913, solicitor, former Master of University College Oxford, a Life Peer and Companion of Honour. He is outstanding among contemporary solicitors for his negotiating ability and eloquence which have given him incredible contacts which he uses successfully, but properly, for the benefit of his clients.

GOODWILL. An intangible asset of a business which can take years to develop and minutes to destroy. It is nothing more than the probability of old customers resorting to the old place; it is the reputation and connection; the result of hard work or lavish expenditure of money. It represents the difference between the price paid for a business or company and the value of its net tangible assets. SSAP 22 requires that purchased goodwill must be written down in the accounts of a company either immediately or over its useful economic life. It is an asset for the purposes of capital gains tax and inheritance tax.

The sale of goodwill does not stop the seller from carrying on a competing business, but he may be restrained from soliciting customers of the former business.

Practical advice – always get a non-competition covenant from a seller of goodwill.

GOVERNMENT BROKER. The senior partner of Mullens & Co., stockbrokers, has since 1786 handled the sale of government securities on behalf of the government. When Big Bang takes effect the present senior partner will become a Bank of England official but will retain the title of Government Broker.

GOWER, PROFESSOR. Laurence Cecil Bartlett (call me Jim) Gower, solicitor, research adviser to the DTI on company law, and consultant to Goodman Derrick & Co. (of which Lord Goodman is senior partner). Born 29 December 1913, he was responsible for reviewing investor protection. His book on company law is the most stylish ever written, now, unfortunately, out of date as a result of his most recent writings – as draftsman of the Companies Act 1985.

GRANTOR TRUST. Another example of the cat and mouse game played worldwide by revenue authorities and taxpayers (hoping to become non-taxpayers presumably). In this instance, the playing field is the USA and the term is used to describe a form of trust where the person making it (the grantor) retains a right to the income, or some sufficient means of control over the trust to ensure for himself the possibility of benefiting at some later time from its income. The US Revenue requires the trust income to continue to be taxable in the grantor's hands.

It soon became apparent to those who think about these matters that these anti-avoidance rules could be turned to the taxpayer's advantage. Hence, this type of trust is, in practice, often used to protect US situated assets and US beneficiaries from taxation by the device of a grantor who is not liable to US taxation. As the grantor trust has become a weapon in the armoury of the taxpayer and not the tax collector, the rules are due to be changed.

GREEN BOOK. A publication of The Stock Exchange, so called because of the colour of its covers which distinguishes it from the *Yellow Book.* It contains the terms and conditions which govern entry of a company's securities to the Unlisted Securities Market and the provisions with which a company must comply following the commencement of dealing in its shares on the USM.

GUARANTEE COMPANY. A private company under which each member guarantees to pay a specified amount (which can be as derisory as 1p) to the assets of the company should it be wound up while he is a member or within one year after he ceases to be a member. It is thus a limited liability company, the liability of the members being limited to the amount of their guarantee. It may receive dispensation not to use the word 'limited' after its name. There is nothing to prevent it issuing debentures to the public.

A person does not necessarily have to pay to become a member. There are no shares, as transfers of membership and distribution of profit are not contemplated. For these reasons and because it is more versatile than a trust, it is the constitutional vehicle of organizations with charitable purposes and quasi-charitable purposes such as the friends of museums and learned societies.

GUARANTEES. The best advice that can be given to a person who wants to give a guarantee is the same as to those about to do an illegal act – 'don't'. But, despite this, guarantees continue to be given as security for a contractual obligation or a loan. The guarantor contracts with a creditor of a debtor to be responsible to him for the whole or part of the debt if the debtor defaults. The creditor to whom the guarantee is given has no obligation of disclosure towards the guarantor, but silence about a relevant fact may amount to a misrepresentation which can justify the guarantor repudiating the contract. A guarantee contract must be in writing.

In the absence of specific provision, the liability will continue after a guarantor's death. A guarantee given by a partnership to a third person in respect of its transactions is revoked by any change in the constitution of the firm, or of the firm in respect of which the guarantee was given.

Although not on its inception a contract of good faith, once it has been entered into the creditor must observe the utmost good faith towards the guarantor. There must be no dealings behind the guarantor's back or variations of terms with the debtor, or unauthorized extension of time to the debtor to discharge his debt. See CONTRIBUTION, INDEMNITY, MANUFACTURERS' WARRANTIES AND GUARANTEES, SUBROGATION and WARRANTIES AND CONDITIONS.

H

HART-SCOTT-RODINO. The US Hart-Scott-Rodino Antitrust Improvements Act of 1976 (HSR) requires a filing with both the Antitrust Division of the US Justice Department and the Federal Trade Commission, and a waiting period of generally up to 30 days before a purchase of voting securities worth not less than $15 million, or which would result in a holding of 50 per cent of the voting stock of a target company which had annual net sales or total assets of at least $25 million, provided that one of the parties meets a relatively modest size test and the other has minimum annual net sales or total assets of $100 million.

Although it is a US federal law it has extra-territorial application, e.g. it would apply if a US company bid for an English company with sales of $25 million or more into the USA or assets in the USA of $15 million or more. It also applies to purchases of assets.

HARVARD LAW JOURNAL. One of the most respected of all law journals; the best Harvard students aspire to 'join' the *Journal*, though whether for academic status or to enhance job prospects is unclear.

HEARSAY EVIDENCE. A statement, other than one made by a witness giving oral evidence, is inadmissible as evidence of any opinion or fact stated. For instance, if Jane gives evidence that John said he saw Charles steal an *Economist*, Jane's evidence of what John said is not admissible evidence of theft. Evidence of the fact that a statement was made is not hearsay. Hence the evidence given by Jane is inadmissible hearsay in a trial of Charles for theft but admissible to prove that John made his remarks in an action brought against him by Charles for slander. The reasons for excluding hearsay evidence are that the absent person cannot be cross examined and the court has no opportunity to observe his demeanour or the accuracy with which his words have been repeated.

There are many exceptions, particularly in civil proceedings, to the basic rule that hearsay is inadmissible.

HIGH COURT OF JUSTICE. Its central office is in the Law Courts in the Strand, London. It has 128 District Registries in cities through-

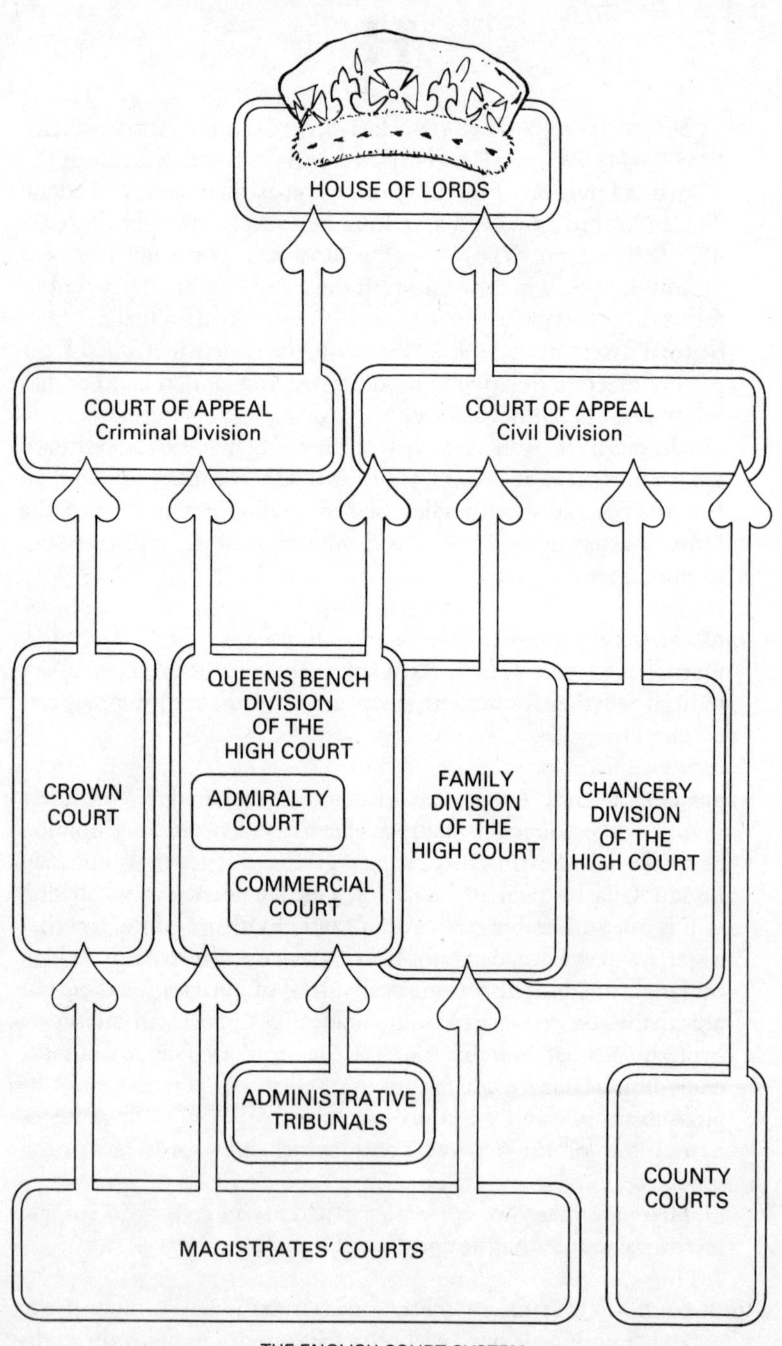

THE ENGLISH COURT SYSTEM

out England and Wales. Together with the Court of Appeal it makes up the Supreme Court of Judicature.

The High Court is the first port of call for litigants with civil claims worth £3,000 or more. Any claims below this sum should, for costs reasons, be brought in the County Court (though County Courts have jurisdiction to deal with claims up to £5,000). It also has jurisdiction in (amongst others) criminal, matrimonial and probate matters, and hears applications for judicial review and appeals from inferior courts.

The High Court has three divisions: Queen's Bench, Chancery and Family. Trials and more important applications are presided over by High Court judges (His Honour Mr Justice . . .). Other interlocutory applications and summonses are heard by Masters (in London) and District Registrars (outside London).

Civil actions brought in the High Court are usually dealt with more quickly and efficiently than those in the County Court, owing to more efficient procedures and a greater degree of professional representation; however they are considerably more expensive. In all applications before a High Court judge in open court, litigants must be represented by barristers (but, if they are individuals, they may appear in person).

HIRE-PURCHASE. An agreement to hire goods with an option for the hirer to purchase them when he has paid a prescribed number of instalments of hire.

Hire-purchase agreements appear most frequently in the context of purchases made with the assistance of finance houses, where no contractual nexus exists between the trader (who sells to the finance house) and the hirer (who makes the hire-purchase agreement with the finance house). Where this arises the Consumer Credit Act helps consumers by deeming representations made by the trader during negotiations to be those of the finance house: consequently the hirer is not denied a remedy for misrepresentation or breach of implied conditions. See CREDIT SALE.

HOLDING COMPANY. The parent company of one or more subsidiaries. It must submit group accounts to the Registrar.

England, unlike West Germany, has no general law governing the relationship between groups of companies; the ordinary rules of company law apply to them and they are treated as distinct legal entities. The directors of a holding company owe no duty as such to a subsidiary. The converse is true and a director of a subsidiary cannot justify transactions between parent and subsidiary to the detriment of the subsidiary by showing that a holding company has benefited.

HOTCHPOT. A mixing together of assets in order to ensure an equal division amongst those entitled to a share in them. If a particular fund is to be divided amongst a group of which one member has already received a share, that share must be notionally added to the total in quantifying his remaining entitlement.

HOUSE OF LORDS. The court of final appeal in the UK for all civil and criminal matters. Constitutionally it is identical to the upper House of Parliament, but is in practice confined to the Lord Chancellor and a maximum of 11 Lords of Appeal in Ordinary. The last time a lay peer ventured to give a judgment on an appeal was in 1883.

There is no right of appeal to the House of Lords: leave must always be obtained and will not always be given.

Decisions of the House of Lords are binding on all lower courts and it normally considers itself bound by its own earlier decisions. However, since 1966, it has allowed itself to depart from them in the interests of justice or the proper development of the law, but not merely if they were wrong or illogical. See LEAP-FROGGING APPEAL and PRIVY COUNCIL.

I

ILLEGAL CONTRACTS. Contracts which infringe a law specifically forbidding them (such as restrictive trade practices) or which are forbidden by common law on the grounds of public policy.

There are some contracts which offend public policy by ousting the jurisdiction of the courts or by restraint of trade; these are invalid and unenforceable, but not illegal. The broad categories of illegal contracts are those to commit a crime, a tort or a fraud on a third party; a contract that is sexually immoral; a contract to the prejudice of public safety (such as trading with an enemy alien in time of war); those prejudicial to the administration of justice (such as an agreement that a person who aids in litigation shall receive a share of damages in an action); a contract that tends to corruption in public life (such as an agreement to procure a title for a person for money); and a contract to defraud the taxman.

Illegal contracts are void; it is as though they never existed. Save in exceptional circumstances gains and losses remain where they have accrued or fallen. Sometimes, however, a person is allowed to recover what he has paid if the illegal contract has not been wholly performed or if he is the person whom a statute was intended to protect.

IMPACT DAY. The day on which a public offering is announced (which normally coincides with the day on which a prospectus is signed and filed with the Registrar) before release to the investing public. So called because it 'impacts' upon the market in the sense of committing funds by virtue of the related underwriting; hence the regulation of 'impact days' by the Government Broker. See CONTROL OF BORROWING ORDER.

IMPLIED AGREEMENT. If the parties to a contract do not expressly agree on a particular matter, the courts may pretend that they have so agreed in order to make the contract work. This is done on the basis that the parties would have agreed on the point had they thought about it. English law thus tries to uphold contracts, which is a good thing, but it imposes an unfair burden on parties who have to think of everything in case they would not in fact have agreed if they had thought about it!

IN PERSONAM. Actions or proceedings directed at a particular person are described as '*in personam*', in other words 'personal'. A court cannot entertain actions or proceedings against a person unless it has 'personal' jurisdiction over him, usually, but not exclusively, because he is in England (for however short a time) or submits to jurisdiction. *In personam* actions are archetypically injunctions compelling someone to do or not to do something, but practically all actions or proceedings are *in personam* unless, exceptionally, they are *in rem*. Companies are regarded, by a convenient legal fiction, as persons in their own right and therefore *in personam* jurisdiction can be exercised against them. See EQUITABLE JURISDICTION.

IN REM. An action or proceeding against a 'thing' (rather than a person or company). Under English law the only *in rem* action is an Admiralty action against ships or things (such as cargo or freight) connected with ships or, despite the name of the action, aircraft. It is the ship or aircraft, rather than its owner, which is 'arrested', to enforce payment of a debt.

A 'non-recourse' secured lending (which is popular in the USA) limits the amount recoverable to the value of the security but an action to enforce payment is strictly a limited *in personam* action rather than one *in rem*. See LIEN.

INCOME TAX. One of the two certainties of life, according to Benjamin Franklin; death being the other. It is a tax levied on income at rates which currently go up to 60 per cent but have been known to touch 98 per cent in recent years.

The UK taxes individuals who are residents on their worldwide income, regardless of their citizenship, unless they are domiciled outside the UK. Income with a UK source is taxed even if the source is owned by a person who never intends to go and never has been to the UK. The USA, as a general rule, taxes the worldwide income of its citizens, even those residing permanently outside the USA and its resident aliens, as well as most income which has a US source.

A UK resident receiving interest from the USA would, in the absence of the US–UK Double Tax Convention, be taxed on it twice: by the UK because he is resident and by the USA because the interest has a US source.

INDEMNITY. Arises where a person incurs a debt or liability and a third person promises to be primarily responsible for its payment. The word 'indemnity' is often interchanged with the word 'guarantee' as if there were no difference in their meanings, which is not the case. However, the practical result is likely to be the same – if you guarantee someone's debt you will probably end up paying and if you indemnify them you certainly will. Usually the person giving the indemnity will require to have the right to contest the claim. Indemnities are often given on the sale of shares of a private company against taxation, and sometimes against other specific items. See WARRANTIES AND CONDITIONS.

INDEPENDENT CONTRACTOR. A person who is his own master in the sense that he is engaged to bring about a given result in his own manner and not by methods specified by another. Sub-contractors, insurance salesmen and consultants are usually independent contractors; contrast an employee, who can be told how and when to do his job. Independent contractors do not usually have power to create binding commitments on the persons for whom they work.

INDIVIDUAL. Under English law an individual is a human being but the word 'person' includes individuals as well as companies.

INDOOR MANAGEMENT RULE. When a person deals with a company he does so through its agents who are its directors, secretary or other authorized person, and the normal rules of agency apply. As the Memorandum and Articles are public documents, an outsider has constructive notice of them and of the powers of the company's officers; yet he does not know what internal documents exist limiting their authority.

The rule in *Royal British Bank* v *Turquand* aids commercial activity, for an outsider need not delve into a company's internal workings before dealing with particular officers if they act in a manner consistent with the Memorandum and Articles; the outsider (but not a director) may assume, without further enquiry, that the acts are legitimate and regular.

The rule does not apply where it is apparent from an inspection of the Memorandum and Articles that an authority does not exist; or where an outsider knew or ought reasonably to have known of the lack of actual authority or is put on enquiry by any suspicious circumstances; or the document on which a person seeks to rely is a forgery.

INFANT. See MINOR.

INHERITANCE TAX. Introduced by the Chancellor in his 1986 budget, it replaces capital transfer tax. The fundamental change is that there is no tax on transfers between individuals if the transferor survives for seven years. If death occurs after three years but within seven, the tax charge will be tapered. Gifts involving companies and most trusts, will be fully taxed. The tax will also be payable on a person's estate on death.

Where a donor reserves a right over property which he has given away, the gift will generally be treated as ineffective for inheritance tax purposes until the reservation has been cancelled. A classic case would be the gift of a house to a child with the parents being allowed to live there for the rest of their lives: the value of the property would be included in the parents' estate.

INJUNCTION. An equitable remedy ordering a person to refrain from doing, or threatening to do, an act of some kind or, more rarely, to require him to do something.

The range of its application is wide. Examples are restraints on publication of defamatory statements, interference with contractual relationships and holding a general meeting. Being an equitable remedy it is granted at the discretion of the court only if it is just and convenient to do so. It will be refused where the applicant is not suffering much inconvenience, or damages would be an adequate alternative, or greater hardship would be caused by its grant than by a refusal.

The courts can deal with urgent cases very quickly *ex parte*. A temporary or interlocutory injunction may be given pending the full hearing of the dispute. The plaintiff must normally give an undertaking to pay all necessary damages arising from the grant of an interlocutory injunction. This acts as a considerable disincentive to the capricious applicant.

A perpetual injunction, which relieves the applicant from

having to seek relief on each fresh infringement of his rights, is granted only after a full hearing.

A breach of the terms of an injunction is a contempt of court.

INLAND REVENUE, THE COMMISSIONERS OF. The statutory body responsible for the care and management of UK taxes. They appoint Inspectors and Collectors of Taxes.

The Commissioners enjoy a Crown immunity from legal action, but if an Inland Revenue official acts unfairly, it is possible to seek judicial review.

The Inland Revenue are not immune from criticism for taking an overbearing attitude. Mr Justice Walton in one case said '. . . the whole submission, however, is so far removed from reality, from even the most rudimentary notions of justice and fair play, that one had no more than to state it for it to be abundantly obvious that it cannot be maintained. Yet here was the Solicitor-General [counsel for the Revenue], whom we all know as one of the most amiable of men, voluntarily casting himself in the role of Count Dracula'.

INNS OF COURT, THE. The Honourable Societies of Lincoln's Inn, the Inner Temple, the Middle Temple and Gray's Inn. They rank equally, have similar constitutions and are composed of benchers, barristers and students. Matters of common interest are dealt with by the Senate, a joint body which deals with legal education, discipline and the overall running of the profession. Admission or expulsion from a particular Inn is the responsibility of its benchers, as is the property of the Inn which is held on trust by them.

A pleasingly monastic atmosphere of scholarship and diligence prevails throughout the Inns. This carefully fostered illusion has deluded many members into thinking that they are not so much a profession as a vocation, though this has never inhibited them from offering their services at a professional rate.

INSIDER DEALINGS. Dealings in securities by persons who have, or are treated as having, inside knowledge. The Company Securities (Insider Dealing) Act 1985 contains a number of detailed and complex provisions prohibiting individuals from dealing in the securities of companies on the basis of information which they have derived from their connection with a company or which, without being so connected themselves, they have derived from persons who are in that position. The rules apply to dealings on a recognized stock exchange and to certain off-market deals.

There were only two prosecutions for insider dealing in 1984 and both were dismissed by the courts.

The City Code forbids persons who are privy to confidential price-sensitive information concerning an offer from dealing in the relevant securities between the time when there is reason to suppose that an approach or an offer is contemplated and the issue of an appropriate press announcement. See INSIDER INFORMATION and MODEL CODE.

INSIDER INFORMATION. Information possessed by persons who participate in 'insider dealings'. It includes information which *inter alia* it would be reasonable to expect a person connected with a company not to disclose, except for the proper performance of the functions attaching to his position, and which he knows is unpublished price-sensitive information in relation to the securities in question. See PRICE-SENSITIVE INFORMATION.

INSOLVENCY. Insolvency is the state of being unable to pay one's debts in full as they fall due. It may result in bankruptcy for individuals under the Insolvency Act 1985.

A company may be wound up by the court if it is unable to pay its debts and is treated as being unable to do so in certain specified events; for example, if a creditor owed more than £750 has made a written demand for payment and the company has neglected to pay within three weeks; or the value of the company's assets is less than the amount of its liabilities, taking into account its contingent and prospective liabilities. See DISQUALIFICATION OF DIRECTORS, WINDING UP and WRONGFUL TRADING.

INSOLVENT LIQUIDATION. The terminal illness of a company by winding up by the creditors, or the court, when the company is unable to pay its debts as they fall due.

INSPECTION AND INVESTIGATION. The DTI has powers to inspect a company's books and papers, to appoint an Inspector to investigate a company's affairs; to make an investigation into the ownership and control of companies; to investigate dealings by a director in options to buy or sell shares and his interest in its shares or debentures. These may lead to civil or criminal actions in the court. In 1985 there were nine successful prosecutions and 20 companies wound up on the DTI's petition, following investigations. See DISQUALIFICATION OF DIRECTORS and MINORITY SHAREHOLDERS.

INSTITUTIONAL INVESTORS. Companies or funds (typically, insurance companies, pension funds and investment trusts) which manage or own their investments for the benefit of other people. The move to indirect investment has been induced for tax reasons as much as for investment expertise, and institutions now represent the biggest investors in The Stock Exchange. Their 'herd' mentality, under which they act in the same way at the same time, makes life very difficult for market-makers and causes big swings in prices; it was one of the underlying causes of the jobbers' need for extra capital that led to the City revolution.

Successive governments have excluded institutional investors from statutory investor protection, although it is unclear whether this is because they are regarded as capable of looking after themselves or because they are fair game.

INSURABLE INTEREST. A person who insures another person or an asset will have no right to claim under his policy unless he has an insurable interest; he must not only have a legal or equitable interest in the property or matter to be insured, but he must also lose a benefit or incur a liability if the insured event happens.

INSURANCE. A contract of insurance provides for the payment of a sum of money on the occurrence of a particular event. There must be a degree of uncertainty either as to whether the event will occur or, if (as with death) it is inevitable, as to when it will occur. For precisely this reason insurance payable on death is more properly called assurance.

The person taking out the insurance must have an insurable

interest in the event: normally he must suffer some loss as a result. If there were no insurable interest, the contract would be equivalent to a wager and would be legally unenforceable.

Most contracts of insurance provide for the insured to be indemnified against the amount of his actual loss; the sum insured then merely represents the maximum potential liability of the insurer. However some contracts, such as those for life insurance or personal accidents, provide for the payment of a specified sum on the occurrence of the event insured against; there is then no need to prove the amount of any resulting loss.

All contracts of insurance involve a duty of good faith on the part of the insured, who must disclose to the insurer all matters which could be material to the insurer's decision to enter into the contract.

Insurance companies are subject to the control of the DTI.

INTELLECTUAL PROPERTY. A generic term which includes letters patent, trademarks, copyright and registered designs, all of which can be described as products of the intellect rather than hand, hammer or sickle. Commonly, though less correctly, used to include any rights in know-how.

INTENTION TO CREATE LEGAL RELATIONS. Parties to a commercial contract are presumed to intend that it should not be the sport of an idle hour but one to be taken seriously and to be enforceable at law unless the party denying it proves the contrary.

If a contract states that it is not 'a formal or legal agreement and shall not be subject to legal jurisdiction in the law courts of the USA or England' the courts have held that it is not enforceable. A party agreeing to pay '*ex gratia*' or 'without admission of liability' simply indicates he does not admit any pre-existing liability on his part, but those words do not warrant the conclusion that a promise duly made, and accepted for valuable consideration, was not intended to be enforceable by the parties at law.

With family agreements the presence or absence of an intention to create legal relations, hence an enforceable agreement, depends upon the circumstances and language used.

INTER VIVOS. A legal phrase most commonly used in relation to gifts of property made between living persons, as distinct from a gift made by a testator in a will.

INTER-BANK MARKET, THE LONDON. A nebulous term referring generally to all of the recognized banks operating in the London money market. There are 293 in the UK. It is best known for the London Inter-Bank Offered Rate (LIBOR), a fluctuating rate which may vary from bank to bank. The rate published by banks at 11 a.m. every day is normally used for the calculation of interest rates under loan documentation.

INTEREST IN POSSESSION. An interest under a trust where the holder has the right to receive the trust income and there is no power to accumulate income. A transfer of assets by a person to a trust where he has an interest in possession did not attract capital transfer tax and will not be subject to inheritance tax. This has encouraged the creation of many such trusts with overseas trustees, who are also exempt from capital gains tax, and possibly protected from future exchange controls in the UK.

INTEREST IN SHARES. A right which a person may have over shares when he is not the absolute legal and beneficial owner. Where shares are held by a nominee, the beneficial owner will have an interest in those shares. An interest, such as a mortgagee's security, can amount to less than full beneficial ownership.

The right must be one against the shares themselves (a right '*in rem*') and not merely a personal contractual right to require the owner of the shares to dispose of a number of them. Thus, the question of whether an option over shares amounts to an interest in shares will depend on its terms. See DISCLOSURE.

INTEREST RATE SWAP. An immediate exchange between a fixed rate and a floating rate borrower of the same principal amount of their respective liabilities, effected by making, either directly or through an intermediary (usually a bank), compensating payments from time to time. It may be combined with a currency swap, with or without a physical exchange of the principal amount.

Interest rate swaps work by exploiting the credit spread differential between the public capital markets and the inter-bank market. The swap market has been considerably boosted by the increased liquidity generated by the commencement of trading in swaps and the invention of option contracts on swaps.

INTERNAL REVENUE SERVICE (IRS). The US equivalent of the UK Inland Revenue. Unlike the Inland Revenue the IRS is prepared to give rulings on projected proposals, therefore helping the taxpayer to know where he stands 'taxwise' if not otherwise.

INTERNATIONAL ARBITRATION. Contracting parties from different political, economic, cultural and legal backgrounds are frequently distrustful of foreign national courts. Hence arbitration has developed in recent years as the preferred mechanism for resolving disputes arising out of international commerce.

There are certain specialist international arbitration institutions, including the Court of Arbitration, International Chamber of Commerce, the London Court of International Arbitration, and the American Arbitration Association. The United Nations Commission on International Trade Law (UNCITRAL) has developed arbitration rules for use in *ad hoc* arbitration. These rules were adopted by the US–Iran Claims Tribunal in The Hague.

Although international arbitration will generally be governed by some national law, various international conventions have sought to facilitate the recognition and enforcement of arbitration agreements and awards. Most notable is the New York Convention on the Recognition and Enforcement of Foreign Arbitral Awards 1958, to which currently 69 states are party, including the UK.

The Washington Convention 1965 established the International Centre for the Settlement of Investment Disputes which aims to provide a forum for arbitrating disputes between states and private corporations arising out of nationalization or expropriation of the private company's assets. Almost 100 states are now party to this Convention.

International arbitration is also used by sovereign states to settle disputes between them, most notably border disputes.

INTERNATIONAL BUSINESS LAWYER. The monthly journal published in London of the Section on Business Law of the International

Bar Association which is a federation of national bar associations. The Section on Business Law was founded in 1970 to promote the exchange of views and information on business law and practice throughout the world.

INTERNATIONAL COURT OF JUSTICE. Situated in The Hague, Holland, this court, sometimes known as the World Court, is the successor to the Permanent Court of International Justice, which was set up in 1920 under the auspices of the League of Nations. Following World War II it became, and remains, the principal judicial organ of the United Nations under the UN Charter. Its function is to hear disputes between member states and to give advisory opinions on questions of public international law and custom.

Unlike the European Court of Human Rights and the European Court of Justice, the court does not have jurisdiction to hear disputes involving individuals: only sovereign states may appear. See PUBLIC INTERNATIONAL LAW.

INTERNATIONAL LAW. See CONFLICT OF LAWS, PUBLIC INTERNATIONAL LAW and TREATY.

INTESTACY. Dying without leaving a valid will. A will which disposes of part, but not the whole, of the deceased's estate results in a partial intestacy. Administration of the estate is obtained by a grant of probate (where there is a will which appoints executors who do not renounce this office) or, more commonly, by letters of administration which give administrators their power to act. Any part, or the whole, of the deceased's estate which does not devolve under his will (if any) is dealt with and distributed (once any inheritance tax payable has been paid) according to the rules in the Administration of Estates Act 1925, which are supposed to approximate to an 'average will'. For example, on a total intestacy, if the deceased leaves a widow and a parent but no children, the widow is entitled to his personal chattels, a statutory legacy of up to £85,000, and half of anything left over, all of which is exempt from inheritance tax. The parent takes the remainder. To avoid the intestacy rules and minimize tax liability, spouses are advised to leave valid wills, and die in an organized fashion.

INVESTMENT BANK. The US near-equivalent of a merchant bank. Salomon Bros, Goldman Sachs and Drexel Burnham Lambert are among the leaders.

The US Glass–Steagall Act creates, theoretically, a rigid demarcation between the activities of commercial banks and those of investment banks, whose main role was the marketing and underwriting of securities. However, the demarcation lines

have blurred in recent years. Investment banks usually have greater financial muscle than their poorer English counterparts: their future impact on the UK stock markets and take-over scene may exceed all present expectations.

INVESTMENT COMPANY. A company which has notified the Registrar of its intention to be an investment company and has since then carried on the business of investing its funds mainly in securities, with the aim of spreading investment risks and giving its members the benefit of its management of funds.

No investment (except in another investment company) may exceed 15 per cent by value of the company's investments. The distribution of capital profits must be prohibited by its Memorandum and Articles and it has to distribute 85 per cent of the income it derives from securities. The irreverent will avoid both these problems by the judicious use of subsidiaries.

An investment trust is an investment company whose shares are listed on The Stock Exchange with the additional conditions that, at the time of acquisition or addition to an investment, no holding may exceed 15 per cent of gross assets and that an aggregation of investments and loans to subsidiaries does not exceed 15 per cent of gross assets at the time of making the investment. The company can become an authorized investment trust if the Inland Revenue so approves.

An authorized investment trust is not subject to corporation tax on realized chargeable gains, and cannot purchase its own shares.

INVESTMENT TRUST. See INVESTMENT COMPANY.

INVESTOR PROTECTION. The traditional market philosophy in the UK until 1985 was that competition and the probity of practitioners were sufficient to protect investors in the securities and commodities markets. There were minimal statutory requirements which had their greatest impact in the case of the marketing of investments by circular, and also certain rules of conduct imposed by the DTI; as a matter of law the latter applied only to licensed dealers, who were perceived as the less reputable end of the market.

Several scandals highlighted the need for reform of the principal regulatory statute (first enacted in 1939), and reform was made essential by the Big Bang which removed the fundamental protection for Stock Exchange investors of the previous separation of function. The proposed FSA 1986 emphasizes the need for full disclosure, fair dealing and best execution if a dealer wants to meet its clients' needs 'off its own book'. Full disclosure sits uneasily with the concept of chinese walls.

Contrary to the system of transaction regulations favoured by the USA and Canada, the English system is based on practitioner regulation by non-statutory self-regulatory organizations.

INVITATION TO TREAT. An invitation to make an offer which must be contrasted with an offer. The distinction between them is often difficult to draw, and generally is said to be a matter of intention. It is, however, fairly well settled that a display of goods at a fixed price in a shop window, a menu in a restaurant, an auctioneer's request for bids, and a share offer on a flotation, are all invitations to treat, and not offers capable of acceptance.

ISSUED CAPITAL. That part of the authorized (nominal) capital of a company which is issued (outstanding). It can consist of paid-up capital representing the total payments made in respect of issued shares, and uncalled capital representing the difference between the amount paid and the nominal amount of issued shares.

ISSUING HOUSE. Any dealer in securities, not necessarily a member of the exclusive Issuing Houses Association, who raises capital for a company on a flotation.

A responsible Issuing House has a split duty to advise the company on the best possible terms of issue, while at the same time guarding the interests of potential investors. Its name is thought to be a contributor to the success of an issue, but this is by no means a foregone conclusion, although some would like to think so. The advantage of dealing with a reputable house is exemplified by Baring Brothers who bought back all the shares in Home Counties Newspapers, following an issue sponsored by them when, through no fault of Baring's, the company failed to meet its profit forecast. Barings are said to have made a profit at the end of the day!

J

JOINT VENTURE. An arrangement, which is not always satisfactory, between two persons or companies to conduct a business, venture or transaction together. The participation in the joint venture is usually not the main activity of either party (unlike a partnership). Often the joint venture is carried out by a company, formed specifically for the purpose, in which the participants hold shares. The terms of participation are governed by a shareholders agreement and the Articles.

Where a joint venture is not carried on through a separate company, the joint venture operation may constitute a partnership although, if the contributions by each of the participants are different and their rewards are separately calculated, no partnership may be implied.

JUDGES. The Lord Chancellor bears full responsibility for recommending to the Crown individuals for appointment as judges of the High Court. They are selected from barristers. Solicitors who have more than 13 years' experience can be appointed circuit judges (Crown Court and County Court) and then, theoretically, High Court judges. Judges continue in office during good behaviour which is the basis upon which a prisoner merits remission of a sentence.

Judges are allegedly insulated from politics and enjoy an exemption from liability for all acts done in the exercise of their jurisdiction. See JUDICIAL NOTICE, JUDICIAL PRECEDENT and *OBITER DICTA*.

JUDICIAL NOTICE. A declaration by the court that a fact at issue exists even if its existence has not been established by evidence.

Judicial notice will be taken of facts of public notoriety; facts known to the judge from his general knowledge or as a result of inquiries from proper sources; English and EEC law and other matters specifically referred to by statute.

Judicial notice has been taken of the fact that the University of Oxford exists for the advancement of learning, that criminals do not lead happy lives and that two weeks is too short a period for human gestation.

Judges are, however, duty-bound to ignorance of mundane matters. Mr Justice Darling, a judge much given to witticisms from the bench, once asked counsel, 'who, pray, is Mr George

Robey?'. Robey was an immensely well-known music-hall comedian, and the judge received the well-merited reply, 'My Lord, they call him the Darling of the Halls!'.

JUDICIAL PRECEDENT. Although judicial decisions are colloquially referred to as precedents, it is correctly the principle of law (the *ratio decidendi*) on which the decision is based which is a precedent. It is binding on lower courts when the facts occur again; for instance a High Court judge is bound by precedents set by the Court of Appeal and the House of Lords, but in turn his decisions are binding on a County Court and a Magistrates Court.

The sport of judges and lawyers is attempting to distinguish one precedent from another, or in arguing that a particular precedent does not apply to the facts of a particular case. This has led to a mass of case law, some conflicting, others rigid in application, and many containing legal principles that do not match the changing needs of society.

JUDICIAL REVIEW. The most effective way of challenging administrative decisions and actions. It becomes more important as the lives of citizens are increasingly circumscribed by complex laws.

Unlike the right of appeal, which is only conferred in particular circumstances by statute, the right to judicial review is an inherent right in every person to invoke the supervisory jurisdiction of the High Court to review the way in which government ministers, local authorities and other public bodies come to decisions which affect their lives or livelihood. Such decisions can be challenged on one of three grounds: illegality, irrationality and procedural impropriety.

As well as applying the normal remedies of injunction and declaration, the Divisional Court can deal with offending decisions by means of three of the ancient prerogative writs, *certiorari*, prohibition and *mandamus*. *Certiorari* quashes the offending decision; prohibition prevents a decision or action being taken; and *mandamus* directs a body to act in a particular way.

JUNK BONDS. The heavy artillery of the US corporate raider. They are securities which are not rated as investment grade by the credit rating agencies and are issued to finance take-overs. The Federal Reserve Board wishes to curb the use of these bonds, of which it is estimated that over $15 billion were issued in 1985.

JURIES. The traditional constitution of the jury as 12 good men and true has experienced some modification in keeping with changing social and political attitudes. However, the need for a social sanction on the administration of justice and the discretion of the judiciary has remained. Thus the institution of the jury has survived, although in civil litigation its role has been substantially limited and in complex cases of fraud it is likely to disappear.

Anyone on the electoral role between the ages of 18 and 65 who has been ordinarily resident in the UK for five years since attaining the age of 13 can be a juror. Ineligible persons include the judiciary, the clergy and the whole population of Northern Ireland for whom jury service can prove fatal.

In civil actions, trial is without a jury unless the court in its discretion orders otherwise. The court must order a jury on the application of either party in cases of defamation, malicious prosecution, false imprisonment and fraud.

In a criminal prosecution the accused may usually elect to be tried in the Magistrates Court or the Crown Court. If the latter, trial will be by jury unless the accused is pleading guilty. In the Magistrates Court the justices take on the role of both judge and jury.

The jury decides questions of fact (as to which the judge applies the relevant law) and the final question of guilt or innocence. It may acquit the accused even if the judge directs that he should be convicted.

JURISPRUDENCE. The philosophy or theory of law. Originally concerned almost exclusively with the analysis of the formal structure of law and its concepts, jurisprudence today is concerned with a wider variety of legal questions and ideas. In contrast to substantive law which describes, for example, how rights and duties are acquired, jurisprudence considers the nature of rights and duties and their role in different branches of law.

JUSTICES OF THE PEACE. The fourteenth century introduced both the

Black Death and the Justice of the Peace (JP) into English society. The former phenomenon moved mercilessly through the country inflicting a terrible toll of death and suffering on a largely undeserving public, but eventually had the good sense to retire gracefully into the history books. The latter still exists. JPs need not retire until they are 70. They sit in Magistrates Courts with a local, limited, civil and criminal jurisdiction.

K

KNOW-HOW. Information, usually but not necessarily technical, which is valuable because it is known to one person, wanted by another and not available to the general public. Unless covered by letters patent or reduced to some permanent form in which copyright subsists, there are no proprietary rights as such in know-how under English law; the first line of defence for know-how is, therefore, commercial security. Once know-how has reached the public domain, it may freely be used; but if it is disclosed by one person to another in conditions of confidence, and has the necessary quality, an equitable duty of confidentiality will arise, giving the person whose information it is the right to restrain unauthorized use or disclosure.

Know-how is commonly licensed for general or limited purposes, often in conjunction with a patent or trademark licence. Even where a commercial product can be 'reverse engineered', the manufacturing know-how will remain protected in equity during the 'springboard period' which an independent manufacturer would require to introduce a similar product.

L

LACHES. A delay, after knowledge of the circumstances giving rise to a claim, in bringing an action which is sufficient to prevent a person from obtaining an equitable remedy in cases where the Limitation Act 1980 does not apply. A substantial lapse of time coupled with circumstances (such as loss of evidence or agreement to abandon a claim) which make it inequitable to grant relief, will bar claims for remedies such as specific performance, injunction, rescission and rectification. See LIMITATION OF ACTIONS.

LAW COMMISSION, THE. Established by the Law Commission Act 1965 for the purpose of promoting the reform of the law. It consists of a chairman and four other Commissioners appointed by the Lord Chancellor for a term not exceeding five years.

The Commission's duty is to review the law with a view to its systematic development, simplification and modernization. Its reports are models of clarity and sometimes surprise.

The Commission's recommendations have led to many changes in the law including exemption clauses in contracts, financial provision in matrimonial proceedings and criminal liability for damage to property. Many of their recommendations, such as on penalties and liquidated damages and positive and restrictive covenants, have not been implemented and continue to gather dust.

LAW REPORTS. They contain the texts of the judgments in selected cases which are thought to include significant points of law. Some also summarize arguments advanced by counsel on each side. There is an official series of reports, known simply as *The Law Reports*, published by The Incorporated Council of Law Reporting in England and Wales. The reporters are barristers. There is an increasing number of other reports produced by commercial publishers, such as the *All England Law Reports*, *Lloyd's Reports*, and *Common Market Law Reports* containing decisions of the European Court and the European Commission. See JUDICIAL PRECEDENT and *OBITER DICTA*.

LAW SOCIETY, THE. The solicitors' trade union as well as their governing body. It exerts enormous disciplinary powers over solicitors from a beautiful building in Chancery Lane adjacent to the Law Courts. It has a powerful sense of its own dignity and importance, and little sense of public relations. The Society has over 40,000 members and in 1984 received 6,800 complaints and requests for assistance from lay clients as well as 1,950 complaints by solicitors. A Lay Observer is appointed by the Lord Chancellor to provide an independent review of the way the Society handles complaints, and issues an annual report.

LEADING QUESTION. It either suggests the desired answer or assumes the existence of disputed facts upon which a witness is to testify. The answers are not always admissible in evidence.

LEAP-FROGGING APPEAL. An appeal in civil proceedings direct from the High Court or Divisional Court to the House of Lords, leaving out the Court of Appeal. Available where a point of law of general public importance is involved, provided that the parties consent and both the lower court and the House of Lords approve.

LEASE. It can be an agreement governing the use, for a fixed period, by a lessee of goods or equipment rented from the lessor against regular payments, which are tax deductible if the goods are for business use. It relieves the lessee of finding the purchase price 'up front'.

When land is leased, the owner gives the lessee possession with the right to use the property under specified conditions and on payment of a rent. On its expiration the right to possession reverts to the lessor or freeholder. A lessee may, unless the lease prohibits it, sub-let the property to a sub-lessee. See CROSS BORDER LEASING and FEE SIMPLE.

LEGAL ESTATE. An interest in property which entitles the holder to exploit the property: the holder is the owner as far as third parties are concerned. This should be contrasted with the beneficial interest which can be separated from the legal estate: the holder of the legal estate must account to the beneficial owner for income, the proceeds of sale, or other results of any dealings.

It also has important implications in determining priorities, particularly in relation to rival mortgages. It is a legal right enforceable against any person who takes property, whether or not he has notice of it, except where the right is void against him because it should have been, but was not, registered. Subject to certain statutory exceptions a purchaser for valuable consideration who obtains a legal estate at the time of purchase without notice of a prior equitable right is entitled to priority in equity as well as in law. See TRUSTS.

LEGAL OPINION. In its widest sense a legal opinion is simply any view expressed by a lawyer on a matter of law. The view of a barrister on a legal point is called an 'opinion'.

In major commercial, financial and particularly international transactions a formal opinion is often given by lawyers confirming the legal position on relevant points: e.g. that a corporation has been duly incorporated according to the law of the country of incorporation, that the persons signing the relevant documents have been duly authorized to do so and that the obligations undertaken by the parties will be legally binding on them.

The habit of seeking formal opinions seems to be of US origin but has been creeping into other jurisdictions like a contagious disease.

LEGAL TENDER. A person is not obliged to accept a payment unless it is tendered in cash. A tender by bill, cheque, or notes of a bank other than the Bank of England, is not strictly a legal tender. A creditor waives his right to be paid in cash when he asks for payment by cheque. Coins made by the Mint are legal tender under the Coinage Act 1971 up to specified (relatively minor) amounts.

LETTER BEFORE ACTION. A letter written by or on behalf of a prospective plaintiff, making a claim against the recipient and indicating that proceedings may be commenced if the claim is not satisfied within a specified period. A letter before action is not obligatory, but its absence may result in a successful plaintiff not being awarded costs.

LETTER OF ALLOTMENT. A temporary document of title recording the allotment of new shares in a company to a named person. Until the Finance Act 1986 it was capable of renunciation free of stamp duty to someone else for a stated time ('the renunciation period').

A provisional letter of allotment on a rights issue confers a right to shares provided that their subscription price is paid; failing payment the letter becomes valueless. It is transferable either in nil-paid or fully-paid form during the renunciation period. When the renunciation period ends a share certificate will be issued.

LETTER OF CREDIT. An arrangement for financing international trade. A bank acting at the request of a customer (the buyer) agrees to make payment against presentation of specified documents to or to the order of the beneficiary of the credit (the seller). Payment is subject to strict compliance with the terms and conditions of the credit. The payment may be made directly or through an advising bank.

The letter may provide for sight (i.e. immediate) or deferred payment; or for acceptance and payment of drafts drawn by the beneficiary; or for negotiation of the credit, i.e. payment, without recourse to any party to the credit other than the issuing bank, of drafts drawn by the beneficiary.

Letters of credit are generally issued subject to the International Chamber of Commerce Uniform Customs and Practice for Documentary Credits, the current edition of which came into force in October 1984.

LEVERAGED BUY-OUT. The acquisition in the USA and the UK of a company for cash by persons who finance the transaction mainly by borrowing. Used extensively when a company wishes to divest itself of a subsidiary to management, and by many private companies as a more palatable alternative to a take-over or the demands of public ownership. The acquisition debt is repaid by the internally generated cash flow of the acquired company.

Management usually have a substantial stake in the equity of the business at minimal cost, the finance being provided by secured lenders and subordinated (or mezzanine) financing, so called because it ranks below the secured lenders but above the equity investor, who is generally unsecured.

The real skill involved in a leveraged buy-out is the ability to capture a company at a price which does not lessen its potential to develop and prosper. See MANAGEMENT BUY-OUT.

LEXIS. The 'in thing' for English and US lawyers. It is a computer-assisted legal research facility linked to a database library containing case law and statutory material.

LICENCE. A permission to carry out some act given by a person who otherwise would have power to prevent it. Licences are common in intellectual property franchising and land law, and the word is extensively used in the area of government regulation.

A licence under letters patent or copyright is preferable to an outright assignment because the rights will automatically revert to the licensor on termination arising from breach or insolvency.

LICENCE OF RIGHT. The 1977 Patents Act, which brings English patent law into line with the European Patent Convention 1975, provides for the terms of all 'new existing patents' to be extended from 16 to 20 years subject to such patents, during the four-year extension, being endorsed 'Licence of Right'. The patentee must, during this period, license all-comers on terms which, if not agreed, must be settled by the Comptroller-General of Patents.

LICENSED DEALER. See DEALERS IN SECURITIES.

LICENSED DEPOSIT-TAKER. See BANK.

LIEN. The right of a person to retain possession of another person's goods until his claims are satisfied. It is lost by waiver or parting with possession; there is generally no right of sale.

A general lien is the right to retain goods until their owner pays all claims against him, whether or not they relate to those particular goods. It is created by custom or agreement, and by custom it is available to solicitors, stockbrokers, bankers and agents.

A particular lien is the right to retain goods until fees or charges have been paid. An auctioneer has a particular lien on goods sold, as has an accountant on his clients' papers.

All the above are liens at common law. They are different from equitable liens which arise, independently of possession, because of the relationship between persons. The principal equitable liens are the purchaser's lien for his deposit, the vendor's lien for his purchase money and the lien of trustees and personal representatives on the trust property for their expenses. It is hardly surprising that a solicitor has an equitable lien on moneys recovered by his exertions. See *IN REM*.

LIFE INTEREST. The right to have the income of a trust paid to a person during his life. His death or his release of the interest gives rise to a charge to inheritance tax on the whole of the trust fund. If the interest is sold, the disposal will normally be free from inheritance tax, but capital gains tax will be levied on the difference between the value of the trust fund and the proceeds of sale. See INTEREST IN POSSESSION.

LIMITATION OF ACTIONS. Statute and equitable doctrines which ensure that stale claims are not litigated. They are now largely concentrated in the Limitation Act 1980, which extinguishes the right to bring an action outside specified time limits commencing from the date a cause of action accrues, as amended by 'the clumsy draftsmanship' of the Lantent Damage Act 1986.

Time limits are extended for infants, mental patients and negligence actions in respect of latent damage which do not involve personal injury. Fraud, concealment, or mistake misleading the plaintiff, may prevent time running. A cause of action accrues upon the breach being committed in contract and torts which do not require proof of damage to be actionable. With other torts (including negligence), the general rule is that time runs from the date of the damage. See LACHES.

LIMITED LIABILITY. In the case of a club there will generally be an implied term that the members are not personally liable for debts incurred on its behalf beyond their subscriptions; the officers will, however, be personally liable. In a partnership each partner (other than limited partners) is an agent of the other and, therefore, unless a creditor knows of a limitation placed upon a partner's authority, all the partners will be liable for the debt.

The liability of the members of a limited company for its unpaid debts is limited to the unpaid nominal value of their shares. In practice, their shares are likely to be paid up in full. See CORPORATE VEIL, GUARANTEE COMPANY, LIMITED PARTNERSHIP and UNLIMITED COMPANY.

LIMITED PARTNERSHIP. A tax-efficient method both in the USA and the UK of making investments, or trading, while taking advantage of limited liability. In the UK, the partnership cannot exceed 20 in number of whom at least one must be a general partner with unlimited liability for all debts and obligations, and responsibility for management. Curiously, there is no objection to the general partner being a company with limited liability.

The limited partners contribute a specific amount of capital to the firm, which is their only liability for its debts and obligations. Limited liability is lost if a limited partner takes part in the management of the business, or if the firm is not registered as a limited partnership with the Registrar.

The arrangements between the partners should be regulated by a partnership deed and not left to the vagaries of the Limited Partnership Act 1907, which would apply in its absence.

Limited partners' capital will sometimes take the form of loans to avoid the payment of capital duty.

LIPTON, MARTIN. Fronted by thick glasses, he is one of the shrewdest and most innovative legal brains on the US corporate scene who is credited with having conceived the poison pill. His charm of manner belies a battling inner core. Unlike his competitor, Joe Flom, his deliberate policy is to keep his firm Wachtell Lipton as small as possible.

LIQUIDATION. See WINDING UP.

LIQUIDATOR. The person who takes control of a company's assets and affairs from its directors on its winding up. Appointed by the creditors in a voluntary winding up and by the court in a compulsory winding up, his job is to ensure a fair distribution of the remaining assets to shareholders after payment of all debts and liabilities to creditors.

A liquidator must now be duly qualified and authorized by the DTI which also exercises control and supervision of some of his activities, e.g. in a compulsory winding up he must notify the DTI of any fraudulent trading by directors.

A liquidator also needs the approval of the court (or committee of inspection) in order to exercise some of his powers, such as bringing legal proceedings in the company's name, or to recover money wrongfully paid by the company to one creditor in preference to another prior to winding up.

Accountants who are impervious to anguish and pressure tend to engage in this field of work. The Insolvency Act 1985 refers to them as insolvency practitioners. See DISCLAIMER OF ONEROUS PROPERTY.

LISTING. The admission of a company's shares, or other securities, to the Official List of The Stock Exchange. It is also commonly, but wrongly, used to describe the quotation of, and dealing in, shares or other securities on the Unlisted Securities Market or the Over the Counter Markets. See FLOTATION and LISTING REGULATIONS.

LISTING REGULATIONS. The Stock Exchange (Listing) Regulations 1984 incorporated into English law the European Community Directives on the admission of securities to listing on The Stock Exchange, and on the continuous reporting requirements applicable to companies and other bodies with listed securities. The regulations specify the disclosures required for a listing and apply both to capital raising and take-overs. They are considerably more wide reaching than the prospectus requirements of the Act.

The Stock Exchange is responsible for enforcing the regulations and they are incorporated in the *Yellow Book*. Prospectuses which comply with the listing regulations are exempt from the general requirements otherwise applicable to the issue of prospectuses.

The regulations do not apply to open-ended investment companies, even if listed on The Stock Exchange, or to securities dealt in on the Unlisted Securities Market. The regulations will be superseded by comparable provisions in the proposed FSA 1986.

Listing particulars have to be filed with the Registrar and there are fines for failure to do so.

LOAN NOTE/STOCK. See DEBENTURES.

LOCK UP. In the USA and UK any device which is designed to increase the likelihood of the successful acquisition of a target company by one particular bidder and to discourage or prevent competing offers by other potential bidders, except by price competition or litigation. Sometimes known in the UK as a 'shut out' when irrevocable commitments to accept an offer are given by shareholders owning a substantial proportion of a target company.

LORD CHANCELLOR. A member of the legislature, judiciary and the executive. He is the chief judicial officer in Britain. He is appointed by delivery of the Great Seal, of which he is the keeper, and which derives from his original role as the King's Secretary. He is the president of the Supreme Court and of the House of Lords sitting as the final court of appeal. He also is a cabinet minister, and Speaker of the House of Lords.

M

MAGISTRATE. See JUSTICES OF THE PEACE.

MAGNA CARTA. The charter granted by King John at Runnymede in 1215. It was later re-enacted by Parliament and now appears at the commencement of the statute book as Statute 9 Hen 3. Its purpose was to limit the royal prerogative in matters of arbitrary arrest and imprisonment.

MANAGEMENT BUY-OUT. The purchase of a business by (usually) a combination of management (who put up relatively little funding and are given a strong financial incentive to succeed) and outside investors.

In the UK, government has improved the legislative environment for MBOs: interest on borrowings by managers to invest in their company is allowable for income tax on a more generous basis than before, and the assets of the acquired company can be used to assist in the payment of the purchase price. See LEVERAGED BUY-OUT and PURCHASE OF OWN SHARES.

MANAGING DIRECTOR. A justifiably magnificent title, for he is a director to whom is delegated power of management without reference to the board of directors: his authority in dealing with third parties is thus greater than that of any other director. The Articles must authorize such an appointment, and his service agreement will normally ensure that if the company fires him as a director, he is deemed to have been wrongfully dismissed from his executive appointment.

MANDAMUS. See JUDICIAL REVIEW.

MANDATORY BIDS. The City Code regards an acquisition of 30 per cent or more of the voting shares in a company as being effective control, so that it would be unfair to the remaining shareholders if they did not also have the opportunity to sell their shares when control changed.

The Panel therefore requires a person, upon reaching the magic 30 per cent figure, to make a cash offer (which can only be subject to two limited conditions) to all shareholders. This must be at the highest price paid by him, or any concert party, for shares of that class within the preceding 12 months. This is not very welcome, particularly as where there is more than one class of shares comparable offers must be made for each class, whether it carries voting rights or not.

A mandatory bid will also be required if a person holding not less than 30 per cent but not more than 50 per cent of the voting rights increases that holding by more than 2 per cent in any period of 12 months. See ACTING IN CONCERT, COMPULSORY ACQUISITION and TAKE-OVERS.

MANUFACTURERS' WARRANTIES and **GUARANTEES.** Unless the consumer has been injured or his property damaged by a defect caused by the manufacturer's negligence, he must usually look for his remedies to the person from whom he bought the goods, and to the terms implied by law into his contract with that person, not to the manufacturer.

Many products are supplied with guarantees or warranties offered by the manufacturer promising to replace or repair them if they are faulty. The legal status of such guarantees is uncertain: they may well not be enforceable on the grounds that there is no consideration for the manufacturer's promise. Yet manufacturers rarely refuse to honour them, and the courts have very rarely had to deal with questions concerning their legal effect. For producers, guarantees are good selling points; for consumers it is often cheaper and more effective to rely on a guarantee than on statutory rights against the retailer. However, guarantees sometimes involve the consumer in added expense, and they rarely offer to compensate for damage or personal injury. In such cases the person supplying the goods should always be approached – the supplier is not entitled to insist that a consumer relies on the manufacturer's guarantee.

Under recent EEC 'product liability' legislation, the UK is introducing new laws, expected to come into force in 1988, which will greatly enhance the availability to consumers of remedies against manufacturers for damage caused by defective products.

MAREVA. An order, developed since 1975, preventing a defendant from removing assets from the jurisdiction until trial. It will be granted only where the plaintiff has a good arguable case and the court is satisfied that there are assets within the jurisdiction which the defendant is likely to remove or dissipate in order to frustrate the claim, or its execution after judgment. A recent development is the grant of a Mareva in support of an overseas judgment enforceable in England: it must now be regarded as an essential option for a foreign judgment creditor.

MASTER OF THE ROLLS. Presides over the Civil Division of the Court of Appeal. He was a Chancery judge sitting at first instance with responsibility for the rolls of solicitors and the records of Chancery, until in 1881, the then formidable Master of the Rolls, Jessel, was translated to the Court of Appeal because of the difficulty of finding judges of sufficiently high calibre to sit on appeals from his decisions.

MATERIAL. A word much used by lawyers which, some would say typically, has alternative meanings: either (perhaps more correctly) relevant or (more loosely) substantial. Under the test of relevance, material facts, in the context of a court or tribunal hearing, include all those likely to affect the outcome of that hearing. Under the test of substantiality, there are no hard and fast rules as to what arithmetical proportion is appropriate; this very imprecision is a warning as to the dangers of its use.

MAXIMS OF EQUITY. The 12 general principles upon which the old court of equity based its jurisdiction. They are applied, even in this modern world, by the High Court. All of them may be encompassed by two: 'equity will not suffer a wrong to be without a remedy' and 'equity acts on the person'. Each of the 12 has its own peculiarity, although they are not mutually exclusive.

Equity will not suffer a wrong to be without a remedy: see INJUNCTION and SPECIFIC PERFORMANCE.

Equity follows the (common) law: which it did in numerous ways 'but not slavishly and not always'.

Equity acts *in personam*: see EQUITABLE JURISDICTION.

Where there is equal equity the law shall prevail: see PRIORITY.

Where the equities are equal the first in time shall prevail: see PRIORITY.

He who seeks equity must do equity.

He who comes to equity must come with clean hands: in the USA, the maxim was applied to a state trooper's pre-marital fornication so as to prevent him from obtaining a decree of nullity, but equity does not demand 'that its supplicants should lead blameless lives'.

Delay defeats equity, or equity aids the vigilant and not the indolent: see LACHES.

Equality is equity: see CO-OWNERSHIP.

Equity looks to the intent rather than the form: it will treat an unauthorized transaction as valid if it could lawfully have been effected by going through two or more separate transactions.

Equity looks on that as done which ought to be done: particularly with contracts.

Equity imputes an intention to fulfil an obligation: the most favourable construction is put on a person's conduct where he does some act which is not, but which can be, regarded as the fulfilment of his obligation.

MEMORANDUM OF ASSOCIATION. The written constitution of a company incorporated under the Act. The Articles are subordinate to and cannot modify the Memorandum. The Memorandum, with the Articles, constitutes a contract between the company and its members as well as between the members as shareholders. See *ULTRA VIRES*.

MEMORANDUM IN WRITING. A memorandum containing or evidencing all the material terms of an agreement which is signed by the person to be bound. Such a memorandum is required for a contract of guarantee under section 4 of the Statute of Frauds 1677, and for a contract for the sale or disposition of land under section 40 of the Law of Property Act 1925. The memorandum may consist of several documents. If it was necessary, a binding contract for the sale of a house could be created with half the conditions written on the back of a ticket, and the remainder on a beermat. This is not a recommended practice.

MERCHANT BANKS. A company need not be one of the elite Accepting Houses to merit being known as a merchant bank. They are bankers, fund raisers, investment advisers, and experts or quasi-experts in all possible related activities. The City Code gives them the inside track on mergers and take-overs.

MERCHANTABLE QUALITY. A condition implied when goods are supplied in the course of a business, that they are as fit for the purpose for which goods of that kind are commonly bought as it is reasonable to expect, having regard to any description applied to them, the price (if relevant) and all other appropriate circumstances. The condition does not apply to defects specifically brought to the buyer's attention before the contract is made or, if the buyer examines the goods beforehand, as regards defects which that examination ought to reveal. The condition is not limited to goods sold by description.

MERGER. A take-over of one company by another, normally where the directors of the target recommend the offer.

Where a consequence of one taking over the other would be a dilution of the assets or earnings of the bidding company, the merger is usually effected by forming a new company which offers its shares (and possibly loan stock and/or warrants) in exchange for the shares of each of the existing companies. This obscures the disadvantages and highlights the advantages. This route will usually operate in favour of merger accounting, with its attendant advantages, as well as receiving favourable tax exemptions. See MERGER CONTROL.

MERGER ACCOUNTING. Permitted under the Act where one company acquires at least 90 per cent of the equity shares of another in exchange for an issue of shares. The principal advantage is that pre-acquisition profits of the acquired company, which are distributed to the acquiring company, form part of its distributable profits (which may in turn be paid to shareholders).

MERGER CONTROL. Merger control in the UK is governed principally by the Fair Trading Act 1973.

Two conditions have to be satisfied before 'a merger situation qualifying for investigation' arises. The first is that two or more enterprises, at least one of which is carried on in the UK or by or under the control of a UK corporation, cease to be 'distinct enterprises'. The second is satisfied if either the gross value of the assets taken over exceeds £30 million, or the merged enterprise will have at least a quarter share of goods of any description in the relevant UK market.

It is usual to consult the Office of Fair Trading (OFT) about a proposed bid or merger, and its expected effects. There is no obligation to do so, and it is lawful to complete a merger without reference to the OFT. A private merger without notification may result in a merger reference within six months of the date when the fact of the merger becomes public. If the merger is to be effected by means of a public offer, the OFT will certainly have knowledge of it and the bidder can rely on the OFT to contact him if he does not contact them.

The OFT will recommend to the Secretary of State whether the merger should be referred to the Monopolies and Mergers Commission (MMC). The Secretary of State is not bound to follow the advice but, when he did not do so in the case of the contested offer for Sotheby's, there was something of a public furore. The Secretary of State himself may make a reference to the Commission. A reference is not only made because of its anti-competitive effects, but also on more general grounds such as the method of financing a bid. If a reference is made to the MMC, a take-over offer will lapse.

The Industry Act 1975, which has never been applied, may prevent a non-UK resident taking over an important UK manufacturing undertaking. See ARTICLES 85 AND 86, COMPETITION LAW and TAKE-OVERS.

MINIMUM SUBSCRIPTION. The amount which, in the opinion of the directors, is the minimum required to be raised on an issue of shares to finance the purchase of property to be paid for out of the proceeds of the issue, any underwriting commissions, preliminary expenses, the repayment of any monies borrowed for those purposes and working capital.

Unless the minimum subscription has been raised and paid, a company cannot allot shares offered to the public, the object being that an applicant for shares should not be landed with them if the company cannot raise the amount needed for its business.

'MINI-TRIAL'. Although so called, it is not a trial at all, but a session designed to clarify the claims of the parties and to arrive at a solution which will not harm on-going business relationships. Originating in the USA, it has been adopted by the Zurich Chamber of Commerce to settle international commercial disputes in the space of one or two days. Lawyers are not discouraged, nor are they encouraged! See CONCILIATION.

MINOR. An individual is, in the context of commercial law, a minor until his eighteenth birthday; the only contracts which are absolutely binding on a minor are contracts for necessaries. Contracts entered into for the repayment of a loan or for goods supplied or to be supplied (other than necessaries) are absolutely void.

MINORITY SHAREHOLDERS. Any shareholder who does not own or have under his control a majority of the voting shares of a company. Some measure of protection is afforded them: against 'fraud on a minority'; when class rights are altered; by the exceptions to the rule in *Foss* v *Harbottle* and the indoor management rule; by DTI inspections and investigations; and the duties of good faith imposed upon directors.

MINUTES. A record of the decisions taken at meetings. Companies have to keep minutes of the proceedings at general meetings and directors' meetings. If signed by the chairman of that meeting or the next succeeding meeting, they are evidence of the proceedings and, until the contrary is proved, the meeting is deemed duly held and convened. There is a presumption that a matter was not brought before the board if there is no reference to it in the minutes, but this presumption can be rebutted by express evidence to the contrary.

Any shareholder of the company can inspect the minute book of general meetings but not the more interesting minutes of directors' meetings.

MISFEASANCE. Wrongfully failing to carry out an obligation and, in particular, a breach of fiduciary duty consisting of misapplication or misappropriation of a company's assets.

An action for misfeasance may only be brought by a

liquidator or creditor of a company which is in liquidation against its officers, auditors or persons engaged in its formation. If misfeasance is proved, the guilty person may be ordered to repay or restore money or property or make a contribution to the assets of the company.

A misfeasance claim is a chose in action which forms part of the company's assets and can be sold by a liquidator.

MISREPRESENTATION. An untrue statement of fact made by one party to a contract to the other which induces that other to enter into the contract.

Such a representation must relate to an existing fact or past event, and not be one of opinion, intention or law. However, an expression of opinion or intention may constitute a misrepresentation of fact if the intention does not exist or the opinion is not actually held.

A misrepresentation normally gives rise to a right of rescission. If the misrepresentation amounts to fraud, the representee may alternatively (or additionally) claim damages. A negligent misrepresentation (made carelessly, or without reasonable grounds for believing it to be true) gives rise to a claim for damages if the circumstances would have justified an award of damages for fraudulent misrepresentation. Damages are not normally available for an innocent misrepresentation (made without fraud or negligence).

MISTAKE. A mistake of fact (but not of law) may be relevant in two circumstances: the law of contract, and the criminal law.

At common law a contract is void for mistake only if the mistake is such that there is nothing to contract about, either because the subject matter does not exist or because the subject of the sale already belongs to the buyer. Equity may hold that a contract is voidable whenever it is founded on some fundamental mistake where justice requires that a party should not be held to his contract. In such a case he may be released on such terms as the court may think it proper to impose.

In criminal law, a defendant who convinces a jury that he made a mistake of fact is entitled to have his guilty intentions adjudged accordingly. In one case, an intending rapist was welcomed into the bedroom of his 'victim', who thought the visitor was her boyfriend. Although convicted at first instance, he successfully appealed.

MODEL CODE. 'The Model Code for Securities Transactions' is a code of conduct for directors of companies whose shares are listed on The Stock Exchange or dealt in on its Unlisted Securities Market.

It cautions directors and connected persons from dealing in their company's securities when an exceptional announcement is to be made and during a two-month period prior to the announcement of results and dividends. The Code does not affect the law on insider dealing.

MODIFICATION OF RIGHTS. The Act contains special provisions relating to the variation of the rights attached to any class of shares in a company whose share capital is divided into shares of different classes. Subject to provisions in the Memorandum or Articles, such rights may be varied only if either the holders of 75 per cent in nominal value of the issued shares of the class give their written consent, or an extraordinary resolution is passed at a separate general meeting of the holders of the relevant class approving the variation.

Some protection is given to minorities who did not consent or vote for the resolution: within 21 days those holding at least 15 per cent of the shares of that class may apply to the court to have the variation cancelled. The court will do so if satisfied that the variation would unfairly prejudice the shareholders of the class.

MONOPOLIES AND MERGERS COMMISSION. The investigative body to which the Director General of Fair Trading or the Secretary of State can refer potentially anti-competitive activities for enquiry as to whether they are against the public interest.

Of the nine monopoly, merger or competition references in 1984, four were adjudged not to be against the public interest, one was abandoned, three are still (in 1986) continuing, and only one reference (that relating to the supply of Ford car parts) was considered to be against the public interest – but legislation would be needed to effect any change. In 1985 there were ten references: five were cleared, two abandoned and three continue; none has yet been found to operate against the public interest.

The system is riddled with uncertainty, both in the all-encompassing vagueness of key terms such as 'public interest' and 'market share' and in the dominant role played by political discretion. See COMPETITION LAW, MERGER, MERGER CONTROL and TAKE-OVERS.

MORATORIUM. When the rights of creditors are temporarily suspended or the remedies which are available to the creditors resulting from a default are temporarily barred.

MORTGAGE. A charge or security over property which is created where a creditor requires security for the payment of monies advanced by him.

Mortgages can be either legal or equitable. A legal mortgage may be created by the borrower granting a long lease, or term of years in his property, to the lender; or by a legal charge 'by way of legal mortgage' over the property.

If the mortgagor is in default of any of his obligations the mortgagee can take action on the personal covenant to repay or alternatively will have the right to sell or take possession of the property or appoint a receiver. These rights may also be enforceable against a third party.

The courts may invalidate any term in a mortgage transaction which restricts or negates the borrower's right to discharge his obligations, or which proves to be extortionate or oppressive. The borrower is deemed to retain an interest in property despite having mortgaged his rights to it. See EQUITY OF REDEMPTION, EQUITABLE MORTGAGE and FORECLOSURE.

MOTIVE. When a detective looks for a motive he looks for the reason for a crime, e.g. jealousy, fear or greed. When a lawyer talks of motive he means purpose, object or end; and in law a person's motive, unlike his intention, is usually irrelevant. So if a person blows up an aeroplane in mid-flight he will be said to intend to kill all the passengers even though his purpose or motive may have been to kill only one of them; and he will be guilty of murdering them all.

However, a legitimate motive can provide a defence to the tort of conspiracy: when dockers on the Island of Lewis in the Outer Hebrides were instructed by their union not to handle non-union, hand-spun Harris Tweed, they were not liable for conspiracy because their motive was to establish a closed shop, which was believed by the union to be in the best interests of the industry as a whole.

N

NAME (CORPORATE). A company – unlike an individual – must be given a name before it is born. Freedom of choice is limited in a number of ways: the name must indicate whether it is a public or private company; it cannot be the name of an existing company or one that is offensive or unlawful. Some names may be used only with the consent of the Secretary of State who may also require a change of name within 12 months of incorporation. Registration under the Act does not provide protection against passing off or trademark infringement. A company may change its name by special resolution. See BUSINESS NAME, CERTIFICATE OF INCORPORATION, PRIVATE COMPANY and PUBLIC COMPANY.

NAPOLEONIC CODE. The grandiose idea of the diminutive dictator: the codification of the whole of the civil law. As a result, a continental lawyer can carry all his substantive law of civil obligations in a handy paperback, whilst a common (Anglo-Saxon) lawyer would need a library full of case reports and could still not be sure he had everything.

NATIONALITY. Nationality arises from membership of a country or state and determines the political status and allegiance of an individual. Acquisition of nationality is normally through birth, descent, marriage or naturalization, but may also arise exceptionally through annexation of territory. See CITIZENSHIP.

Corporations also have a nationality: under English law this is determined by their country of incorporation; under most continental laws a company's nationality depends on the location of its centre of management.

NATURAL JUSTICE. A code of procedure to ensure that justice should not only be done but should be seen to be done. It applies to any body acting in a judicial capacity, and any administrative process which affects individual rights. The main tenets are that no man may be a judge in his own cause; a person should be told of the charge against him and both sides should be heard.

Judges or quasi-judicial bodies cannot hear a case in which they have a personal or pecuniary interest in the outcome, or where they may otherwise be fairly suspected to be biased. Moreover, each party has the right to have notice of the other's case, to bring evidence and to advance argument. It is the duty, not only of the court, but also of any other body or society with the power of affecting a person's rights, to act fairly.

The English courts will never enforce a judgment of a foreign court if the decision was reached following a procedure which denied one party natural justice.

NECESSITY. There is a vague but undeniable principle that acts which would otherwise be a tort may be committed for the reasonable protection of life and property. This is an exception to the general rule that a person is responsible for damage intentionally caused. For example, a house on fire may be demolished to protect adjacent property but, as Lord Denning said in a squatting case, 'the courts must, for the sake of law and order . . . refuse to admit the plea of necessity to the hungry and the homeless, and trust that their distress will be relieved by the charitable and the good'.

NEGLIGENCE. The tort of causing, or failing to avoid or prevent, damage which is not too remote, in breach of a duty of care owed by the defendant to the plaintiff.

The defendant must owe the plaintiff a duty not to cause the particular type of damage suffered; he must have failed to discharge that duty to the standard required of a hypothetical 'reasonable' man; and that failure must have caused the plaintiff damage that was reasonably foreseeable. The court will, so far as is 'just and equitable', reduce damages awarded against the defendant to the extent that the plaintiff was contributorily negligent.

Modern product liability may be traced to a 1932 case concerning the purchaser of a bottle of ginger beer who became ill after drinking most of its contents, which contained the decomposed remains of a snail. However, there is no general duty to avoid causing others economic loss, unless it flows directly from physical damage or (where there is a special relationship) careless written or oral mis-statements.

A person will be liable, irrespective of the existence of a duty of care, for damage caused by inherently dangerous things such as a loaded gun, underpants containing sulphites, or petrol.

See OMISSION, PRODUCT LIABILITY, PROFESSIONAL NEGLIGENCE, REMOTENESS OF DAMAGE, *RES IPSA LOQUITUR* and *VOLENTI NON FIT INJURIA*.

NEGOTIABLE INSTRUMENT. A chose in action which may be transferred by mere delivery, or by endorsement and delivery, from one person to another, with the result that the complete ownership of the instrument, and all the property it represents, passes free from equities to a transferee who takes it *bona fide* and for value and with the right to sue in his own name all parties to the instrument.

Negotiable instruments divide broadly into undertakings to pay (e.g. promissory notes) and orders to a third party to make payment (e.g. bills of exchange). They were created to facilitate domestic and international trade, and were originally governed by the corpus of law and procedure internationally recognized as the law merchant. The common law, and prior legislation on the topic, were finally codified in the Bills of Exchange Act 1882. This has been adopted as a basis of the law in the UK and other Anglo-Saxon countries.

Other forms of negotiable instruments are cheques, banker's drafts, dividend warrants, interest warrants, bearer bonds and debentures payable to bearer.

'NO ACTION' LETTER. The rendering of non-binding interpretative advice in the USA by the SEC. The commission offers 'interpretation and advisory assistance to members of the general public, prospective registrants, applicants and declarants. For example, persons having a question regarding the availability of an exemption may secure informal administrative interpretations of the applicable statute or rule as they relate to the particular facts and circumstances presented'.

NO PAR VALUE SHARES. Common in the USA, prohibited in the UK where each share must have a fixed nominal value which is the par value. With NPV, each share represents a fraction of the whole share capital of the company, and that in turn fluctuates with the value of the underlying business. Professor Gower has said that NPV would render the true nature of a share more intelligible, and would prevent unsophisticated people being misled by the unscrupulous.

NOMINEE DIRECTOR. See NOMINEES.

NOMINEE SHAREHOLDING. The ferocity with which House of Fraser pursued possible links with Lonrho, which led to protests from Swiss and Luxemburg bankers acting as nominees for their clients, is a good example of the effectiveness of a relatively new change in UK corporate law. A person cannot now secretly acquire voting control of a company or a significant block of shares, unless, of course, the directors are particularly dozy, in which case a requisition of shareholders holding one-tenth of the paid-up capital can spur them into action.

A public company can require a shareholder to disclose whether he is the true owner of shares, as well as any voting arrangements in respect of them; and, if he is not the beneficial owner, to identify that person. The starting point need not be a shareholder, it can be anyone who is believed by the company to have been interested in shares within the previous three years. It is a criminal offence to fail to give the information.

In addition a court may impose restrictions on the transfer of shares, payment of dividends and the exercise of voting rights. Companies may also impose restrictions in their Articles. See NOMINEES.

NOMINEES. A nominee director is one who has been appointed by a particular interest, usually a substantial or institutional shareholder. This does not detract from his responsibility to all shareholders. He must not put the interests of the person he represents before those of the company as a whole.

A nominee shareholder holds shares on behalf of another person, normally under a declaration of trust, which will require him to act in accordance with the directions of the beneficial owner. No notice of any express, implied or constructive trust may be entered on the register of members of a company in England. This protects the company: it is not liable for registering a transfer which is in breach of trust, or concerned with priorities of equitable mortgages on shares of the company. See NOMINEE SHAREHOLDING.

NON EST FACTUM. 'This is not my deed.' It is a plea in the law of contract that a person did not consent to the terms of the document which he has signed. If the plea is successful the contract is void and therefore cannot be enforced against the signatory, even by a third party who has acquired the benefit of the contract in good faith and for value.

The claimant must show that, through no fault of his own, he has been induced by the false statement of another, to sign a contract that is fundamentally different in character from that contemplated.

Those out in the commercial world should not think that they can stop reading the contracts placed before them and rely on this plea: it can only hold out much prospect of success to little old ladies and illiterates.

NON-EXECUTIVE DIRECTORS. See DIRECTORS.

NOTARY PUBLIC. A notary must possess a practising certificate issued by and registered with the Court of Faculties of the Archbishop of Canterbury. His principal role in the UK is to certify shipping and ecclesiastical documents, translations and original documents for use abroad.

Notaries in Continental Europe have a monopoly and key role in many areas of the law; they also act for both parties in many transactions, even where there may be conflicts of interest. See AVOCAT.

NOVATION. One of the methods by which a contract may be discharged or obligations under a contract transferred. It is, in effect, a form of assignment in which a new contract is substituted for an existing one. Often a new person becomes a party to the new contract and a person who is a party to the former contract is discharged from further liability. It is sometimes favoured over an assignment of a contract as it can save stamp duty!

NUISANCE, PRIVATE. The tort of unreasonably causing indirect damage to land or interfering with the use or enjoyment of, or a right over, land. It is often called a tort of 'strict liability', as the act complained of by the plaintiff need not be caused either intentionally or negligently.

Where statute has authorized something to be done which necessarily involves commission of a private nuisance, any resulting harm may not be actionable if the harm is not excessive. For this reason, Parliament sometimes expressly preserves nuisance liability when empowering corporations to carry out certain operations.

NUISANCE, PUBLIC. An act which obstructs or causes inconvenience or damage to the public. If a plaintiff can establish that a public nuisance has been committed, he may obtain damages in tort by proving that he suffered substantial damage or inconvenience over and above that suffered by the general public.

The most common tortious claims for public nuisance relate to personal injuries sustained while passing along the highway, which does not have to be completely obstructed for there to be a successful claim. For instance, in 1947 the Court of Appeal held that, when Mr Almeroth tripped over a small pile of slates left by builders against the kerb of a road in West Ham, the builders were liable for his personal injuries.

O

OATH. Lawyers are renowned for their swearing! An oath is a sworn statement to the court. Almost all oral evidence given in court is upon oath and all affidavit evidence is given under oath. Affidavits have to be sworn before a solicitor or a commissioner for oaths, for which a fee is charged. Conscientious non-believers may affirm. See PERJURY.

OBITER DICTA. 'Things said by the way' are statements by a judge which are not essential to decide the case before him. As judges are frequently caricatured as verbose in the extreme, it may be thought that most of what they say could be considered to be *obiter dicta*. This is not the case; the phrase describes those statements of opinion relating to hypothetical facts which, while not necessary for the disposal of the case before them, can be used as a persuasive authority in a later case which has similar facts to the hypothetical case. By this method judges (particularly the more influential members of the Court of Appeal and House of Lords) can deliberately influence the development of the law.

OBJECTS. Provisions governing the nature and extent of the business of the company. They are contained in the objects clause of the Memorandum.

A company has no capacity to do any act or carry on any business which is not part of its objects: hence, out of caution, they usually run to some thirty clauses, most of which will never be required or used.

Although modern objects clauses invariably provide that each object is self-standing, many objects (e.g. to borrow) are more properly viewed as powers to facilitate the principal objects.

The objects clause may be altered by special resolution for any of seven purposes, which in practice would cover any enlargement or reduction of the objects. See *ULTRA VIRES*.

OFFER AND ACCEPTANCE. Two of the essential elements required to form a legally binding contract. An offer is an expression of willingness to contract which is made with the intention that it shall become binding as soon as it is accepted by the person to whom it is addressed. An acceptance is a final and unqualified assent to the terms of the offer which is communicated to, and brought to the notice of, the offeror.

Acceptance must be unequivocal. If it is made subject to terms not included in the original offer, it will constitute rejection of that offer and, possibly, a counter offer, but not acceptance.

A postal acceptance takes place when the letter is posted, not at the time the letter arrives. A telex is governed by the general rule that an acceptance must be actually communicated.

The place where acceptance occurs can be of critical significance in identifying the proper law of the contract and, if the contract is a trading contract, the place in which that trading is done for tax purposes. See INVITATION TO TREAT.

OFFER FOR SALE. See FLOTATION.

OFFER TO PUBLIC. See FLOTATION.

OFFER FOR SALE BY TENDER. A variation of an offer for sale at a fixed price. Applicants are invited to buy shares at the higher of a fixed minimum tender price or the highest price at which sufficient applications are received for all the shares on offer to be fully taken up. This method ensures that all shares are issued at the same price, and that the punter who applies for shares at an absurdly high price does not have to pay in full for his absurdity.

The idea of tender offers for companies was pinched, in the early 1970s, from the water companies, who had historically issued securities by the tender method. They were introduced in order to frustrate stags who applied for shares in order to make a quick profit, and to ensure that the price was pitched at the best possible level.

It is unfair to accuse those Issuing Houses who adopt the tender method of abdicating their responsibility to fix a price. See FLOTATION.

OFFICIAL RECEIVER. An officer of the DTI who is attached to the court for the purposes of bankruptcy and liquidation. He can be appointed a trustee of a bankrupt's estate and investigates the conduct and affairs of a bankrupt and the cause of the failure of a company subject to a winding up order by the court.

OFFICIAL SECRETS ACTS. They represent the tireless (tedious) efforts of government to impose the restrictions on freedom of expression and access to information which are felt necessary to protect the interests of the UK. They cover a wide variety of matters, ranging from serious breaches of national security, such as spying, to the unauthorized disclosure of any official information. A prosecution for an offence under the Acts may only be instituted by or with the consent of the Attorney-General. Their application to the media is governed by a voluntarily accepted code of censorship known as the 'D' notice. See CONFIDENTIAL INFORMATION.

OFFICIAL SOLICITOR. The Official Solicitor to the Supreme Court who is appointed by the Lord Chancellor. His duties include acting as guardian *ad litem* (in litigation) to persons under disability; conducting sales by order of the court if the parties to an action cannot agree upon an independent solicitor; acting as a judicial trustee; and generally assisting the court where the judge considers that the assistance of a solicitor is required.

OLD BAILEY. The name by which the Central Criminal Court is affectionately known by police, legal practitioners and other villains. The courts are famous for the notorious cases that they hear, being all major criminal cases and all major crimes in the London area. Perched on the roof of the building is a figure holding the scales of justice, ensuring that the full weight of justice is felt by those most deserving of it.

OMBUDSMAN. The Parliamentary Commissioner for Administration. He investigates maladministration in the central government machine (local government has its own Ombudsman). Maladministration is not defined in the legislation but would cover bias, neglect, inattention, delay, incompetence; in fact all those qualities for which civil servants are most frequently caricatured. Complaints can be investigated by the Ombudsman only when they have been referred to him by a member of the House of Commons. The Ombudsman may lay a special report on the case before each House of Parliament if an injustice is not remedied.

OMISSION. A failure to act. There is no general duty in English law to act positively for the benefit of others. There are exceptions, such as the duty of the occupier of premises to ensure that his visitors are safe and that of an occupier of land to prevent the escape of things likely to do mischief. Where a person undertakes to help or care for another he accepts a duty of care towards that person. If he then omits to carry out that duty he may face tortious or, in extreme cases, criminal liability. See NEGLIGENCE and REASONABLENESS.

OPTIONS. An offer to buy or sell property of any kind, which is irrevocable if given for some consideration (or under seal), and which remains open to acceptance in accordance with its terms.

When the option is exercised (by acceptance) it becomes a contract which creates rights and obligations on both sides. The price to be paid for the property need not be fixed in advance, provided there is some machinery for determining it by objective standards. An option giving the grantee the right to buy is known as a call option. If the grantee has a right to sell it is a put option. Some options (other than those to renew a lease) are subject to the rule against perpetuities.

Options are traded in established markets around the world, the largest of which is the Chicago Mercantile Exchange. A traded currency option contract, for example, gives its holder the right to buy or sell currency at a predetermined price ('strike price') on or before a specified maturity date. The holder pays the issuer ('writer') of an option a 'premium' and the writer is then obliged to buy or sell the currency at the holder's request. The option holder's potential loss is restricted to the size of the premium paid if the option is allowed to lapse, but the potential gain is unlimited. See DISCLOSURE OF INTEREST IN SHARES.

ORDINARY RESOLUTION. A resolution passed by a majority of those voting at a general meeting of which at least 14 clear days' notice has been given. Special notice has to be given for certain ordinary resolutions. See EXTRAORDINARY GENERAL MEETING, PRE-EMPTIVE RIGHTS and SPECIAL RESOLUTION.

ORDINARY SHARES. These generally carry the voting rights of the company and, subject to the prior rights of preference shares, the right to any dividends declared and to the surplus of assets on a winding up. They are sometimes known as equity shares.

Despite institutional objections, it is possible to have ordinary shares which have limited, or even no, voting rights. There are still companies listed on The Stock Exchange in which a small number of ordinary shares control a company with a preponderance of non-voting, or limited voting, ordinary shares.

ORIGINATING SUMMONS. A summons which commences proceedings, It contains a statement of the questions on which the plaintiff asks for determination or direction, and the relief he seeks.

It is used where the principal question is one of construction of a statute, document, or some other dry question of law, where there is no substantial dispute on the facts.

OVER THE COUNTER MARKETS. In the UK, the market which exists outside the centralized market place of The Stock Exchange, although some shares quoted on an OTC market may also be dealt in under The Stock Exchange's auspices. At the end of 1984, some 150 companies had their shares quoted on an OTC market.

In the USA the OTC market has about 4,800 companies quoted, of which about 300 are foreign companies. The system is based on the ability of 5,800 members of the National Association of Securities Dealers to obtain immediate stock price information over their automated quotation system (NASDAQ).

OVERSEA COMPANIES. There is no serious hindrance to a foreign company carrying on business in the UK: perhaps that is why so many do so. The Act applies conditions to be observed by any company incorporated outside the UK which establishes a place of business in the UK; any company which does so submits itself to the jurisdiction of the English (or where appropriate Scottish) courts.

When an oversea company has established a place of business in the UK it must within one month deliver a certified copy (plus English translation if appropriate) of its constitution and certain other information to the Registrar. Naturally changes to this information, as well as the company's annual accounts, have to be filed with the Registrar.

Whether or not a foreign company has established a place of business in the UK, the distribution in the UK of a prospectus offering its shares or debentures must comply with somewhat wider prospectus requirements than those relating to UK companies. These provisions are relaxed when a foreign company issues a prospectus in connection with shares uniform with shares already listed on The Stock Exchange (although there may then be a requirement to file listing particulars).

P

PANEL. See CITY PANEL.

PART PERFORMANCE. In the case of a contract for the disposition of an interest in land, the Statutes of Frauds render the contract unenforceable unless there is a sufficient memorandum in writing signed by the party to be charged. To mitigate the rigors of this rule, equity developed the doctrine of part performance, under which a party who acted to his prejudice on the basis that such a contract would be performed was held entitled to require the other party to complete the contract.

Generally a party must perform all his obligations under a contract: any less can give rise to an action for breach, or rescission, with the guilty party being unable to claim anything for what he has done. However, where a contract has been substantially performed, the agreed price can be recovered, subject to an action for damages. A contracting party may recover a reasonable price, on a *quantum meruit* basis, for work done or goods supplied if his performance is accepted, or the other party waives, or forbears to require, full performance.

PARTLY-PAID. Shares or other securities where only part of the issue price has been paid (the US equivalent expression is 'assessable'). In the UK there is no requirement for a minimum amount to be paid up on shares.

The holder of a partly-paid share is usually bound by the Articles to pay the balance of the issue price at specified dates, or on demand. If payment is not made the shares can be forfeited or the company can exercise a lien over them. See CALLS ON SHARES.

PARTNERSHIP. Unlike a company 'which has no soul to be saved or body to be kicked', a partnership is not a legal entity separate from its members. It is the relationship which subsists between persons carrying on business 'with a view of profit'. Whether a partnership exists is a question of fact. The joint ownership of property, sharing gross returns, or the receipt of a payment varying with profits, do not, of themselves, constitute a partnership.

There is no limit on the liability of each partner for the debts and obligations of the firm unless he is a limited partner. Each partner is an agent of the others, and his acts done in carrying on the business bind all the partners.

The Partnership Act 1890 applies in the absence of an agreement between the partners; its principle is to treat partners equally. Each is entitled to take part in management, to share equally in the profits, and is bound to contribute equally to capital and losses. Accordingly partners are well advised to have an agreement.

In the absence of agreement a partner is not to compete with the firm, and is accountable for any profit or benefit arising from the use by him of the partnership property, name, or business connections. See FIDUCIARY DUTY and LIMITED PARTNERSHIP.

PASSING-OFF. The means afforded by the law of ensuring fair trading based on the old maxim that nobody has any right to represent his goods as the goods of someone else. The common law tort of passing-off has now moved far beyond mere goods to cover many misrepresentations made in the course of trade. To succeed, a plaintiff must show some reputation in the UK usually, but not necessarily, gained by trading here; that there is a common field of activity between his activities and those of the defendant; that there is a likelihood of confusion; and actual or threatened damage. See SERVICE MARKS.

Passing-off commonly arises from the use of similar names, marks or get-up and the plaintiff may be entitled to damages, an account of profits and, most importantly, an injunction to restrain further acts. The law of trademarks can be seen as a statutory extension of the principle of the law of passing-off; but it is of narrower application.

PATENT. The grant by the Crown or state to an inventor of a 20-year monopoly to manufacture or use some new product or industrial process in exchange for the publication of details of his invention. In President Lincoln's words, they add 'the fuel of interest to the fire of genius'.

In the UK, patents are available for new inventions capable of industrial application in which there is an 'inventive step' over the available art in that field. They may not be obtained for discoveries, methods of treatment of humans and animals, mathematical processes or pure software.

Patents are granted after exhaustive examination by national (or, increasingly, international or Pan-European) patent offices. The patentee may apply to the courts to restrain the manufacture or disposal of products falling within the patent or the use of patented processes. When doing so he usually has to face a challenge to the validity of the patent which can lead to a long and expensive legal process.

PATENT AGENT. One of the 1,400 members of the Chartered Institute of Patent Agents. As the name implies they act for their clients in all matters relating to the technical aspects of patents. They usually have a technical degree and must pass a complex, hybrid examination on procedure, and drafting. They also enjoy the title 'European Patent Attorney'. The term 'Patent Attorney' is usually applied to American patent lawyers who, unlike English patent agents, are fully qualified lawyers and who may practise at the American Bar.

PATENT CONVENTIONS. The four principal patent Conventions show a steady trend towards internationalism and the avoidance of duplicated effort.

Under the Treaty of Paris, most industrialized countries permit foreign applicants to apply for local patents, and also allow them a period of 12 months in which to apply for a patent in the 'foreign' country that will enjoy the same priority date as it does in the country in which the person's first application was made.

The Patent Co-operation Treaty allows a single filing in one patent office and a single search of the prior art. That search report is made available to national patent offices.

The European Patent Treaty provides a regional system within 'greater Europe' by allowing single filing, single search and single examination of validity, the results being communicated to national patent offices for final processing and the grant of a national patent.

The Community Patent Treaty will provide for a single community patent extending to all member states of the European Community in place of national patents.

PAYMENT INTO COURT. A defendant may pay into court a sum which he considers satisfies the plaintiff's claim. If that amount is not accepted by the plaintiff within 21 days it remains in court until an order for payment out is made. The payment cannot be revealed until after judgment when it becomes relevant to the issue of costs. If the plaintiff does not recover, on trial, an amount exceeding the amount paid in, he may be liable for all the costs of the action from the date the money was lodged.

Payment into court is also a means by which a person can relieve himself of the responsibility of administering or distributing funds.

PENALTY AND LIQUIDATED DAMAGES. Parties to a contract may provide that, if there is a breach, a sum of money shall be paid by the recalcitrant party to avoid the need and expense of proving actual damage before the courts. That sum may be liquidated damages, which are recoverable, or a penalty, which is irrecoverable. The name that is used is not conclusive of its real nature.

The essence of a penalty is a payment of a sum of money stipulated as *in terrorem* of the offending party; the essence of liquidated damages is a genuine pre-estimate of damage.

PER INCURIAM. A decision by a court (or anybody else!) which has been given in ignorance of relevant authority or statute. Such a judgment is not a binding precedent.

PER SE. 'By itself'. Normally a tort requires proof of actual damage to the plaintiff. Torts actionable '*per se*' do not. Examples are:

- trespass to land and goods
- trespass to the person
- private nuisance affecting rights over property
- libel
- special categories of slander

PERFORMER'S PROTECTION. It is an offence under the Performer's Protection Act 1963 for a person knowingly to make a record or a film directly or indirectly from the performance of a musical or dramatic work without the consent in writing of the performers, or to sell or let such a work on hire or to use it for public performance. The court also has power to restrain the commission of such acts.

PERFORMING RIGHT. The performance in public of musical, literary or dramatic works is restricted under the Copyright Act 1956 and known as the 'performing right'. The phrase is most common in relation to musical works in which composers and music publishers traditionally assign or license performing rights to the The Performing Right Society Limited ('PRS'), which arranges collection of fees from broadcasters, concert halls, hotels and all other places in which music may be publicly performed. Disputes as to fees may ultimately be referred to The Performing Right Tribunal. Similar organizations to PRS exist in many countries.

PERJURY. A person on oath commits perjury if he deliberately makes a material statement which he knows to be false or does not believe to be true. A half-truth is said to be no better than a downright falsehood, and a person can even commit perjury by saying something which is in fact true, but which he believes to be false. See AFFIDAVIT.

PERPETUITIES RULE. A technical rule which renders void and of no effect any gift, or interest in property, which may vest (i.e. take effect) outside the traditional period of lives in being and a further 21 years, or a specified fixed period not exceeding 80 years.

PERSONAL REPRESENTATIVE. Persons appointed by a testator to administer his estate, or who administer the estate of an intestate. Their authority flows from the will or, in the case of an intestacy, from the grant of letters of administration.

They owe a duty to creditors and beneficiaries to carry out their obligations with due diligence.

PERSONALTY. All forms of property whether movable or immovable, tangible or intangible, other than freehold estates or interests in land, and things fixed to and forming part of land. Leasehold is personalty but has quasi-realty status. See REALTY.

PETITION. One of the prescribed methods of beginning proceedings in the High Court. There are no petitions in the Queen's Bench division except election petitions to challenge a parliamentary or local petition. It is used as an application to wind up a company and on a variety of other applications relating to companies.

PLACING. A means of selling a company's securities to a limited number of (usually) institutional investors when there is no need or desire to reach the public generally.

A vendor placing arises when a listed company agrees to buy, in exchange for its securities, assets or shares of another company. The vendor (understandably) may prefer cash to shares or other securities. The company's brokers will, therefore, place the securities through the stock market, or with clients, as soon as they are allotted: the vendor receives the cash that is raised.

If it is possible to place securities verbally, a prospectus is not required. Nor is it required in a placing to a limited number of people where each offer is made to a particular person who warrants that he is acquiring the securities for himself as a long-term investment and no renounceable documents of title, but only the share certificate, are issued, payment is made in full and, even if the securities are to be listed, there is no doubt that the securities will be held as an investment and not with a view to resale. See FLOTATION and PROSPECTUS.

PLAINTIFF. The person who brings an action in the civil courts against another, the defendant. If he appeals, he becomes an appellant, and if appealed against, he becomes a respondent. See PLEADINGS.

PLANT VARIETY PROTECTION. A plant breeder who creates a new, distinct, uniform and stable variety of certain species of plants may, after official testing of the variety's reproduction or propagation, be entitled to monopoly protection for between 15 and 25 years under the Plant Varieties and Seeds Act 1964. A new variety name is usually required.

The monopoly right extends to the marketing of seeds, tubers and cuttings intended for reproduction of the variety, and may be licensed.

PLEADINGS. Formal documents prepared by each side to a civil action which contain all the material facts on which each party relies, and in which admissions and denials of the other's case are made.

They enable each side to see the substance of the other's case. Judgments and settlements are often achieved on the strength of what a party has pleaded. The exchange of pleadings is an obligatory part of any action and is the next stage in most actions following the issue of the writ. When pleadings close, preparations are made to bring the case to trial. See DISCOVERY AND INSPECTION.

PLEDGE. A delivery of possession of goods for the purposes of granting security for a loan or other obligation, effected either by making physical delivery of the goods pledged, or by constructive delivery, e.g. by handing over keys to the warehouse in which the goods are kept. A delivery of documents of title to goods does not usually constitute a pledge of the underlying goods although a lien may arise.

If the pledgor defaults, the pledgee has, under common law, an implied right of sale over the pledged goods.

POISON PILLS. Properly known as rights plans, they are a corporate defence in the USA against future unwelcome take-overs. They are lauded by corporate directors, loathed by predators, and were lambasted by the *Wall Street Journal* which prophesied, on 21 November 1985, that they could eventually lead to European-style ossification of the nation's economy.

There are many variants but, typically, it is a right issued by way of dividend to stockholders enabling them to acquire corporation stock at an exercise price substantially above the market price of stock at the time of the dividend. The right has a 10-year term, trades with the common shares and is exercisable on the announcement of a tender offer for 30 per cent of the voting stock. The directors can redeem the rights for a nominal sum until the acquisition of 20 per cent of the stock by a person or group.

Rights plans therefore make a corporation much more expensive for the predator in two-tier mergers. They would not be much use in England where, under the City Code, the same price has to be offered to all shareholders of the same class – as has been the case in the USA from 18 August 1986.

POLL. See VOTING.

POWER OF APPOINTMENT. Normally a power given to trustees to appoint settled property in favour of a beneficiary; or to appoint new trustees. Being a fiduciary power, it must be exercised in the best interests of the beneficiaries and without any influence from a third party.

Powers of appointment amongst a specified class are called 'special powers'; those that can be made to persons (including himself) specified by the donee of the power, are known as 'general powers'.

POWER OF ATTORNEY. A deed appointing an agent which may contain limited or extensive authority to act on the donor's behalf. It also enables the agent to execute a deed on behalf of the donor of the power. It will be revoked on the instruction of the donor, or on his death, mental incapacity or bankruptcy, unless it is irrevocable and given to secure a subsisting proprietary interest of the donee, or the performance of an undischarged obligation owed to the donee.

A donee who acts after the power has been revoked will not incur any liability if, at the time, he did not know of the revocation. A transaction in favour of a person without knowledge of revocation is as valid as if the power had not been revoked.

The Enduring Powers of Attorney Act 1985 creates a new type of power which will continue in force despite the donor's mental incapacity.

POWER OF SALE. A right to sell the goods or property of a third party without the need for his consent or co-operation and, by such sale, to pass good title to a purchaser. Examples include a mortgagee acting under an express or implied power; a bailee exercising a statutory power of sale over uncollected goods; a bailiff selling duly seized goods; and a trustee in bankruptcy selling goods of a debtor in respect of whom a receiving order has been made.

PRACTICE DIRECTIONS. Periodic statements by judges and masters on matters of court practice and procedure. They are intended as a guide to the legal profession and courts, and supplement the various rules of court; but they do not have statutory authority. See *WHITE BOOK*.

PRE-EMPTION. A mechanism, usually contained in the Articles of a private company or a shareholders' agreement, which requires any shareholder wishing to transfer his shares to offer them first for purchase by the other shareholders (and sometimes other persons whom the directors may introduce) usually at an agreed price or in default of agreement at a fair value determined by the company's auditors. It is only if the shares are not purchased by those persons that they may be transferred to a third party.

Pre-emption is different from an option as it can only take effect on an action triggered by a vendor.

PRE-EMPTIVE RIGHTS. A right of first refusal, most commonly encountered in connection with the issue by companies for cash of securities having an equity element. The right allows members to maintain their percentage interest and to take advantage (if any arises) of any price movement resulting from the issue of the securities. Existing members are offered the new securities in proportion to their existing holdings on no less favourable terms than they are to be issued to non-members. Members can waive their rights by resolution in general meeting; or, the Articles may contain a waiver of statutory rights. Guidelines issued by institutional investors recognize that some limited waiver of the statutory rights may be of assistance to listed companies.

PREFERENCE. See FRAUDULENT PREFERENCE.

PREFERENCE SHARES. Shares in a company which usually give the holders priority rights, over ordinary shares, to fixed dividends and the repayment of capital in a winding up. They are not normally entitled to vote except on a resolution for winding up, or on a proposed modification of their rights. There is a presumption that dividends on preference shares are cumulative, so that if dividends are not paid in one year they will be payable later when profits are distributed.

Redeemable preference shares were, until 1981, the only class of shares that could be redeemed by a company. Redeemable shares of any class may now be issued.

The precise rights of preference shares are governed by the Articles or by the resolution creating them.

PRE-INCORPORATION CONTRACT. A contract made before the date of incorporation of a company. A company has no power to enter into such a contract – because the company does not exist – and therefore a person purporting to act for the company, or as its agent, is personally liable on the contract. The personal liability can be avoided if the company, after its formation, enters into an agreement in the same terms.

PREROGATIVE ORDERS. See JUDICIAL REVIEW.

PRESIDENT (OF COMPANY). The chief officer of a US corporation generally charged with its direction and administration under powers conferred by statute, corporate charter, bye-laws, or by the board of directors.

The post in the UK is of an honorary nature, normally bestowed upon a retiring (or retired) chairman.

PRICE-SENSITIVE INFORMATION. The statutory definition has arisen from the need to prevent the misuse of corporate property by those people who are entrusted, or more cogently cannot be trusted, with confidential information relating to company affairs. Essentially, it is knowledge of important factors relating to a company which is not available to the public (or, more significantly, to people who are likely to deal in the company's securities) but which would, if generally known, have a material bearing on the price of the securities in question. See INSIDER DEALINGS.

PRINCIPAL. See AGENCY.

PRIORITY. What every creditor would like when a company or individual becomes insolvent. Generally, the order of priority is:

firstly, the persons having fixed charges over assets of the insolvent to the extent of their security; secondly, the preferential creditors specified in the Insolvency Act 1985; thirdly (in the case of companies only) the holders of debentures secured by any floating charge created by the company; lastly the other unsecured creditors.

Priority also arises between persons who take security for different debts over the same asset. The general rule is that priority arises according to the date on which the security is created and the degree of formality employed (particularly whether the security creates a legal interest or merely an equitable one). Possession of the documents of title to the charged assets, or the assets themselves, and compliance with registration and notification formalities are often important in establishing the priority of a security interest.

Exceptions to the general rule occur by agreement amongst the holders of security interests, often in a letter of priority or a subordination agreement, and where a holder of security is able to tack further advances. See CHARGES and LEGAL ESTATE.

PRIVATE COMPANY. Any company which is not a public company. It is prohibited, under pain of criminal sanction, from offering shares or debentures to the public. If it has limited liability status its name must end with the word 'limited'. If its registered office is in Wales the equivalent word is 'cyfyngedig'. See PURCHASE OF OWN SHARES.

PRIVATE INTERNATIONAL LAW. See CONFLICT OF LAWS.

PRIVILEGE. A witness is said to be privileged when he cannot be compelled to answer a question or supply information in judicial proceedings. The three important heads of privilege are:

- the right in civil or criminal cases not to answer questions or produce documents which, in the opinion of the judge, may tend to expose the deponent to any criminal charge or penalty (in civil proceedings one spouse cannot be compelled to answer questions which may tend to incriminate the other);
- confidential communications between a client and his legal adviser if made for the purpose of legal advice or with

reference to litigation either taking place or contemplated. This also extends to communications between the solicitor or client and a third party if for the purpose of litigation;

- 'without prejudice' communications.

The privilege between a client and his professional adviser extends only to legal advisers (except 'in-house' lawyers in competition investigations by the European Commission): the priest can be compelled to reveal the secrets of the confessional, the doctor secrets of his couch and the accountant his client's tax planning. This may argue for a wider use of lawyers.

Parliament claims rights and privileges for its members (individually and collectively) to maintain independence of action and 'the dignity of its position'. Examples are not to attend as a witness in court and freedom of speech, even if defamatory, in parliamentary debates and proceedings.

PRIVITY OF CONTRACT. The relation between the immediate parties to a contract. As a general rule, a contract cannot confer rights or impose obligations on any person except the parties to it. The most important and firmly established result of this rule is that only a party to a contract can sue on it.

PRIVY COUNCIL. There has been one Privy Council for Great Britain since 1708. It was the Crown's chief advisory council before that function was assumed by the cabinet. All acts of the council are expressed as orders in council or proclamations signed by the Sovereign. It makes government orders, which obtain the force of law without being subject to previous parliamentary criticism.

The Judicial Committee of the Privy Council was at one time the ultimate court of appeal, but its jurisdiction is now limited to being, principally, the final appellate court from courts in a diminishing number of Commonwealth states, and the ecclesiastical courts. As Law Lords sit on the committee its decisions are of importance as persuasive precedents. See SUBORDINATE LEGISLATION.

PROCURING A BREACH OF CONTRACT. The tort of intentionally procuring or inducing one party to break his contract with the other.

The tort emerged from the ancient form of action brought by a master to enforce proprietary rights in his servant. Along with related torts protecting economic interests, it still plays a prominent role in the employment field, in particular by offering a remedy for the enticement of an employee away from the services of his employer. The tort made its debut in 1852, when Johanna Wagner contracted to sing for three months exclusively for one Mr Lumley at the Queen's Theatre but was enticed away by a Mr Gye to sing for him instead. Lumley was granted an injunction and, in a later action, was awarded damages.

Its expansion into other areas of contractual relations followed quickly. Most controversial has been its use in relation to industrial disputes and a 1976 Act removes liability where the tort was committed in contemplation or furtherance of a trade dispute. The Employment Act 1980 has restored liability in cases brought in respect of: unlawful picketing; secondary action; industrial action calculated to impose union membership or recognition; and official industrial action taken without a secret ballot of union members.

PRODUCT LIABILITY. The EEC Product Liability Directive is potentially one of the most significant developments in Community legislation. It will introduce into UK law strict liability for damage caused by defective products. Damage is defined as covering death or personal injury and also damage to goods. The commercial object of the Directive is to ensure that all manufacturers of products can be subjected to the same rules of liability for products marketed in any member state. The Directive must be brought into force in the UK (as in all other member states) by 30 July 1988. The Directive renders the 'producer' liable for such damage. This will normally be the manufacturer or importer but can also be a distributor who markets the product by placing its own brand name on it. The test for defectiveness is wide and is cast in terms of whether the product 'provides the safety which a person is entitled to expect taking all circumstances into account, including the presentation of the product, the use to which it could reasonably be expected to be put and the time the product was put into circulation'. A defence open to the producer will be to show that the state of scientific and technical knowledge at the time of manufacture was not such as to enable the defect to be discovered. See NEGLIGENCE.

PROFESSIONAL NEGLIGENCE. Doctors, solicitors, accountants and members of other professions are exposed to claims for negligence which they regard as a scourge of the modern world. Some professionals have already run, and others are contemplating running, for the cover of limited liability as fast as they can.

The duty of the professional man or woman to his client is to exercise the care of a normal professional man or woman in that profession by the exercise of reasonable skill and judgment. A claim for negligence will arise when a breach of the duty results in loss to the client. A person who is not a client, but who is in a special relationship of such a nature that the professional should know that his advice will be relied upon by that person, is also owed a duty of care.

Apart from the excessive cost of insuring against negligence, a damaging consequence of the recent spate of negligence claims, particularly in the USA, is the tendency for the professional not to take risks, by the practice of 'defence medicine'. See AUDITORS.

PROFIT FORECAST. The City Code requires statements to be treated as profit forecasts even if they contain no figures, e.g. 'profits will be somewhat higher than last year'. Companies are wise not to make forecasts of future profits, not only because they look so foolish if expectation does not match reality, but also because a profit forecast made shortly before a take-over must be repeated in the offer documents.

The City Code refers to the hazards attached to the forecasting of profits. It requires them to be to be compiled with scrupulous care and objectivity by the directors. The accounting policies and calculations must be examined and reported on by the auditors and financial advisers.

Similar requirements are imposed in the case of profit forecasts included in listing particulars or in documents published in connection with the sale of shares which are to be dealt in on the Unlisted Securities Market. See LISTING REGULATIONS and PROSPECTUS LIABILITIES.

PROHIBITION. See JUDICIAL REVIEW.

PROMISSORY NOTE. Defined for the purposes of English law by section 83(1) of the Bills of Exchange Act 1882 as 'an unconditional promise in writing made by one person to another signed by the maker, engaging to pay, on demand at a fixed or determinable future time, a sum certain in money to, or to the order of, a specific person or bearer'. See NEGOTIABLE INSTRUMENT.

PROMOTER. The term jingles with unsavoury undertones, which may have been true in the distant past, but are not these days. A promoter has been described as 'one who undertakes to form a company with reference to a given project and to set it going, and who takes the necessary steps to accomplish that purpose'. He also undertakes responsibility for the provision of its capital.

A promoter stands in a fiduciary position towards the company; he must not make a secret profit for himself at its expense. To avoid liability full details of any benefit he receives must be given either to an independent board of directors or, if that is impossible, to all persons who subscribe for shares.

A prospectus must disclose details of any benefit given to a promoter within the two preceding years, and the consideration for its payment. Promoters are liable to pay compensation to persons who subscribe for securities in reliance on a prospectus containing an untrue statement.

PROPER LAW. It is important for the parties to a contract to know its governing law. The proper law is shorthand for whether a contract is to be governed by a foreign, or English, law. There is a presumption in favour of a single system, but different parts of the contract may be governed by different systems of law.

The English courts, in theory, find the proper law by looking at the intention of the parties, that is the law the parties intended to apply when making the contract. As this is subjective and difficult to apply, the practice tends to be for judges to look at connecting factors between the contract and the various countries involved, and find where in factual terms the most ties exist. Examples of connecting factors could be the place where the contract was made, the country of its performance, or the currency in which payment is made.

Modern business practice is to state in a contract the law which is to be applied: unless there are urgent reasons of public policy to the contrary, the courts will apply that law. See CONFLICT OF LAWS.

PROPERTY IN GOODS. A term tantamount to ownership. When the property in goods passes to the buyer there is transferred to him the title to the legal interest in the goods sold. The buyer can then deal with the goods and pass a good title to any other person.

The time when property passes is crucial to determining who will bear any risk if the goods are lost, deteriorate, are damaged or destroyed. The general rule is that goods remain at the seller's risk until property passes, although there are many important exceptions.

Property will normally be transferred on delivery of goods, but this may be varied by conditions in the contract such as safe arrival, or payment of the purchase price in full. If any pre-condition is not satisfied, property will remain in the seller whether delivery has been made or not.

Bailees who have possession, and not ownership, and other people with limited interests, are said to have a 'special property'. See SALE OF GOODS.

PROSPECTUS. The prospectus requirements of the Act were designed to protect the gullible public against the unscrupulous promoter and director. A prospectus is given an extremely wide and partially circular definition and is 'any prospectus, notice, circular, advertisement, or other invitation, offering to the public for subscription or purchase any shares in or debentures of a company'.

Although the definition does not say so, there must be a document. An offer to any section of the public is a prospectus (but see PLACING) unless it is solely of domestic concern to the persons making or receiving it. Where a private company offers securities to its existing members, debenture holders, or employees, it is regarded, unless the contrary is proved, as being solely of domestic concern.

A take-over offer document, where the offeror is to issue shares in exchange for shares in the offeree company, is not a prospectus since it is not an offer for subscription or purchase.

The Act contains detailed regulations specifying matters which have to be included in every prospectus. If securities being sold are to be listed on The Stock Exchange, any document offering them must comply with the listing regulations. Every prospectus must be signed by, or on behalf of, all the directors and registered with the Registrar. Listing particulars must also be registered. See FLOTATION and PROSPECTUS LIABILITIES.

PROSPECTUS LIABILITIES. Any statement included in a prospectus is deemed to be untrue if it is misleading in the form and context in which it is included.

Criminal actions in respect of untrue statements are rare. Civil claims are more common. Compensation is payable to all those who subscribe for securities for the loss or damage sustained by reason of any untrue statement included in a prospectus. The persons liable are directors, promoters and others who authorized its issue. Civil claims for compensation may also be brought for negligent mis-statement or deceit. In addition there might be a possible claim for damages against the company itself for breach of contract or under the Misrepresentation Act 1967.

PROTECTION OF TRADING INTERESTS. US courts seek to extend their jurisdiction extra-territorially: manifestations of this long-arm jurisdiction resulted in the UK passing the Protection of Trading Interests Act 1980.

The Secretary of State may prohibit any person carrying on business in the UK, from complying with foreign process or orders which damage or threaten to damage the trading interests of the UK. Disobedience is a criminal offence.

PROTECTIVE TRUSTS. The perfect gift for a spendthrift child. They are trusts where the principal beneficiary receives the income for his life on protective trusts as defined in section 33 of The Trustee Act 1925. If the beneficiary attempts to dispose of his interest or becomes bankrupt, it automatically terminates and discretionary trusts of income spring up; the trustees have a discretion to distribute income between the principal beneficiary, his spouse, children and remoter issue.

PROVISIONAL LETTER OF ALLOTMENT. See LETTER OF ALLOTMENT.

PROXY. The agent appointed by a member to vote on his behalf in a poll taken at a general meeting of a company, as well as the document of appointment.

A member of a private company is entitled to appoint only one proxy and he has the right to speak, but a proxy of a member of a public company cannot speak except to demand a poll. A proxy must vote in accordance with his instructions.

A company may appoint a natural person as its representative and is best advised to do so for he can speak and, having a human structure, can vote on a show of hands as well as on a poll. See VOTING.

PROXY FIGHT. Primarily a US practice. It is a battle to secure proxy votes from shareholders in a company in favour of or against a proposed merger or some corporate transaction. In the USA, unlike the UK, a merger may be effected by a vote of shareholders, instead of an offer for the shares, in one of the companies. Consequently the importance of obtaining proxy votes is much heightened. In the USA professional proxy solicitation agents engage in the business of seeking proxy votes on behalf of contending companies. Their actions in so doing are subject to detailed regulation by the SEC.

PUBLIC COMPANY. It can be distinguished at a glance from a private company, as its name must end with the words 'public limited company' or its abbreviation 'plc' unless its registered office is to be in Wales, where the Welsh equivalents are 'Cwmni Cyfyngedig Cyhoeddus' or its abbreviation 'CCC'.

The only thing a plc can do that is forbidden to a private

company is to raise money from the public by an issue of shares or debentures. There are other, more onerous, obligations placed upon a plc, principally in the area of public reporting. See AUTHORIZED CAPITAL and REDEEMABLE SHARES.

PUBLIC INTERNATIONAL LAW. The rules governing the conduct of states towards each other and each other's nationals, the law of the sea, air space and even outer space. The sources of these rules are treaties, custom, generally recognized principles (such as those of natural justice) and, to a limited extent, judicial decisions and the opinions of eminent jurists. International law lacks a legislature, courts of compulsory jurisdiction, and proper means of enforcement. It relies ultimately on the recognition and consensus of the community of nations, which can be very fickle. See TREATY.

PUBLIC POLICY. The ideas which prevail in a community as to what is necessary for its welfare; but, as Mr Justice Burrough said in 1824, it is 'an unruly horse, and when once you get astride it you never know where it will carry you'.

The courts will not enforce what is against public policy. This includes unreasonable restraints of trade, marriage brokerage, perpetuities, gaming contracts, an agreement by a newspaper not to comment on a creditor company or its directors and, in a 1908 case, a condition in a will that a beneficiary must not join the army or navy.

PURCHASE OF OWN SHARES. It is a truism that every rule has an exception and this is so with the basic rule of company law that a limited company may not acquire its own shares.

A limited company can purchase its own shares out of distributable profits if authorized by its Articles. A private company may also purchase its shares out of capital.

If a listed company purchases its shares on The Stock Exchange there is no taxable distribution and the selling member will only be liable to pay capital gains tax on any gain. Otherwise, generally, there is a taxable distribution for both company and seller.

Enthusiastic judges applied a highly rigorous interpretation of a prohibition in the Companies Act 1948 (as amended) on a company giving financial assistance in connection with the purchase of its shares by others. The Act recast those restrictions by making it unlawful and criminal for a company or its subsidiaries to give financial assistance directly or indirectly for the purpose of:

- an acquisition of shares in the company if the assistance was given before or at the time of acquisition;
- discharging or reducing a liability incurred by any person for the purpose of an acquisition of shares in the company by that or any other person.

Financial assistance includes a gift, guarantee, idemnity and the release or waiver of rights or obligations, but not the payment of dividends. The purpose for which a company gives financial assistance is now paramount. If the principal reason for a company (acting in good faith and in its interest) making a payment is to acquire an asset or a benefit, there will be no breach of the prohibitions. Private companies are given an additional exemption from the prohibitions, determined by reference to the source of funds as opposed to the primary purpose of the assistance, but special procedures are involved.

Q

QUALIFIED PRIVILEGE. Protects the maker of an untrue and defamatory statement if he has acted honestly and without malice. The defence includes fair and accurate reports of parliamentary and public judicial proceedings, and statements where the maker has a legal or moral duty to the recipient, e.g. a past employer giving a reference about an employee to a new employer.

QUANTUM MERUIT. The amount merited in the circumstances. Where someone has been asked to provide a service, without remuneration being specified, but clearly intending that he should be paid, there is an implied promise to make a reasonable payment for the services provided. See BREACH OF CONTRACT and PART PERFORMANCE.

QUIET ENJOYMENT. The right of a purchaser or tenant of land to remain there without any disturbance by the vendor or landlord. This is the common law protection against harassment of tenants, which in recent years has been strengthened by statutes creating criminal offences.

QUIET POSSESSION. The warranty, implied by statute in every sale of goods, that the buyer's possession will not be disturbed by anyone except under a charge of which he is aware, or if it is clear that the seller is only transferring such rights as he may have. The warranty is wider than the implied warranty of quiet enjoyment in relation to land.

QUORUM. The minimum number of persons present at a meeting to ensure that it is not a nullity. In England a quorum must be present at the beginning of a meeting but possibly not for its entire duration (as is the case in the USA) and more than one person must remain throughout. Two members present personally or by proxy will suffice as a quorum for both a public and private company.

One person cannot be a quorum at a general meeting unless it is convened by the court or the DTI. If there is only one director, he may be able to operate by making resolutions in writing.

QUOTATION. See LISTING.

R

RATIFICATION. Retrospective approval or confirmation. Ratification can be express or implied from any act showing an intention to adopt a transaction; it may be inferred from silence or mere acquiescence. Written ratification of a written contract is unnecessary but ratification of a deed must be by deed.

The process only adds the authority of the ratifying body to the transaction and so cannot render lawful anything innately unlawful, *ultra vires* or void. Its effect is to place all parties in the same position as they would have been had the transaction received prior authorization.

It is also a method of creating an agency.

RATIO DECIDENDI. Literally, the reason for the decision. The *ratio decidendi* of each case is the essence of the judgment for which that case forms the precedent to be followed or, as the case may be, distinguished in subsequent litigation. See JUDICIAL PRECEDENT and *OBITER DICTA*.

REALTY. A synonym for real property (known as 'real estate' in the USA). It includes land and fixtures attached to and forming part of the land, and rights and interests in land that are freehold in nature, such as rights of way and the right to receive profits from the leasing of land.

The distinction between realty and personalty is almost synonymous with the distinction between immovable property (land) and movable property (goods), but with one important exception: leasehold land, being derived out of a freehold estate in land, does not constitute full realty, but is immovable personalty.

REASONABLENESS. A concept which is used in many branches of English law. For example, in the leading case of negligence, *Donoghue* v *Stevenson*, the court stated that 'you must take reasonable care to avoid acts or omissions which you can reasonably foresee would be likely to injure your neighbour.'

Reasonableness is an objective measure of a person's behaviour in judging whether that behaviour is culpable, and the courts enlist the help of that fictitious animal 'the reasonable man'. They do not judge the case by the standards of a saint or sinner, but on the basis of the behaviour they would expect from the reasonable man 'on the Clapham omnibus'. See NEGLIGENCE and RESTRAINT OF TRADE.

RECEIVER. Securities, such as debentures and mortgages, usually contain powers for a receiver to be appointed by the lender to safeguard the security and to sell assets to repay the loan obligations.

The receiver is usually a hard-headed chartered accountant and under a debenture can be given powers to take over the management of a company from its directors until the debt is recovered, or (more likely) the company is put into liquidation. He acts as agent for the company and not the creditor appointing him.

Under the Insolvency Act 1985, the receiver/manager appointed under a floating charge is called an administrative receiver and must be an authorized insolvency practitioner. The statute clarifies and regulates the receiver's role, extending his powers, liabilities, duties to the court and to other creditors. For example, he must now notify other creditors of his appointment and must prepare a report for them on his proposed actions and the prospects for repayment. See OFFICIAL RECEIVER.

RECHTSANWALT. West German attorney admitted to practice in a '*Land*' (or state) court or in higher federal courts. Lawyers fees are prescribed by statute (*Geburenordnung*) based on the amount in dispute and the level of court activity. Also lawyers in Austria and the German-speaking areas of Switzerland.

RECITALS. Explanatory or introductory statements to the operative part of a legal document.

RECONSTRUCTION AND AMALGAMATION. Reconstruction is a procedure whereby the share capital of a company, or the ownership of a business, is reorganized: but continues to be owned by the same persons as before.

An amalgamation is a reorganization where two or more businesses (or companies) are merged so that the owners of each business (or the shareholders of each company) end up holding substantially all the shares in a single entity (which may be one of the existing entities or a new company formed for the purpose). The new entity carries on both businesses (or owns both companies).

The terms are particularly relevant to capital gains tax reliefs available on a share for share exchange. It appears to be a requirement of an amalgamation, at least for capital gains tax relief, that the businesses of the companies involved are carried on together through a single company as a result of the amalgamation.

There are many technical methods by which reconstructions and amalgamations can be effected. See SCHEME OF ARRANGEMENT.

RECTIFICATION. If a document contains a manifest typing or drafting error and the correction is obvious, there is no need to have it rectified: the courts have a duty to construe documents correctly and would always give it its correct meaning.

When a written agreement fails to reflect what was agreed by the parties in the negotiations leading up to it, and neither was aware of the mistake at the time of execution, either party can apply to the courts to rectify the document, and the other cannot resist. The courts will only correct the document. They will not add improvements which were not agreed or would not have occurred to the parties at the time. Rectification will not be granted when a document correctly records an agreement even though the parties misunderstood the words used.

The courts will also rectify a document if it contains a mistake benefiting one party which was noticed by him when the document was signed, but which he failed to bring to the other's notice.

If the parties rectify a document, the rectification operates only from its date and not from the date of the original document.

REDEEMABLE SHARES. A limited company may issue redeemable shares of any class, if it has existing shares which are not redeemable: this prevents a company redeeming all its shares and by doing so effecting an informal winding up to the detriment of its creditors. Existing shares cannot be converted into redeemable shares, but may be purchased by the company.

The method and terms of redemption are subject to the

Articles and the Act but generally the shares to be redeemed must be fully paid, payment must be made on redemption and, in the case of public companies, payment must be made out of distributable profits or out of the proceeds of a fresh issue of shares made for the purpose. A private company may redeem shares out of capital. Any premium payable on redemption must normally be paid out of distributable profits.

Shares are cancelled on redemption and the company's issued capital is diminished by their nominal value. See CAPITAL REDEMPTION RESERVE, PURCHASE OF OWN SHARES and SPECIAL RESOLUTION.

REDEMPTION. The re-possession of property which has been pledged, deposited, transferred or charged to another by way of security against a loan or other obligation, by the discharge of that loan or obligation.

REDUCTION OF CAPITAL. A company limited by shares may reduce its share capital in any way. The authority to do so must be in the Articles, a special resolution to reduce capital must be passed, and the reduction must be confirmed by the court.

While the court will not question the wisdom of a reduction, if it is unfair then even a few objectors can resist it. The court will exercise its discretion to ensure that creditors are protected, that the reduction is fair and equitable as between the classes of shareholders, and that the terms for modification of all class rights have been strictly observed.

The purposes of a reduction are manifold. They have ranged from returning capital to shareholders where the company is over-capitalized, to cancelling or repaying share capital, or cancelling share premium account out of the reserves of the company, or out of borrowings. A cancellation of paid-up share capital which is lost, or unrepresented by available assets, followed by a new share issue, is a way of restructuring a company's capital without paying capital duty on the new capital.

REDUNDANCY. Arises where an employer has stopped, or intends to stop, carrying on business or where a plant or factory is closed, or a particular department or job function is extinguished or reduced. Employers are under a duty to consult with relevant trade unions before effecting substantial redundancies.

Most employees with two years' continuous service have the right to receive a payment when dismissal is caused by redundancy. Selection of an employee for redundancy may constitute the basis for an unfair dismissal claim, although the employer will be exonerated if he acted reasonably.

REFRESHER FEES. Daily fees paid to barristers for each day, other than the first, of any trial, thereby exciting further interest in the case and refreshing those parts that brief fees cannot reach.

REGISTER OF MEMBERS. A list of the names, addresses and shareholdings of each member of a company with the dates of becoming and ceasing to be a member. A member is defined in the Act as a person who agrees to become a member and whose name is entered on the register of members. The register must be kept at an office notified to the Registrar and must be open at least two hours a day for inspection by anyone. Members can see it without payment. A non-member must pay not more than 5p. The company must send a copy of the register within 10 days to anyone who requests it – normally a sure precursor of a hostile take-over bid. See NOMINEES.

REGISTERED DESIGN. A design, consisting of new or original features of shape, configuration, pattern or ornament, intended to appeal to the eye, and applied to an article by an industrial process, which is registered under the Registered Designs Act

1948. A registered design confers a 15-year monopoly and, in any proceedings, the onus is on the defendant to prove dissimilarity.

Registered designs lie uneasily with the separate copyright in artistic works applied industrially.

REGISTERED OFFICE. Every British company must have one, even if it is not resident in the UK for tax purposes. The Memorandum must state whether the registered office is to be in England, Scotland or Wales. That cannot be changed, although its situation within those countries can. The registered office is where all communications and notices to the company must be addressed and where it keeps its charges register and register of directors and secretary. The location must be mentioned in all business letters and order forms. Any change must be notified to the Registrar.

REGISTRAR OF COMPANIES. The official appointed by the Secretary of State to carry out the administrative functions involved in the registration of companies and compliance by them with the Act. Documents filed with the Registrar can be inspected by the public.

REMAINDER. A future interest in property. Property held upon trust for John for life with remainder to Jane is property in which John has the interest in possession and Jane has the remainder interest. It is a contingent interest if expressed 'with remainder to Jane if she attains the age of 25 years', so that her remainder interest will not fall into possession unless she attains 25.

Most remainder interests are excluded property for inheritance tax purposes, so they may be given free from tax.

REMOTENESS OF DAMAGE. The concept used to establish those acts or omissions for which a defendant is legally responsible.

A plaintiff must normally prove that the damage he suffered was not too remote a consequence of the act or omission of the defendant. The exceptions to this rule are torts actionable *per se*.

In negligence, the principle is that damage must have been of a kind that is reasonably foreseeable as occurring, although neither the extent of the damage, nor the precise way in which it occurred, need have been foreseeable.

A person will be liable for losses resulting from breach of contract which, at the time the contract was made, were within the reasonable contemplation of the parties, having regard to their knowledge of special circumstances. The parties will be assumed to have contemplated all loss that arises from the breach in the usual course of events and more remote loss if it was foreseeable in the circumstances.

RES IPSA LOQUITUR. 'It speaks for itself': a maxim which is used to impute negligence to a person in circumstances in which damage, arising from an unexplained occurrence, can be reasonably attributed to no other fact than his negligence. The presumption of negligence can be rebutted if he can show that the cause was one consistent with the absence of negligence.

RES JUDICATA. The full maxim is *res judicata pro veritate accipitur*: 'a thing adjudicated is received as the truth.' Its practical effect is that a judicial decision is conclusive until reversed and its correctness cannot be contradicted. Once a matter or issue between parties has been litigated and decided, it cannot be raised again between the same parties, but other persons are not so bound.

RESIDENCE (COMPANIES). Under UK law, companies are resident in the place where their central management and control are exercised. This is normally where the board of directors meet and take decisions of policy and general strategy.

A company incorporated in the UK is not resident there if its central management and control are outside the UK. Hence the use of non-resident UK companies as tax-haven vehicles for a variety of aliens.

It is illegal for a company to emigrate from the UK without Treasury consent but it is a matter of doubt whether a UK company needs that consent to emigrate to another country within the EEC. See CORPORATION TAX and DOUBLE TAX CONVENTIONS.

RESIDENCE (INDIVIDUALS). Individuals may be either resident and/or ordinarily resident in the UK. There are no statutory rules defining the term but, if a person spends more than six months in a year of assessment in the UK, he will be treated as resident for the whole of that year. If he spends, on average, three months a year in the UK over a period of four consecutive years he will be treated as both resident and ordinarily resident.

If a person has accommodation available for his use in the UK and visits for as little as one day in that year, he will be treated as resident. The rule generally does not apply to a person who works full time outside the UK and whose performance of duties in the UK is merely incidental to the performance of overseas duties.

These UK domestic rules may be overriden by the provisions of Double Tax Conventions. See DOMICILE, INCOME TAX and TRUSTEES.

RESCISSION. When one party to a contract expresses, in an unequivocal manner, his refusal to be bound by it because of fraud, misrepresentation, or mutual mistake, which induced him to enter the contract, the contract may be avoided and the parties restored, as far as possible, to their original positions.

The right to rescind is lost if the aggrieved party, with knowledge of the facts giving rise to the right to rescind, affirms the contract; or if there is an unreasonable lapse of time; or if restoration of the parties to their original positions is not substantially possible; or if rescission would deprive a third party of goods or other things which are the subject matter of the contract, which he has acquired in good faith and for value.

The term is also sometimes used to refer to the termination as opposed to the avoidance of a contract. See TERMINATION OF CONTRACT.

RESTITUTION ORDER. An order made by a court with the objective of compelling a person to return property to its rightful owner.

RESTRAINT OF TRADE. Contracts which are excessively restrictive of a party's freedom to trade are void and unenforceable at common law. A court will uphold a contract only if its restrictions can reasonably be considered to be in the interests of the parties and the public.

Contracts attracting scrutiny are those possessing unusual characteristics and where there is an obvious inequality of bargaining power; particularly those which contain covenants limiting competition between employee and employer; or restrict the future activities of a vendor of a business; or regulate the conduct of members of trade associations; or take the form of selective sales or a 'solus' agreement.

Whether a restraint, or restrictive covenant, is reasonable is a question of fact in each case and will depend largely on the length of time for which the restriction is imposed and the geographical area concerned. If an obligation is severable and can stand independently of others, a court will be likely to ignore or 'blue pencil' the offensive restriction in a particular clause in order to construe the rest as valid and enforceable. The court will not use this approach as an excuse to insert new words or adopt a meaning other than that originally intended. See ARTICLES 85 AND 86 and RESTRICTIVE TRADE PRACTICES.

RESTRICTIVE COVENANT. See RESTRAINT OF TRADE.

RESTRICTIVE TRADE PRACTICES. A limitation accepted by a person engaged in the business of supplying goods or services, on his freedom to decide certain matters relating to his business, whether by reason of a specific contract, or an informal arrangement or understanding, or a recommendation. Those matters include prices, the terms on which business is done, quantities, specification, customers or geographical concentration.

The Restrictive Trade Practices Acts 1976 and 1977 identify restrictive trade practices as being *prima facie* against the public interest and require (generally before any restriction comes into force) the registration of certain restrictive trading agreements and information agreements. These agreements can be referred to the restrictive practices court: if it finds any restriction to be contrary to the public interest, then the agreement is void in respect of that restriction. See ANTITRUST, COMPETITION LAW and RESTRAINT OF TRADE.

RETAINER. A fixed amount of money paid to secure the services of an attorney. Particularly prevalent in the USA, it permits a client to call upon his lawyer for an unlimited amount of services (whether litigious or not) in return for a fixed fee paid as a periodic lump sum.

A retainer is often structured to enable the lawyer to seek additional remuneration after a specified time – an arrangement which may be less attractive for the client.

REVOLVING FACILITY. Bank facility under which the borrower is permitted to borrow, repay, and re-draw monies on a continuing basis throughout the life of the facility, provided that its maximum permitted amount is not exceeded and the full amount outstanding at the maturity date is then repaid.

RIGHTS ISSUE. Method by which a company raises additional capital from shareholders by offering them the right to subscribe further securities in proportion to their existing holdings.

The Act requires that any offer by a company of equity securities for cash must be made in the first instance by way of rights, except where the requirement is specifically disapplied either by special resolution or in the Articles. See PRE-EMPTIVE RIGHTS.

ROMALPA CLAUSE. Contractual clause enabling a supplier of goods to reserve his title to them validly until he receives payment. If the goods are sold, the supplier may be able to claim the proceeds of sale in preference to secured creditors. If the goods are unsold when the company goes into liquidation the supplier can recover the goods. The reservation is ineffective if the goods supplied are wholly changed in character because of some manufacturing process.

The retention of title may amount to a charge requiring registration in the charges register.

ROMAN LAW. The codified system of law developed by the ancient Roman jurists. It forms the basis of the civil law systems of several European countries (as contrasted with the common law system originating in England) and, by historical accident, has strongly influenced Scottish law.

ROYAL CHARTER. Document whereby the Crown exercises the

royal prerogative of forming corporations. Once a common means of incorporation e.g. The East India Company, the Bank of England and the notorious South Sea Company. Nowadays incorporation by Royal Charter is rare and confined to charities, learned institutions, and non-trading bodies such as the Institute of Chartered Accountants and the BBC.

In contrast to companies, chartered corporations have all the powers of a natural person and are not fettered by the *ultra vires* rule.

ROYAL COMMISSION. Government-appointed inquiry intended either to achieve, or to avoid, a new policy. Once described as a device which 'takes minutes and wastes years'. Subjects covered have ranged from charities to gambling. See TORT.

ROYALTY. A term regularly used in legal agreements which has, however, no legally defined meaning. It may be a fixed sum paid in advance, or more frequently a per unit amount, or a mixture of the two, in respect of a license to manufacture goods under someone else's patent, industrial design or know-how, or to sell goods carrying their trademark or tradename, or to publish or reproduce a book, picture, film, musical score or record, where the copyright belongs to another, or to use any other intellectual property belonging to someone else. It may also be payments which owners of land obtain in respect of the taking of some substance, often gravel, forming part of that land.

An Australian judge has taken the easy, but circular, course of holding that the term 'royalty' is used to signify payments to which business or commercial usage attaches the name of 'royalty'.

RULES GOVERNING SUBSTANTIAL ACQUISITIONS OF SHARES (SARs). The sight of bleary eyed brokers, at an unaccustomed early hour, battling to buy substantial blocks of shares in possible take-over targets came to be known as dawn raids. Whether out of compassion for the brokers, small shareholders, or even the target company, SARs were introduced to restrict the speed at which a person (and those acting by agreement or understanding with him) might increase his holding in UK resident companies to an aggregate of between 15 per cent and

30 per cent of the voting rights of a company. The rules also require accelerated disclosure of the acquisition of shares, or rights over shares, relating to such holdings. The rules are supplemental to the City Code. See TENDER OFFER.

RUSSIAN ROULETTE. Also known in the USA as a Texas shootout. It is a method of resolving deadlocks in joint venture situations. One of the parties (John) may offer to purchase the interest of the other (Jane) at a particular price. Jane may then either accept the sale of her interest at that price or elect to purchase John's interest at the same price. Although seemingly a dramatic remedy, it operates to encourage constructive and reasonable discussion on a sensible resolution to a deadlock: neither party will make an unreasonable offer for fear that the consequences will rebound on him.

S

SALE OF GOODS. Defined by the Sale of Goods Act 1979 as a contract by which the seller transfers or agrees to transfer the property in goods for a money consideration called the price.

The statute substantially codifies the law relating to the sale of goods. Exclusion or limitation of its operation is restricted by the Unfair Contract Terms Act 1977. It implies in contracts for sale of goods a condition that the seller has the right to sell the goods, or will have the right to do so when the property is to pass. There are implied warranties to the effect that the buyer will enjoy quiet possession; that goods sold by description will correspond with their description; that goods sold in the course of a business will be of merchantable quality and are reasonably fit for the purpose for which they have been supplied.

The statute sets out rules as to the transfer of title when there are third party or competing interests to the goods. It also regulates delivery, performance of the contract, and the rights of both parties in the event of non-payment or other breach of contract. See PROPERTY IN GOODS, QUIET POSSESSION and WARRANTIES AND CONDITIONS.

SALE AND LEASEBACK. A common commercial transaction where an owner sells land and/or buildings, usually to an institution, on condition that the property is immediately leased back to him. The principal object is to free for use the capital value of the owner's interest in the property whilst retaining the right to use and occupy it at a rent.

SCHEME OF ARRANGEMENT. A formal arrangement between a company and any class or its shareholders and creditors. It is conditional on approval by 75 per cent (by value) of each class affected, and requires the sanction of the court.

A scheme is generally used either to facilitate the merger of two companies, or undertakings, or as part of the rescue of a company in financial difficulties or for a reconstruction.

The classic comparison between a take-over bid and a scheme of arrangement for merger is that between a taxi and a train; the former is far more flexible.

SCOTLAND. The Scottish legal system is quite distinct from that of

England. It is more closely aligned with the early Roman civil code than a system based on precedents.

Although there is a presumption that every Act of Parliament is operative throughout the UK, Scotland is often specifically excluded.

Scotland has long operated a public prosecutor system where both a decision to prosecute, and the conduct of prosecutions, are the sole province of the Lord Advocate, independent of the police. England and Wales are at last following suit.

The final court of appeal for Scotland as well as England is the House of Lords whose decisions may be as important in English as in Scottish law.

SCRIP ISSUE. See BONUS ISSUE.

SEAL. Every company must have a common seal engraved in legible characters with its name. It equates to the signature of a human being and must be used to execute deeds.

SECRECY. The holy grail of banks. They are required to observe secrecy regarding the affairs of their customers. But there are four broad heads of exception:

- where there is a public duty to disclose, e.g. knowledge of a crime;
- where disclosure is under compulsion by law, e.g. court order or pursuant to a statutory obligation (this does not automatically encompass all requests for information from all authorities);
- where the bank's own interests require disclosure; and
- when the customer's consent has been expressly or impliedly obtained. See BANKERS' BOOKS EVIDENCE ACT 1879 and OFFICIAL SECRETS ACTS.

SECRETARY (COMPANY). The company's chief administrative officer. Anyone who thinks of him as a clerk, no matter how glorified, is mistaken. Every company must have a secretary who cannot be its sole director or its auditor. The secretary of a public company must have the knowledge and experience to discharge his duties, and be properly qualified.

He has ostensible authority to sign contracts connected with the administrative side of a company's affairs, and those which come within the day-to-day running of a company's business.

SECURITIES EXCHANGE ACT OF 1934, THE. A US federal body of law which requires the registration of securities prior to listing and trading on a national stock exchange, as well as the registration of over-the-counter securities in which there is a significant trading interest. Registration with the SEC is also required by broker-dealers, national securities exchanges and associates of securities dealers. The statute also generally regulates trading markets in securities, and counters fraud and manipulation in connection with the purchase or sale of securities. The UK has a system of self-regulation. See SELF-REGULATORY ORGANIZATIONS.

SECURITIES AND EXCHANGE COMMISSION (SEC). A US government regulatory body created by the US Congress under the authority of The Securities Exchange Act of 1934. It is charged with assuring full and fair disclosure to the public investing in securities, and protecting the interests of the investing public against malpractices in the securities and financial markets. There is no equivalent statutory authority in the UK.

SECURITY FOR COSTS. The plaintiff to an action can be required, on the application of the defendant, to lodge in court a sum of money, or provide a sufficient guarantee, to cover the defendant's costs in the event that the plaintiff does not succeed at trial and faces an order for costs against him. Such orders are entirely discretionary, and will only be made where the plaintiff is foreign and has no substantial property within the jurisdiction, or is an insubstantial nominal plaintiff.

Security for costs will not be ordered where the defendant's case is hopeless, or merely because a plaintiff is impecunious, unless that plaintiff is a limited company and sufficient evidence can be produced to show that it will be unable to pay the costs of the defendant if required.

SELF-REGULATORY ORGANIZATIONS. Associations formed by practitioners in a given sector of the securities or commodities market to regulate the conduct of their business. Recognition of an organization by the Securities and Investments Board under the proposed FSA 1986 confers legal authorization on its members to carry on investment businesses without the need to register directly with the Board (as is otherwise required). It works in a similar way to the requirement for US broker-dealers to register with the SEC.

Organizations can be 'recognized' only if their rules of conduct meet the standards set by the Board to provide appropriate investor protection. The use of self-regulatory organizations to police investment businesses is a keynote of the new system of self-regulation within a statutory framework enshrined in the proposed FSA 1986.

SENIOR DEBT. A US term which is creeping into the UK. It is an unsecured debt to which priority is given by agreement between the company and its creditors.

SEQUESTRATION. An ordeal to which UK trade unions have recently become exposed. It is a temporary legal appropriation of property by a sequestrator appointed by the court, pending the purging of contempt of court. The sequestrator is given wide authority to 'ferret out' property – wherever it is.

SERVICE CONTRACT. The provision of services under a contract will not always give rise to the relationship of employer and employee. A contract of service will provide such a relationship, a contract for services will not. The distinction is crucial in terms of the application of the common law, taxation and employment legislation. See DIRECTOR'S SERVICE AGREEMENT, EMPLOYER AND EMPLOYEE, INDEPENDENT CONTRACTOR and SPECIFIC PERFORMANCE.

SERVICE MARKS. From 1 October 1986 it has become possible in the UK to register distinctive marks, names and devices used in relation to the supply of business services in much the same way as one has been able to register trademarks for goods. Registration will enable the owner to acquire a statutory right to the exclusive use of that mark in relation to the service for which it is registered. Enforcement is more straightforward than having to rely on the common law rules of passing-off.

The greatest protection is afforded by registering in Part A and to achieve this the mark must contain at least one of the following:

- the name of the company, individual or firm represented in a special or particular manner;
- the signature of the applicant for registration or some predecessor in his business;
- an invented word;
- a word having no direct reference to the character or quality of the goods and which is not a geographical name or a surname; or
- any other distinctive mark.

SET-OFF. The defence to a monetary claim where there is also a monetary claim the other way. Technical rules govern its availability. It differs from a counterclaim both in its application and effect, for a counterclaim is not limited to money claims.

Banks have an implied right of set-off (sometimes called 'combination') which can be excluded by express agreement with the client to keep accounts separate. The customer has no corresponding right although may, whilst his accounts comply with his agreement with the bank, have a right of appropriation.

Banks frequently extend their implied rights by contract, e.g. to enable a debit on a customer's current account to be set-off against any credit balance on a deposit account in the name of the same customer, which, in the case of a time deposit, could not otherwise be effected until the maturity of the time deposit.

On bankruptcy or the insolvent liquidation of a company, the implied right of set-off is overtaken by the mandatory set-off provisions of the Insolvency Act 1985.

SHADOW DIRECTOR. Not a director at all but, in practice, gives the orders which the actual directors obey. Company law treats him as a director for certain purposes, e.g. disclosure of his interest in a contract with the company, or if it is proposed that he be given a service contract of more than five years.

SHARE CAPITAL. Shares are 'merely a right of participation in the company' on the terms of the Articles. The precise rights and nature of a share are determined by the Memorandum and Articles.

Shares may be divided into separate classes such as ordinary, preference or deferred shares. These will have different rights in respect of such matters as participation in surplus capital, dividends and voting. The share capital may be increased, reduced, divided into different amounts or have the rights attaching to the various classes altered. See AUTHORIZED CAPITAL, BONUS ISSUE, NO PAR VALUE SHARES, PURCHASE OF OWN SHARES and REDUCTION OF CAPITAL.

SHARE CERTIFICATE. The once beautifully, but nowadays starkly, printed document evidencing entitlement of a person to shares in a company. Sometimes companies issue renounceable share certificates; but they no longer enable the shares to be transferred free of stamp duty.

A share certificate is not conclusive evidence of the title of a member to shares. The holder's legal rights depend not on the certificate, but upon entry in the register of members. The certificate is merely a declaration by the company stating what those rights are, and giving *prima facie* evidence of them; but the company may be estopped from denying what it purports to state against someone who has relied upon it. It will be some time before the proposals for transferring shares in public companies without the need for share certificates are implemented.

SHARE PREMIUM ACCOUNT. Where a company is in the fortunate position of being able to raise additional capital by the issue of shares at a price in excess of their nominal value, i.e. at a premium, the total amount of the premium is credited to a share premium account. For most purposes this is treated as though it were share capital and it is, therefore, non-distributable.

SHARE WARRANT. See WARRANT.

SHERMAN ACT. See ANTITRUST.

SLANDER OF GOODS. See TRADE LIBEL.

SLANDER OF TITLE. See TRADE LIBEL.

SLAVENBURG REGISTER, THE. An alphabetical index, maintained by the Registrar, of charges over property in England and Wales delivered for registration against a foreign corporation which has not registered as an oversea company.

***SOCIETE ANONYME* (SA).** The French and Belgian form of public company, as contrasted with the SARL which is the form of private company. The constitutional document of an SA is its 'statutes' and it is normally managed by the 'Conseil d'Administration'. Most strikingly, a French SA has a fixed maximum life of not more than 99 years and, if its assets fall below half of its registered capital, a general meeting must consider dissolution, failing which the SA must reduce its capital.

SOLICITOR. A member of the junior branch of the legal profession. There are over 61,000 in England and Wales. The end of the uncertain metamorphosis from student to articled clerk to qualified solicitor is signalled by the issue of a practising certificate from the Law Society. Once qualified, compulsorily

Ten biggest firms of English solicitors (by partners) January 1986

	Partners
Linklaters & Paines	85
Clifford-Turner	76
Slaughter and May	70
Allen & Overy	66
Norton, Rose, Botterell & Roche	65
Herbert, Smith & Co	63
Simmons & Simmons	63
Lovell, White & King	61
Coward Chance	60
Freshfields	57

Earnings – variable: in a central London firm with more than 15 partners the median net profit share per partner was £81,300 in 1985. By contrast, central London firms of 1–14 partners had a median net profit share per partner of £22,900. The average profit share per partner of all firms in 1985 was £21,300.

insured against professional negligence, and registered on the rolls, the solicitor spends the mature years of his life trying to satisfy two uncompromising codes of conduct: as matters of law, a duty to his clients to exercise reasonable skill and care and to keep his client's affairs confidential; as matters of professional conduct to further his client's interests to the best of his ability so long as those interests do not conflict with the superior duty which he owes as an officer of the court. The solicitor has no right of audience in the higher courts which are for the time being the exclusive territory of the bar except upon a formal or unopposed application. See BARRISTER, MASTER OF THE ROLLS and UNDERTAKING.

SOLICITOR-GENERAL. A principal legal adviser appointed by the government whose primary role is as deputy to the Attorney-General. As a general rule, he will be a member of the House of Commons but not a member of the cabinet. He (but not yet she) is, however, invariably a barrister rather than a solicitor.

SOVEREIGN IMMUNITY. The right of foreign sovereign states to refuse to submit to the jurisdiction of courts of other countries. A distinction has come to be drawn in international law, now reflected both in the US Sovereign Immunity Act 1976 and the UK State Immunity Act 1978, between those activities which the state undertakes *jure imperii*, i.e. in the exercise of sovereign authority, for which immunity persists, and those activities which it undertakes *jure gestionis*, i.e. commercial and trading transactions, for which immunity no longer applies.

SPECIAL NOTICE. A notice required for certain resolutions by the Act; the resolution is not effective unless notice of the intention to move it has been given to a company 28 days before the meeting at which the resolution is to be submitted. The company has to give its members notice of the resolution at least 21 days before the meeting.

Special notice is required of a resolution to remove a director. The company is required to notify the director of the proposed resolution and allow him to circulate written representations to members and to attend the meeting. Other resolutions requiring special notice are those appointing a director over 70 years of age; appointing an auditor other than the retiring auditor; filling a casual vacancy in the office of auditor; reappointing as auditor a retiring auditor who was appointed by the directors to fill a casual vacancy; and removing an auditor before the expiration of his term of office.

SPECIAL RESOLUTION. One passed by a 75 per cent majority of those voting at a general meeting of a company, of which at least 21 days' notice has been given. The notice of meeting must state the intention to propose the resolution as a special resolution, and no amendments of substance may be made to it.

A special resolution is required *inter alia* to reduce the capital (with the consent of the court); to alter the Memorandum or Articles; to change the name of a company; to make a purchase of the company's own shares. A copy of the resolution must be filed with the Registrar.

SPECIFIC PERFORMANCE. A discretionary remedy for breach of contract which may be awarded by the courts when the normal remedy of damages is inadequate. It requires the defaulting party to perform his part of the bargain. The remedy was developed by the courts of equity, and so is only granted if justice requires it and if the injured party has acted properly.

Contracts of employment can never be specifically enforced: 'the courts are bound to be jealous lest they should turn contracts of employment into contracts of slavery.' A contract for the sale of articles of unusual beauty and rarity may be enforced, but not one for ordinary items of commerce where substitutes can be readily purchased.

SPRINGBOARD PERIOD. The period, important in the calculation of the appropriate length of an injunction in a confidentiality case, that it would take a person to reverse engineer some new product placed on the market and bring out a competitive product. A person who unlawfully obtains access to confidential information can often be restrained from selling in competition during that 'springboard' period.

STAKEHOLDER. A person who receives a deposit of money from one or more persons on terms that the principal and interest are to be paid out as pre-directed on the happening of a particular event. The stakeholder is in law the agent of each person concerned.

STAMP DUTY. See CAPITAL DUTY, STAMP DUTY RESERVE TAX and TRANSFER DUTY.

STAMP DUTY RESERVE TAX. Introduced by the Finance Bill 1986 it is a significant departure from a principle dating back to the seventeenth century that stamp duty is a tax on documents. Reserve tax imposes a duty on certain transactions that, broadly, would have attracted duty had a document been brought into existence. It is refundable if a document is subsequently created and transfer duty paid on it. The tax is charged at 0.5 per cent of the sale consideration on transactions after 27 October 1986.

The tax applies to transfers for valuable consideration of most registered shares and loan stocks of UK registered companies or of foreign companies whose register of members is kept in the UK, and of any interest in those securities or rights arising out of them.

STANDSTILL AGREEMENT. Any agreement between a company and an existing or future significant minority shareholder which, by its terms, controls his behaviour and degree of involvement in the running of the company, and limits the circumstances in which, and the means by which, he can increase his shareholding.

From the company's point of view, the principal purpose of a standstill agreement is to prevent the shareholder from taking control of the company without its approval and, often equally important, to prevent the shareholder selling his shares as a block so as to give some other person, who is not constrained by the agreement, a lock-up position in an acquisition of the company.

STATE TAKE-OVER STATUTES. See BLUE SKY LAWS.

STATEMENT OF CLAIM. The opening pleading in most High Court actions, prepared by the plaintiff and setting out all the material facts on which his claim is based. It is a formal document often containing technical legal language.

STATUTE. Parliament has unlimited power by Acts of Parliament to create, alter and repeal English law subject to the requirements of the European Communities. By historical evolution, the word 'statute' has come to denote those Acts.

Parliament is the ultimate law-maker in the UK. The UK courts, unlike those of the USA, cannot challenge a statute's constitutional effect. The judges do, however, interpret statutes and their 'interpretation' may alter the effect that Parliament intended. See SUBORDINATE LEGISLATION.

STATUTORY DECLARATION. A formal declaration normally made before a solicitor or notary public. It is required for various purposes by statute, e.g. that the necessary formalities have been complied with on the formation of a company. Making a false declaration is an offence under the Perjury Act.

STATUTORY INSTRUMENT. See SUBORDINATE LEGISLATION.

STOP NOTICE. A formal notice, sealed by the court, which is obtained by a person who claims to have an equitable interest in stocks or securities. Originally called a 'notice in lieu of *distringas*', it requires that there be no transfer of the securities or payment of any dividend or interest on the securities concerned without reference to the person serving the notice.

SUBDIVISION OF SHARES. The converse of consolidation so that, for example, one 25p share becomes 25 new 1p shares. The power of a company to subdivide is most often used to increase the marketability of its shares when the price on The Stock Exchange is at a high level. Thus if the nominal value of shares is £1 and they are traded at £10, on subdivision of the £1 shares into ten shares of 10p each, the market value will be £1 per share.

SUBJECT TO CONTRACT. See CONDITION PRECEDENT.

SUBORDINATE LEGISLATION. A method of delegating powers under Acts of Parliament which has long been a popular device with governments wishing to enact publicly controversial or politically sensitive laws without a full debate in Parliament. It enables others authorized by Parliament to create legislation by such arcane methods as Orders in Council and ministerial orders, better known as Statutory Instruments.

Subordinate (or delegated) legislation is used extensively in the proposed FSA 1986. In addition to substantive provisions, the Secretary of State is empowered to create the framework for and the supervision of the City revolution by way of subordinate legislation. See CONSUMER CREDIT and PRIVY COUNCIL.

SUBORDINATED DEBT. Debt ranking in order of priority for payment after sums due to other creditors, and particularly loans to companies which rank after all its ordinary unsecured debts. Such loans tend to be regarded by outsiders as virtually equivalent to share capital, although they are of course still debts and have to be repaid before the shareholders are entitled to receive anything in a liquidation.

They have the effect of expanding the company's capital base for the purpose of establishing its credit-worthiness. There is much learned debate as to the effectiveness of subordination against other creditors of a company; the position is not as clear in the UK as it is in the USA.

SUBPOENA. A writ obtainable by either party to a civil action to compel any person to attend at court as a witness (*subpoena ad testificandum*) or to produce documents, films or tape recordings (*subpoena duces tecum*). Literally 'under penalty', because if the witness disobeys the order he will be in contempt of court.

SUBROGATION. A doctrine derived from the equitable principle that a person should not recover more than his loss. Thus if, after payment by an insurer of the loss sustained by an assured, he later recovers an incidental benefit from a third party, that benefit is held in trust for the insurer; and the insurer may 'stand in the shoes' of the assured, to enforce any available remedies against a third party.

The doctrine has been extended to the relationship between guarantor and creditor; and a guarantor enjoys an additional statutory right under section 5 of the Mercantile Law Amendment Act 1856 to stand in the shoes, and sue in the name, of the creditor. A person who deprives his insurer or guarantor of a right in subrogation does so at his peril.

SUBSCRIBERS. The signatories to the Memorandum and Articles on the incorporation of a company: there must be at least two. On formation the subscribers become the first members of the company.

SUBSIDIARY COMPANY. Where the relationship of holding and subsidiary companies exists, they constitute a group, which is treated in many respects as one company. This qualifies the principle that each company is to be treated as a separate entity.

There are alternative tests to determine whether a company is a subsidiary: one of control, the other of economic participation. Broadly a company is a subsidiary of another (the holding company) if the holding company is a member of it, and controls the composition of its board of directors; or holds more than 50 per cent of its equity share capital. The relationship can easily be avoided by creating an odd share structure.

A subsidiary of a subsidiary is treated as a subsidiary of the head holding company. If two companies each hold 50 per cent of the equity share capital of a third company, the latter is not a subsidiary of either and this is so even if each holds 50 per cent of the votes.

If a subsidiary goes bust, the directors of another company in the group are not allowed to assist it, even for the benefit of the subsidiary or the group as a whole, unless an intelligent and honest man, in the position of a director of the company providing the assistance, would believe that it is solely for the benefit of the assisting company.

Proposals are on the way from the EEC to enforce responsibility for a subsidiary's debts on a holding company unless particular notice is given to the contrary.

SUPREME COURT, US. The final court of appeal in the US federal system and for some cases in the state courts. It is composed of a Chief Justice and eight associates nominated by the President of the USA. Appeal to the court is not a matter of right. It selects those matters which it wants to hear. It protects the individual from the unconstrained acts of government and has been described as the national conscience. Presidents hope that, during their terms of office, sufficient of its members will die off so that they can pack it with like-thinking nominees.

The court is not bound by its own decisions, but they are a binding precedent for all lower courts until limited or overruled by the Supreme Court itself.

The court has the right of judicial review over congressional legislation and may declare it unconstitutional or unenforceable.

SURETY. See GUARANTEES.

SURRENDER. Foregoing rights and obligations, either voluntarily, by prior agreement, or by operation of law.

Fully paid shares in a company can be surrendered to the company if it gives no consideration out of its assets in return; they go into abeyance until the company re-issues them. If the Articles permit a company to forfeit shares for non-payment of calls, a company may accept the surrender of partly paid shares if it would be for the company's benefit.

SYNDICATE. A term commonly applied to a group of banks, or other financial institutions, assembled by one or more lead managers for the purpose of lending a large sum of money to an entity or for a project, on the same terms for each member of the syndicate.

T

TABLE A. The Articles prescribed by the Companies (Tables A–F) Regulations 1985. They apply to all companies limited by shares unless expressly excluded or modified by their Articles.

TACKING. A method by which a mortgagee can obtain priority over earlier mortgages for subsequent advances made by him. It was abolished by the Law of Property Act 1925 except, effectively, for mortgages over land, and then only where the original mortgage deed imposes an obligation to make further advances.

TAKE OVER CODE. See CITY CODE.

TAKE-OVERS. As every economics student hastily revising for his finals knows, there are economies of scale and diseconomies of scale. Take-overs assume the former, and blissfully disregard the latter.

From the narrow standpoint, a take-over is merely an offer to purchase the securities of a target company for a consideration consisting of cash and/or the bidding company's paper on terms which comply with the City Code. The offer may (or may not) be accepted by the target company's shareholders. No matter what strategy is adopted or tactics employed, if the consideration offered is insufficiently tempting, the offer will fail, as indeed it may if it is referred to the Monopolies and Mergers Commission. Unlike in the USA, however, there is no right of merger once a 51 per cent interest is obtained.

139 take-over offers were made in 1985 for listed companies, of which 28 failed and 111 succeeded. See BOOTSTRAP BID, COMPULSORY ACQUISITION, MANDATORY BIDS, MERGER, TENDER OFFER and UNITIZATION.

TENDER OFFER. In the USA, an offer to purchase shares of a corporation, with a view to acquiring control, which is communicated to the shareholders by means of newspaper advertisements, and if the offeror can obtain the shareholders' list (which is not often unless it is a friendly tender) by a general mailing to all shareholders. Used in an effort to go around the management of a target company which is resisting acquisition. Tender offers are regulated by state and federal securities laws.

In the UK, a tender offer enables a person to acquire up to 30 per cent of the voting rights of a company without the normal time restraints of the SARs. It requires publishing an offer to acquire shares by paid advertisement in two newspapers. It may be the prelude to a full take-over. See TWO-TIER MERGER and THE WILLIAMS ACT.

TERM LOAN. A loan for a fixed period of time. The lender may not require earlier repayment except on the occurrence of specified events of default, or of specified supervening changes in circumstances.

TERMINATION OF CONTRACT. Ending or discharging a contract either by agreement, or as a remedy for breach of contract. Termination ends the duty of both parties to perform under the contract. An innocent party can also sue for damages for the loss resulting from the breach.

An innocent party is entitled to terminate where the contract contains a right to do so; or where the other party indicates an intention not to perform it; or if there is a breach of a condition of the contract (rather than a warranty); or a breach which is so fundamental as to frustrate the commercial purpose of the contract. See RESCISSION and WARRANTIES AND CONDITIONS.

THIRD PARTY. The person whom a defendant believes should also be liable because of the claim made against him or should contribute to, or indemnify him against, any award for damages. The court will try the issue between the defendant and the third party after trying the original claim, or the third party may be joined as a second defendant to the action.

Also, the description applied to a person with whom there is no contractual (or other) relationship; a stranger.

TIME OF ESSENCE. When the parties to a contract fix a definite time for its performance, the question arises whether the time must be precisely observed: lawyers would ask whether time is of the essence of the contract. Time is critical if it is expressly so stipulated in the contract. If the contract is not performed by the precise date there will be a breach.

Time will also be critical where the circumstances of the contract, or the nature of the subject matter, indicate that the parties intend that it should be. Time, not originally of the essence of the contract, will become critical if one party is guilty of delay and the other gives notice requiring performance within a specified reasonable time.

TORT. The infringement of a right, or the breach of a duty, arising independently of contract and giving rise to an action in the civil courts for damages or, sometimes, an injunction. For purely historical reasons, some torts, such as passing-off, are not actionable unless damage is suffered; others are actionable irrespective of any actual damage.

Most torts require some element of fault or blame to be established, but this involves from the victim's point of view an arbitrariness, which can be unfair, and litigation, which can be costly. There is a growing, if very slow, trend towards strict 'no-blame' liability, especially where insurance is readily available. A Royal Commission has recommended automatic public compensation for injuries at work or on the roads and no-fault liability for defective products, rail transport and other specific categories. Needless to say, this has not been acted on, but even these proposals do not go as far as the New Zealand social insurance reforms whereby, since 1972, tort in respect of personal injury has been abolished. See DEFAMATION, *PER SE*, TRADE LIBEL, TRESPASS TO THE PERSON, and VICARIOUS LIABILITY.

TRACING. A remedy enabling assets to be followed by the beneficial owner into the hands of a third party. It is available where a fiduciary relationship exists, but never against a purchaser in good faith without notice of the owner's equitable rights.

For the court to make a tracing order, the property must be identifiable; therefore tracing would be of no use, for example, against a trustee who has misappropriated trust funds and spent them all on a holiday (although other remedies might be available). Because the property has to be identifiable, special rules have been formulated to deal with tracing sums into a bank account. With mixed bank accounts the rule in *Clayton's* case may be applied: if there is no express appropriation, then each payment is impliedly appropriated to the earliest debt – the 'first in, first out' approach.

In a loan transaction which is *ultra vires* for the borrowing company, the lender can trace and recover the money lent if it is still held by the company in the form of investments or property.

TRADE DESCRIPTION. An indication, by any means, of the properties of goods sold – including quantity, method of manufacture, composition, fitness for purpose, conformity with standards, place or date of manufacture and other history.

Under the Trade Descriptions Acts 1968 to 1978 it is an offence to apply a false trade description to goods. The statutes are widely drafted and even the most reputable manufacturer may sometimes be caught out. However, perhaps the most common offence is still the 'clocking' of car milometers.

TRADE LIBEL. A trader may have a right of action against another if the other, without just cause or excuse, makes untrue statements about the plaintiff's trade, or his goods and causes actual damage. Trade libel, which is sometimes termed 'slander of goods', forms part of the wider tort of malicious or injurious falsehood. When the false statements touch on the plaintiff's right to deal in particular goods, the tort is usually termed 'slander of title'.

Common slanders of goods include suggestions that goods are not genuine or are of poor quality.

TRADE NAME. The name used by a person in the course of his trade and by which his trade is known. A trade name often carries with it the goodwill of the business and, if used in relation to goods, can also be a trademark.

TRADEMARK. Any distinctive name, word, signature or device used in relation to goods to indicate a connection in the course of trade between the goods and the person having the right to use the mark, usually its owner.

Trademarks may be registered under the Trade Marks Act 1938 in respect of named goods in one or more of 34 different classes or categories. The owner of a registered trademark has a statutory monopoly to use it on or in relation to goods, including in advertising, and may obtain an injunction to restrain infringement, and damages.

If the connection between the owner and the goods to which the mark is applied lapses, it may be held to have become 'deceptive'. Thus, a registered trademark may not be licensed casually: the licensor must impose quality standards in respect of goods sold under the mark by the licensee, who is called a registered user, and record the user agreement at the trademark registry.

A person wishing to assign a registered trademark, while continuing to run the business in which it was used, must advertise his intention and is open to challenge if the result might confuse consumers as to the origin of the goods. See SERVICE MARKS.

TRADEMARK CONVENTIONS. The UK is party to the Treaty of Paris, originally concluded in 1883 and revised most recently in Stockholm in 1967. This enables a national of one member state to own trademarks in another.

The Madrid Convention, to which the UK is not yet a party, enables applications in many member states to be made by means of a single deposit at a central office.

There are proposals for a European Community trademark.

TRANSFER OF BUSINESS. A business is a commercial enterprise with employees, assets, liabilities and goodwill. It may be transferred by its owner on a sale with, or without, its liabilities. A registered trademark may be assigned with the goodwill of the business.

The transfer of a business terminates all contracts of employment. However regulations implementing an EEC Directive operate upon the transfer of a commercial business so that all employees are transferred to the purchaser. For this reason the vendor will often be asked to dismiss employees immediately before the transfer so as to avoid the purchaser having to assume statutory and contractual liability for them.

A hive down is a transfer of a business, often carried on by an insolvent company, to a new subsidiary. It is effected by the receiver and it leaves the new company untrammelled by the liabilities of its parent. The transfer of employees is deemed to occur when the shares of the new company are purchased by an outsider. See TRADEMARK and UNDERTAKING .

TRANSFER DUTY. A stamp duty payable on the sale of most kinds of property which can only be transferred by means of a document. If the property can be transferred simply by delivery, e.g. bearer shares or a motor car, no transfer duty is payable.

The duty is payable at the rate of £1 for every £100 of the price paid, except for transfers of stocks and shares, and the transfer of a business on the occasion of certain mergers where the rate is 50p for every £100. There is a minimum threshold of £30,000, below which no duty is payable, for all assets except stocks and shares.

The duty is not payable on gifts; nor on transfers of short-term loan capital which is not convertible into shares. There are exemptions applicable to certain company reconstructions.

TRANSFER OF SHARES. Where shares are represented by bearer warrants, transfer is effected simply by delivering possession of the warrants. Transfer of registered shares is effected by completion of a share transfer form. When registered shares are sold, a number of separate legal transactions are involved.

There will be a contract which passes the beneficial, but not the legal, title to the shares to the purchaser. There is an implied obligation that the seller will deliver to the buyer a validly executed share transfer and the share certificate, against payment of the price. The buyer must pay stamp duty on the transfer before the company can register it. If the directors refuse to register, the buyer cannot get his money back: the seller will hold the shares in trust for him and must account to him for any benefit, but he is entitled to be indemnified against any obligations. If the seller was unwise enough to transfer shares before payment, he can exercise the voting rights.

If a transfer is forged, it is a nullity. The company who registered it will have to put the true shareholder back on the register, make good any loss to him, and may be liable to him for damages. See STAMP DUTY, RESERVE TAX and TRANSFER DUTY.

TRANSMISSION OF SHARES. The automatic transfer of shares to personal representatives which takes place on the death of the holder, or to trustees in bankruptcy. Before any dividends are paid to, or transfers accepted from, the representatives, they have to prove their title by producing probate of the will or letters of administration.

TREASURY, US. The US Department of the Treasury is an agency of the US government which performs four basic functions: formulating and recommending domestic and international economic, financial, tax, and fiscal policies; serving as financial agent for the US government; law enforcement responsibility; and manufacturing coins and currency.

TREATY. An agreement between states, or between a state and an international organization.

Although the provisions of a treaty are legislative in character, its nature is political; this is because sovereign states are not subordinate to any international legal system. However, treaties reflect the practices and conventions of states (recorded in the 1969 Vienna Convention on the Law of Treaties, which has, however, not been ratified) in their relations with each other, and their effect thus becomes entrenched in international relations.

A treaty is binding upon the states that are party to it. However, in the UK, the entering into a treaty is within the capacity of the Crown as an executive act; its implementation, and recognition in the UK courts, require it to be embodied in an Act of Parliament.

Even after a treaty has been signed by the contracting states, it may not be binding until ratified. This will be the case if the treaty itself provides that its effect is subject to ratification; and it may provide that ratification will only follow parliamentary approval or that it will not be binding until ratified by a specified proportion (say two-thirds) of its signatories.

A state may accede (become party) to a treaty that is already in existence and to which it was not one of the original parties, e.g. the accession of the UK to the Treaty of Rome in 1971 which was then reflected in the (UK) European Communities Act 1972.

International law can be enforced by non-judicial means (e.g. by negotiation, mediation or arbitration), or by judicial means before the Permanent Court of Arbitration and the International Court of Justice, so long as the relevant treaty recognizes the jurisdiction of those courts.

TREATY OF ROME, THE. The treaty signed in Rome on 25 March 1957 establishing the European Economic Community.

The Treaty defines the basic legal and constitutional principles that apply to the establishment and functioning of the Common Market.

TRESPASS TO GOODS. The unlawful disturbance of the possession of goods by seizure, removal, or a direct act causing damage.

It is a tort actionable *per se*: no proof of damage or loss is required. However, only nominal damages will be awarded to a plaintiff, who need not be the owner of the goods, unless he proves an element of substantial loss or damage. The defendant must have intended to interfere with the goods. If his interference was unintentional, any claim must be in negligence, and damage must be proved.

TRESPASS TO THE PERSON. This is one of the torts included under the group of trespasses *vi et armis* (with force and arms). It is further subdivided into assault, battery and false imprisonment, all of which involve interference by one person against the personal security or personal liberty of another, giving rise to a civil action by the latter person against the former.

The act complained of must be intentional (or negligent) and the onus of proving this is on the plaintiff. The act must also be against the will of the plaintiff and this is summed up in the expression *volenti non fit injuria* (that to which one consents cannot be considered an injury). Technically, the slightest interference constitutes a trespass, but often there is implied consent on the part of the plaintiff, e.g. one cannot sue for trespass for being jostled in the street in the normal course of pedestrian movement, since one implicitly consents to this. Otherwise trespass to the person is actionable without proof of actual damage.

Damages for consequential pecuniary loss can be recovered in trespass. It has been held that 'provocation is not the slightest defence' to an action for trespass, though it could reduce the amount of damages awarded.

Battery constitutes direct physical interference; false imprisonment involves the restriction of the liberty of the plaintiff by any coercive method and therefore need involve no physical restriction. Assault involves putting the plaintiff in apprehension of a battery (although the term assault is used by the police in a criminal context to mean assault and battery). Nervous shock resulting from assault is also actionable.

TRIAL. The stage in civil or criminal proceedings at which the evidence is examined and judgment is delivered. In most civil trials the judge decides on the facts and law. In trials before a jury the judge's role is to direct the jury so as to let them decide on the facts, and to decide questions of law himself. Trials are usually conducted in public so that justice can be seen to be done.

Fewer than 90 per cent of civil actions go to trial: the prospect of huge legal fees usually persuades the person with the weaker case to make an out-of-court settlement.

TRIBUNAL. Special courts which exercise quasi-judicial functions, often helped by members who are experts in a particular field. The power of a tribunal is delegated under an Act of Parliament and is limited in its extent; a tribunal has no authority to step outside its statutory power.

The decision of a tribunal can be questioned if it is based on a patently erroneous finding of fact, or if the tribunal has not adhered to the principles of natural justice. Other than this a tribunal's decision is final on a finding of fact unless the law provides for the right of appeal against a finding of fact, or the fact at issue is a 'jurisdictional fact', i.e. one which goes to the root of the tribunal's authority to proceed.

A tribunal's decision on a point of law is subject to judicial review by the High Court. General rules as to the operation of tribunals are embodied in the Tribunals and Enquiries Act 1971. This also provides for a Council on Tribunals appointed by the Lord Chancellor which oversees the workings of all the tribunals to which the statute applies, and also reports on more general matters referred to it with respect to tribunals.

A Tribunal of Inquiry is established for a specific purpose by resolution of both Houses of Parliament for investigation of matters of public importance. It is extra-legal in nature, and inquisitorial. An 'industrial tribunal' is an ordinary court.

TRUST CORPORATION. The appointment of certain corporations to act as a trustee is encouraged by statute. They include corporations entitled to act as custodian trustee: that is any UK company, or one incorporated in any EEC member state which has a place of business in the UK, which is empowered by its constitution to undertake trust business and has an issued capital of not less than £250,000 of which £100,000 has been paid in cash, or is incorporated by Royal Charter or special Act of Parliament.

The Public Trustee, the Official Solicitor and the Treasury Solicitor are also corporate trustees. See TRUST INSTRUMENT.

TRUST INSTRUMENT. The deed (often known as a 'trust' or 'settlement') which contains the terms on which trustees hold property for beneficiaries. It gives details of the trustees, the beneficiaries, and the property comprised in the settlement. It need not necessarily disclose information about the settlor.

The instrument will state the precise trusts on which the trust fund is held, and the powers which the trustees have in relation to the fund. Any action for breach of trust against the trustees will be based on its provisions.

Sometimes as an additional safeguard a custodian trustee will be appointed solely to hold trusts assets. The custodian trustee may also be one of the trustees who deal with the management of the trust. See DECLARATION OF TRUST and VARIATION OF TRUSTS.

TRUSTEES. Persons holding property upon trust for beneficiaries. It is an act of kindness to become a trustee, for it is onerous and troublesome.

For tax purposes trustees are treated as a continuing body of persons, distinct from the actual persons who may from time to time be trustees. Capital gains tax rules treat all bodies of trustees as resident in the UK unless the majority of the trustees are resident, and the general administration of the trusts takes place, outside the UK.

The rules for income tax are less clear; if one trustee is resident in the UK he may be assessed to income tax on the whole of the trust income, irrespective of the residence of the other trustees, or of the place from which the trust is administered.

Trustees must not profit from their trust. Hence if they want to be paid, express provision must be included in the trust deed. See FIDUCIARY DUTY, GOOD FAITH and TRUST CORPORATION.

TRUSTS. The relationship which arises whenever a person, called a trustee, is compelled to hold property for the benefit of some persons, called beneficiaries, in such a way that the real benefit accrues not to the trustee but to the beneficiaries.

The trustee has a duty to act in the best interests of the beneficiaries, who can sue the trustee if he is in breach of that duty. Trusts may be fixed interest trusts, where specific beneficiaries have vested interests, or discretionary trusts.

A trust which is otherwise valid will not be enforced if it offends against morality, public policy, or the provisions of any statute, but even so the trust's role in tax avoidance continues unabated. Unlike companies, trusts may be freely exported outside the UK, even though the beneficiaries may remain resident in the UK, with the result that UK income and capital gains tax may be deferred or in some cases avoided completely. See PROTECTIVE TRUSTS, TRUST INSTRUMENT and VARIATION OF TRUSTS.

TWO-TIER MERGER. A typical method used to achieve control of a US corporation. The bidder first makes a partial offer of cash for a bare controlling interest of the target; upon obtaining control the remaining shareholders are forced to exchange their stock for securities.

US federal tender offer laws require that shares tendered in a partial tender offer be purchased on a pro rata basis. Shareholders of sophistication will respond quickly and accept cash, while those who are tardy will often receive junk bonds which may be valued as equivalent to the cash bid on issue but which in fact trade at a deep discount. See HART-SCOTT-RODINO, TENDER OFFER, and THE WILLIAMS ACT.

U

UBERRIMAE FIDEI. See INSURANCE.

ULTRA VIRES. The Latin tag for an act beyond the powers, or capacity, of the person purporting to do it. The expression is used in two different senses in the case of companies.

The first is corporate *ultra vires.* A company has power to do only the things for which it is established, namely those objects set out in its Memorandum. Any transactions it effects outside those objects are void and cannot be enforced. All objects are within the capacity of the company even if they are gratuitous, or not for the company's benefit. The government is reviewing the question of whether it is still sensible to keep the doctrine of *ultra vires* in this sense.

The second sense is director *ultra vires.* Directors are agents of the company; any transactions outside their authority or not for the purposes of the company's business are *ultra vires* the directors. A contract will normally be enforceable against a company, even if *ultra vires* the directors, but the company will have rights against the directors to recover any loss. The two types of *ultra vires* are often confused because all acts *ultra vires* the company are *ultra vires* the directors although the converse is not necessarily true.

UMPIRE. Not a cricketing term, but the person appointed to adjudicate upon an arbitration from two or more arbitrators if they are unable to agree between themselves. He is, in general, in the same position as a sole arbitrator, and possesses the same qualifications or absence of disqualifications. Like the cricketing umpire, he must be strictly impartial.

UNDERTAKING. A person having signed an agreement for the purchase of an undertaking will walk out of the room the owner of a business, but will not always carry out the legal body with him. An undertaking is the whole of a business or enterprise. It is not the legal entity which owns the business; it is the business itself.

An undertaking is also a promise by a person to do, or to refrain from doing, some particular thing. Its legal effect will depend on the application of the law of contract. Breaking an undertaking given to the court is a contempt of court. The breach by a solicitor of his undertaking is professional misconduct.

If a solicitor gives an undertaking personally it may be enforced summarily by the court; for this reason solicitors take care to express undertakings as given on behalf of their clients: only their clients are then at risk.

UNDERWRITING. A company wishing to raise money by an issue of shares or debentures to the public or, indeed, from a more limited selection of people, will wish to ensure that if the issue is not fully subscribed it will have a fall-back position. This is achieved by underwriting the issue with an underwriter who is usually the Issuing House or sponsoring broker. The underwriter agrees, for the payment of a commission, to subscribe the balance of the securities which are not issued.

If the issue is fully subscribed the underwriter's liability ends. If there is a shortfall the underwriter will subscribe the balance. The underwriter will rarely take the whole risk himself. He has his list of favourite people to whom he offers commissions for their sharing the risk as sub-underwriters. The underwriting commission is based on the total number of shares underwritten and is payable whether or not the underwriter has to subscribe for the shares.

UNDISCLOSED PRINCIPAL. A person who instructs an agent to make a contract on his behalf without revealing to the other contracting party that the agent is not the principal. The agent and his undisclosed principal (if perchance he is discovered) are both liable on the contract. The undisclosed principal may sue, even though he is not in a direct contractual relationship with the contracting party.

UNDUE INFLUENCE. People will not be saved from the consequences of their own folly, but equity will save them from being victimized by other people where there is an inequality of bargaining power.

Accordingly a transaction will be set aside where a court is satisfied that it resulted from the actual use of influence and the relations between the parties are such as to raise a presumption that one had used improper influence over the other. This is so even if there is no fiduciary relationship between the parties.

The onus is on the party alleging undue influence to prove it, except in fiduciary relationships where the stronger party must disprove it. Generally undue influence is presumed where there is a fiduciary relationship. It is possible to detect an expansion of the concept of undue influence to situations where there is economic duress.

UNENFORCEABLE CONTRACT. A contract which the courts will not enforce either by compelling its performance or by giving damages to the party disappointed by its non-performance.

This can occur if the contracts are not, strictly speaking, contracts at all, either because they are unsupported by consideration, or because the required formalities have not been observed.

There are some contracts which are unilaterally unenforceable, e.g. with a foreign sovereign, or with international or European organizations, or their representatives, or with persons having diplomatic immunity. Contracts may be unenforceable against them, although enforceable by them, if, in the circumstances, they are entitled to and claim immunity from jurisdiction.

UNFAIR CONTRACT TERMS . See EXEMPTION AND EXCLUSION TERMS.

UNFAIR DISMISSAL. Most employees continuously employed for two years have the right not to be unfairly dismissed. This should not be confused with wrongful dismissal. If an employee considers that his employer acted unfairly in dismissing him, he may apply to an industrial tribunal, which will decide whether the employer acted reasonably in the circumstances, and will determine any remedy.

An agreement to compromise a claim for unfair dismissal is not enforceable unless it is approved by a conciliation officer of the Advisory, Conciliation and Arbitration Service (ACAS).

UNFAIR TRADE PRACTICES. Those activities, principally the creation of monopolies, restrictive trade practices, and anti-competitive practices, which competition law seeks to regulate. Anti-competitive practices are the subject of control in the Competition Act 1980.

Broadly, an anti-competitive practice exists if a person in the course of business pursues a course of conduct which is likely to have the effect of restricting, distorting, or preventing competition in connection with the production, supply, or acquisition of goods, or the supply of services.

The Director General of Fair Trading can investigate possible anti-competitive practices. He may refer them to the Monopolies and Mergers Commission for investigation and decision as to whether the practice operates, or might be expected to operate, against the public interest. The Commission may recommend remedial or preventative action.

UNINCORPORATED ASSOCIATION. A group of persons who have joined together for some common purpose, and who do not have a separate legal personality. Common forms of unincorporated associations are partnerships, syndicates, mutual associations and members' clubs.

UNIT TRUST. See AUTHORIZED UNIT TRUSTS.

UNITIZATION. The conversion of an investment trust company into a unit trust for the purpose of defeating a take-over offer, or to overcome the (usually) substantial discount between the net asset value of an investment company and its market capitalization.

It is achieved by a unit trust exchanging its units for shares held by members of the investment trust by way of a scheme of reconstruction or amalgamation. Under the capital gains tax legislation, capital gains tax is payable not on the exchange, but on the gains on units which are subsequently sold.

Unitization of real property, enabling multiple transferable ownership to non-professional investors of a single building, is virtually impossible under present laws, but may be capable of achievement when the proposed FSA 1986 comes into effect.

UNLIMITED COMPANY. One for the foolhardy or the brave. It is a company whose members are liable, in a liquidation, to meet all its debts.

There are advantages to an unlimited company: it does not have to file accounts with the Registrar (unless it is a subsidiary, or holding company, of a limited company); and there is no liability to pay capital duty on issues of shares. A company may be converted from a limited company to an unlimited company and vice versa.

UNLISTED SECURITIES MARKET. Launched in November 1980 under the aegis of The Stock Exchange as a second-tier market designed to meet the needs of smaller, less mature companies.

A company wishing to be quoted on the USM must generally have traded for three years and need only make 10 per cent of its equity share capital available for sale to the public, as against 25 per cent and a five-year record for a full listing. Flotation on the USM is not always cheaper than getting a full listing, although the usual method of marketing is by placing, rather than an offer for sale, and the prospectus does not have to be advertised in full in two national newspapers.

USURY. Lending money on extortionate terms. Under the Consumer Credit Act 1974 the court may re-open an extortionate credit bargain so as to do justice between the parties. A credit bargain is extortionate if it requires payments to be made which are grossly exorbitant, or if it otherwise contravenes ordinary principles of fair dealing. It applies to all forms of credit, including a cash loan and any form of financial accommodation, and not merely those regulated by the statute.

This provision replaces the narrower provision formerly contained in the Moneylenders Act which applied only to moneylenders and pawnbrokers. It enables the court to strike down harsh and unconscionable bargains.

V

VARIATION OF CONTRACT. The alteration or modification of the terms of a contract.

Any contract may be varied by an oral or written agreement, except those required to be evidenced in writing (for instance, guarantees, or agreements to sell land) which may only be varied in writing. A variation agreement must be supported by consideration unless it is a deed. The consideration can be the abandonment of rights or the creation of new or increased obligations or benefits. See DISCHARGE OF CONTRACT.

VARIATION OF TRUSTS. A trust may be varied if all the beneficiaries are adult and *sui juris*. If there are minor or unborn children as beneficiaries, the court may be asked to approve a variation on their behalf under the Variation of Trusts Act 1958. As each beneficiary, or class of potential beneficiaries, has to be separately represented, this piece of legislation was the Chancery bar's answer to a portable pension. But its use has been reduced by the introduction of more flexible drafting which gives trustees wide powers of appointment (including powers to appoint on sub-trusts) which often make a variation unnecessary.

The court has, in the past, approved many variations where tax avoidance was the chief motive.

VENDOR PLACING. See PLACING.

VICARIOUS LIABILITY. Not a clerical error! An employer is foisted with responsibility to a third party if his employee commits a tort in the course of his employment. The employee is also liable, although in practice the employer is sued because he is more likely to be able to pay any damages. Three matters have to be established for vicarious liability to arise: an employer–employee relationship; that the employee committed a tort; and that he did so in the course of his employment.

An employer can claim from his employee the damages he has had to pay.

VOID CONTRACTS. Some contracts are void: they are of no contractual effect. If they are illegal any transaction which is founded on, or springs from, them is also void. Some contracts, such as those to oust the jurisdiction of the courts, and contracts in restraint of trade, are not wholly void although they are contrary to public policy. It is possible for the court to sever an objectionable clause from the rest of the contract, or to limit its scope by eliminating unreasonable features, so that the remainder of the contract continues. See *ULTRA VIRES*.

VOIDABLE CONTRACT. One which may be rescinded, thus avoiding the contract for the future; or which may be affirmed, thereby making it wholly valid. See MINOR and RESCISSION.

VOLENTI NON FIT INJURIA. This defence could apply where a man ruptures himself by trying to wear trousers which are three sizes too small for him, just because he cannot accept the size of his waist measurement, and then sues his tailor, blaming him for the injury.

In the law of negligence, where a plaintiff relies on the breach of a duty to take care owed to him by the defendant, it is a good defence that the plaintiff consented to that breach of duty or, knowing of it, voluntarily incurred the whole risk entailed by it. Hence the maxim *volenti non fit injuria* – the plaintiff consented to his own injuries. To establish the defence, the plaintiff must be shown not only to have perceived the existence of danger, but also to have appreciated it fully, and voluntarily accepted the risk.

VOTING . There are a variety of voting methods, but within a company there are only two: the show of hands, and the poll vote.

Directors will decide by a majority vote on a show of hands. Votes at a general meeting will also be initially decided by a show of hands, on which each shareholder, or representative of a company shareholder, will be entitled to one vote. A proxy cannot normally vote on a show of hands, but if he is entitled to do so he has only one vote no matter how many shareholders he may represent. A poll may be asked for by the chairman of the meeting, or by not less than five members, or members having not less than 10 per cent of the votes or 10 per cent of the fully-paid capital with the right to vote.

On a poll, a shareholder or proxy is entitled to exercise the votes attached to each share he holds. Members, or proxies, who hold a majority shareholding, but who are a minority in number, should always demand a poll. A proxy should always call for a poll to enable his votes to be counted.

W

WAIVER. A voluntary abandonment or surrender of a right or remedy. Like any promise made without consideration, it is not enforceable unless it is made under seal or the other party acts in reliance on the promise.

A waiver can be oral, written, or implied by conduct. For example, implied waiver would operate where a party having alternative rights or remedies may be taken to have waived one by pursuing the other.

Wealth warning: adverse tax consequences can result from a waiver. See ESTOPPEL.

WARRANT. An authority allowing some action to be taken by the holder of the warrant or recognizing some privilege he enjoys. Share warrants are options granted by a company to subscribe for its shares. A dividend warrant entitles the holder to payment of the dividend, and is often in the form of a cheque. A search warrant allows the holder to search premises.

Certain royal warrants recognize that the warrant holder is the supplier of goods or services to the Queen.

WARRANTIES AND CONDITIONS. A warranty is in effect a minor term, collateral to the main purpose of a contract. Thus, for example, under the Sale of Goods Act 1979, breach of warranty gives rise to a claim in damages only, and not a right to reject the goods and treat the contract as repudiated. Warranties are often given as to the financial position and business affairs in a private company in contracts for the sale of its shares.

A condition is not a warranty. The terms and obligations of a contract are like real life: not all of them are equal and some have more importance than others. A condition is a major or fundamental term, the breach of which will entitle a party, not merely to damages, but to treat the contract as at an end.

The courts have evolved their own practical test in order to evaluate the importance of contractual terms, based on the seriousness of the consequences of the breach, and the probable intention of the parties at the time that the contract was made. See BREACH OF CONTRACT, INDEMNITY and TERMINATION OF CONTRACT.

WHITE BOOK. In the right hands its two weighty volumes can provide a formidable procedural or, in the last resort, offensive weapon. It contains all the procedural rules and directions governing the administration of justice in the Supreme Court of England and Wales. Known as the *White Book*, not for being above reproach, but merely from its colour.

WILL. The written expression of a person's desire to direct how his assets will devolve after his death. The wise person will always have a will for it avoids all the hassles of intestacy. It has to be executed in the presence of two witnesses, who are not beneficiaries under the will, nor spouses of such beneficiaries. A will may be varied by a written codicil which has to be similarly executed. These formal requirements are relaxed in special circumstances, e.g. for members of the armed forces.

A will may be challenged by members of the deceased's family under the Inheritance (Family Provisions) Act 1975 if they feel that the deceased made inadequate provision for them under the will. It may be revoked at any time before death, and only operates from death. See PERSONAL REPRESENTATIVE.

WILLIAMS ACT, THE. A body of US federal law generally consisting of sections 13(d)–(g) and 14(d)–(f) of The Securities Exchange Act of 1934. The section 13 provisions basically require that substantial acquirers of an issuer's securities disclose to the SEC, the issuer and the stock exchange where the issuer's securities are traded, that an acquisition of such securities has occurred; their intent in acquiring such securities; the source of funds used; and other relevant information. The section 14 provisions regulate tender offers of certain equity securities which would result in the person making the tender offer becoming the owner of more than 5 per cent of such class of securities.

WINDING UP. Liquidation and winding up are synonymous terms describing the proceedings under which the assets of a company are realized and distributed, first to meet its liabilities and then amongst the members, according to their interests, prior to the dissolution of the company.

It is voluntary when initiated by the company in general meeting; compulsory when not. A voluntary winding up can be replaced by a winding up by the court. A members' voluntary winding up, which is usually employed as part of a restructuring of a company whether or not there may be tax advantages in doing so, can only be commenced if the directors can make a declaration of solvency.

Any other voluntary winding up is a creditors' voluntary winding up: the creditors approve or appoint the liquidator and, possibly, a committee of inspection.

A court can order the compulsory winding up of a company following the presentation of a petition, usually by a creditor, which can be brought on a number of grounds, the most common being the inability of the company to pay its debts as they fall due. In these circumstances, it is usual for the Official Receiver to be appointed as provisional liquidator, to be replaced in due course by a liquidator appointed by the creditors. See ADMINISTRATOR and WRONGFUL TRADING.

WITHOUT PREJUDICE. When persons in dispute with each other engage in 'without prejudice' negotiations to resolve their differences, the content of their discussions, and correspondence, cannot be admitted as evidence at trial, without the agreement of both.

Although parties are usually careful to designate letters and negotiations 'without prejudice', the courts are not concerned with the form of words; they will be ready to infer that the exchanges are privileged, as part of public policy to encourage settlement of disputes. An agreement reached in 'without prejudice' discussions or correspondence is fully enforceable, and admission of matters irrelevant to the dispute is not covered by the privilege and may be used by the other side. 'Without prejudice' negotiations cannot be used as a cloak for making illegal threats.

WORLD COURT. See INTERNATIONAL COURT OF JUSTICE.

WRIT. A document in the Queen's name and under the seal of an officer of the Crown requiring someone to do or to forbear from doing something.

A writ of summons is the usual form for the plaintiff to commence an action in the High Court. It originally bore a command from the Sovereign to the defendant requiring him to 'enter an appearance' to the writ. While a writ of summons still bears the royal arms, the command from the Queen no longer appears as it, not unnaturally, was found to cause confusion in the minds of unsuspecting recipients.

WRONGFUL DISMISSAL. The dismissal by an employer of an employee in breach of contract of employment either before its date of expiration, or without giving the required notice. The employee's remedy is to bring an action for damages for breach of contract.

The damages for wrongful dismissal are the value of remuneration and other benefits which would have been received during the outstanding term of the contract, less whatever the employee could be expected to earn from new employment during such term, or unemployment benefit. Other factors which will be taken into account are income tax saved, accelerated receipt of income and sometimes redundancy and unfair dismissal awards.

Termination payments on a contract of employment, including damages for wrongful dismissal, are free of income tax up to a maximum of £25,000 and subject to reduced rates of tax up to £75,000. See DIRECTOR'S SERVICE AGREEMENT and UNFAIR DISMISSAL.

WRONGFUL TRADING. This arises where a director knew, or ought to have known, that there was no reasonable prospect of his company avoiding insolvent liquidation and he cannot show that he took every step which ought to have been taken to mimimize the potential loss to creditors. The court can order the director to contribute out of his own pocket to the company's assets, and may also disqualify him from acting as a director.

The facts which a director ought to have known, and the steps which he ought to have taken, are those of a reasonably diligent person having both the general knowledge, skill and experience which could have been expected of a director carrying out his functions, and the general knowledge, skill and experience which he actually had. Thus an experienced finance director may have a higher duty than others, as would a managing director with financial experience. See DISQUALIFICATION OF DIRECTORS, FRAUDULENT TRADING and INSOLVENCY.

Y

YELLOW BOOK. The colloquial term for the rules of The Stock Exchange relating to the admission of securities to listing; it contains both the procedures and disclosures required for admission and the continuing obligations imposed on companies whose securities are listed.

Alternatively, used by cognoscenti to refer to the private publication which incorporates the current statutory provisions relating to income tax, corporation tax and capital gains tax.

Z

ZEBRA BOND. The acronym for zero-coupon Euro-sterling bearer or registered accruing securities. These are deep discount bonds, backed by UK government stocks, from which the interest has been stripped. It is the latest in a series of bond-stripping exercises started in the USA in 1983 with US Treasury Bonds with acronyms like CATS and TIGRS.